Houses of my Consciousness

Waking From Religion to Spirit

Adelaide Woodcook
as told to Maridel Bowes

Outskirts Press, Inc.
Denver, Colorado

Houses of my Consciousness
Waking From Religion to Spirit

V4.0

Outskirts Press, Inc.
http://www.outskirtspress.com

ISBN: 978-1-4327-1018-7

PRINTED IN THE UNITED STATES OF AMERICA

Dedication

This book is dedicated to the
memory of my parents

Richard Wallace Blauvelt
and
Elizabeth Frances Blauvelt

Table of Contents

Acknowledgments

- To Maridel Bowes, my beloved daughter and talented biographer. Your ability to intuit my feelings and "write between the lines" makes this story shine. My gratitude for reaching back your hand and taking you with me into the light.
- To Linda Beard, my loving daughter for almost fifty years. Your faith in me and the sharing of our journeys is one of my life's greatest treasures.
- To Nikki Bowes, my granddaughter and graphic designer. The cover of this book so beautifully reflects its spirit and your bright heart.
- To Lois Woodcook, my dear, computer-savvy daughter-in-law. Thanks for the many, many hours spent assisting me with this book.
- To the rest of my family: Dale, Jason, Tyler and Amy Woodcook, and Courtney Woodcook Ralls; Justin and Gavin Bowes and Brad and Cindy Bowes; Jerry, Ryan, and Lori Beard. To my four great grandchildren: Jaden, Abigail, and Geren Bowes and Rheanna Ralls. You contribute to my life beyond measure.
- To my support group: Victoria Craig, Shirley Randolph, and Dinah Reilly who have cheered me on in life and through the process of this book. You are my co-conspirators in consciousness.

- To Margaret Heffernan, my editor. Your loving, conscientious attention to my story warmed my heart. Thank you for your expertise and your friendship.
- To Pam Fabbri, my stylist and photographer for this book. Thanks for making me look my best on and off camera.
- To Sharyn Hindley, our last reader. Your bright mind and keen eye put the final polish on these pages.

And lastly,

- To Christiane Schull, who so passionately encouraged me to tell my story. I agree with you that our meeting was "a divine appointment…God and all the angels intended it and made it so."

"The Mystery"

No one expects a miracle standing at the kitchen sink. It's a place of transformation, yes: dishes go from soiled to sparkling, glasses from smudged to clear. But who could imagine that more would arise out of soapy water and fleeting thoughts? Not I.

Perhaps it was the trance of my watery ritual that took my mind from its hopscotching ways and opened another door. Perhaps it was the rising majesty of the Boise Mountains out my window— crowned with snow and sunlight—that let a miracle slip in.

I only know that in the simple act of lifting and rinsing my plate, I heard a voice. It came from within, but so quietly clear that I almost turned to look over my shoulder. I had heard this voice in years past and followed its guidance without regret. But this time, I didn't like the message.

It's easier to negate a message you don't like. Nothing rises up from inside you to greet or bless it. There's no urge to note it in your journal. It's the bud of a flower you don't want in your garden.

To understand my response to this message, you'd have to be reading the end of this book instead of the beginning. *Or*… have a history similar to mine: born into a religious system that with all good intentions, misrepresented God, Life, and Love. And if, like me, you had first given your life to this system, and then left it in order to be whole, you would know why I turned away from these words, "Go to Cathy's church."

"Cathy's church"—it wasn't even *hers* anymore. She was long gone to Arizona, and in the years she'd been my next door neighbor, I'd declined all invitations to go with her. It was good for Cathy. That I could see. Her beloved pastor, George, was obviously a fount of inspiration for her. And I could also see that this church was vastly different from the one of my lineage. Still, it hadn't appealed to me then nor did it appeal to me now. I had the same lack of response to the voice as I'd had to Cathy: no need and no desire. Begin reenacting the decades of obligatory Sunday morning rituals? Give up the quiet, delicious joy of solitude that had replaced those rituals? No.

It had been seventeen years since I'd been to church. In my youth I'd lived in the parsonage because my grandfather, who was the minister, lived with us. In my adulthood, I'd lived in the parsonage because I married a ministerial student. Now, in my eighties, and with my spiritual freedom still relatively new to me, there was no longer a steeple on the landscape of my life. Church had slowly faded—a curled up Polaroid of something I had once lived for, but whose heart no longer lived in me.

And so, on this late winter morning, I let this message go past me like a stranger who had stopped by my house, offered some advice I didn't need, and walked on. The voice itself I chalked up to an old tape impersonating guidance. Besides, I realized with reassuring finality, I *did* go to Cathy's church once to see a film and had even met George. "Thanks anyway," I said to the voice, "but I've already been."

I considered the conversation, such as it was, to be complete. Yet across the next few weeks, the voice returned in another form: an inner, recurring impression to go to Cathy's church. These feelings weren't as resolute as the voice itself had been, but they didn't disappear either. Nor did my response.

Weeks later, in looking over a stack of mail I'd set aside for that infamous "second glance," I came across a small magazine still in its plastic wrapping. Inside was a series of inspirational thoughts—one for each day of the month. The first I read out of curiosity, the rest out of immense satisfaction. Before I knew it, I'd read a week's worth and a few days later, did the same. Having now reached the middle of the booklet, I found to my surprise, a list of churches affiliated with the magazine. *This was a church magazine?* "Science of Mind," it said. I looked to see if there was a local congregation, my eyes scanning the list for Boise. There it was, and with it something else: the address where I'd gone to see the film with Cathy. The pastor's name was listed as George Dashiell. Stunned, I flipped back to the cover to verify the name of these churches. Yes, "Science of Mind." But Cathy had always called it "Center for Spiritual Living." I had never made the connection—until now. Direction stirred in me again, although now it could not be mistaken for an old recording. Nor could I dismiss it.

Still I hesitated. A couple of weeks went by before I got up one Sunday morning, not to the quiet rejoicing of another day of life, another Sunday morning spent alone, but to the odd and deeply familiar nudge to get ready for church. My only motivation was simply this: to pay my respects to the voice, and to see what this was all about. Underneath that motivation, was another: to comply with the voice so that I could get back to my churchless ways.

I arrived to a parking lot completely full of cars, and not one stray soul in sight to consult about alternate parking. I did try the high school parking lot across the street, but was stopped by a sturdy rope across the entry and a menacing sign that read, "No Parking! Cars will be towed!" I hardly needed the admonition. I really didn't want to go anyway.

"Well," I said to myself and to the voice at the same time, "I tried." I felt no triumph, but did ride home in a quasi-state of relief. Maybe the whole thing was just about willingness, a demonstration of openness to a different experience of church than the one still branded on my heart.

As I pulled into the garage, I remembered that I needed to call my son-in-law, Jerry, about reserving a plane ticket for me. Once inside, I dialed the number that was imprinted on my brain from years of continuous use.

"Hello," an unfamiliar voice said. It was the gentle voice of an older man.

"Oh," I replied. "I must have the wrong number."

"This is George," he said.

"I'm sorry, George. I dialed the wrong number."

"Oh I see. Goodbye."

I stood paralyzed with the phone in my hand. *Who gives their name in response to a wrong number?* Then I noticed exactly where I was standing: in the kitchen, staring out the window at the Boise Mountains. The snow was almost gone.

The following week was Palm Sunday. "At least it will be celebratory," I told myself as I dressed for church. My curiosity, I noted, had begun to change places with my reluctance. All week that gentle voice on the phone had come to me when least expected: "This is George." As if the voice that had begun within me calling me to Cathy's church was now echoing back from the outer world. I easily found a parking spot this time, and as I got out of my car, I noticed another person walking toward the door from the opposite direction. It was George. I slackened my step so as not to encounter him, waiting until he got inside the church before I entered.

Inside, over the shoulder of the greeter, I saw a perplexing sight: a crowd gathered around George, waiting to hug him. Surely this wasn't a weekly ritual. The usher seated me toward the front, and as the service started, I noticed that George, too, was taking a seat in the pulsing, warm life of the congregation. My confusion cleared as a vibrant woman introduced herself as Pastor Jackie. She welcomed everyone, but gave a special greeting to George, the visiting *former* pastor.

Sitting in that place I had resisted for so many weeks, I felt that George had come this particular Sunday, not only to see all the people who loved him so dearly, but perhaps just as much for someone he didn't know. His presence was an unmistakable and living confirmation of the direction I'd been given.

In this state, I opened my heart to the music and to Jackie's message. Her lively, passionate words resonated deeply with all I'd been learning for the last many years. Never had the experience of church so fed and vitalized me, so reflected my inner spirit. Never had it met me on the edge of my wending path and beckoned me forward. In the last many years, I had been personally and spiritually transformed. Perhaps now it was time to transform my experience of church.

And so, without making it an obligation, I began attending the Center for Spiritual Living in Boise, Idaho. And every time I went, I left feeling uplifted and renewed. For the first time in my life, I could say that I loved going to church; but even more importantly, I loved how it affected my daily life, supporting me to be more open to the presence of God in all things. Some would say that is enough. Some would say the mystery had been resolved. But inside, I knew there was another reason for the voice, the perfect wrong number, and that one moment alone in the parking lot with George.

I had no idea what the reason was, but I did know this: it would be revealed. As long as I kept following guidance, there's no chance I would miss it.

When I was a child, I had a friend who lived in an abandoned cottage not far from where we lived. Others would have automatically labeled him "imaginary," but to me he was real—whether a product of my creative mind or the actual presence of a spirit, I cannot say. One day, in an unguarded moment, I'd told my mother about my friend, informing her that he was on a trip to Europe. I still remember the spot in our house where I stood before my seated, stern mother while she lectured me on the sin of lying. After that, my friend did not exist for me. His name was "Uncle George."

Without needing to explain or understand this, it's no coincidence that the name George had once again come into my life, creating an experience that some people, just like my mother, would disbelieve. But this time, there was no stern parent to deter me from my reality—without or within.

It has taken me eighty-eight years to come to this place of guidance and grace, of freedom and increasing peace. This book is the story of that late-blooming, but ever-moving transformation. It will lead you one-by-one through the houses in which I've lived, those outer places wherein my inner life found its ultimate home. I call them "houses of my consciousness."

By the end of this story, I trust we will both understand why the voice of Spirit said to me one snow-capped, March morning, "Go to Cathy's church."

HOUSE ONE

Route 45, Spring Valley, New York

I think of myself as having been born in church, though my mother did not deliver me between the pews while parishioners huddled in whispering, concerned clusters in the vestibule. I was born instead in the upstairs bedroom of the parsonage—and as anyone who has lived in a parsonage will tell you, you might as well have been born between the pews.

This was the home of my grandparents, Rev. and Mrs. John Caldwell. It was a modest house, planted right on Route 45, and built in 1916—still new when I was born in 1920. Its style today would best be described as Early Victorian, complete with a long porch that ran across the front of the house and wrapped itself neatly around one side.

My grandfather was a sweet, quiet man and a lover of words. My grandmother, Mary, was by all reports and evidence, a feisty woman and a lover of trouble. Upon delivering her second child, she told her heir-hopeful husband "You got your Johnny." It was six months before the truth emerged: this baby, too, was a girl. My grandmother's "prank" was indicative of her style. As a minister's wife, she had absolutely nothing to do with the church except for attending the ladies' socials, where she positioned herself as the life of the party and held court. Otherwise, she gladly abstained from her husband's ministry. Whatever else might be said of her, one had to acknowledge that such audacity was refreshing in the early 1900's.

Fortunately, for my grandfather's sake, his elder daughter, Elizabeth, was more cooperative, and filled in for my errant grandmother. Thus she became his companion in the ministry: teaching Bible classes, playing the piano for services, and traveling with him by horse and buggy to the remote churches on his itinerary—even in the midst of blinding snowstorms. She married my father, Richard Blauvelt, at the almost unmarriageable age of thirty, and in this, my grandfather was fortunate still: she and her husband continued in the house, and his daughter in her role.

Deep in the bitter cold of a New York winter, just days before Christmas, I was born into this riddle of a household. My parents named me Mary Adelaide after their mothers, and by the time I was two, like my maternal grandmother, I had acquired a reputation for non-compliance. I was a self-proclaimed gypsy. That is to say, I had a habit of roaming—of seeking forbidden freedom. I even had the look: flaming red hair, a face full of freckles, and the defiant stare of one who lets nothing stand in the way of her wanderlust. My mother evidently spent an inordinate amount of time running after me, and when she found that punishment did not deter, she did the only thing she could think of to preserve the life of her firstborn: she tied one end of a clothesline around my waist, and the other to the end of the porch. Two pictures from the family album illustrate both the problem and the solution. The first photo shows me tromping through sepia stalks of corn with my grandfather, hands-on-hips behind me, feigning disapproval. In the second one I'm scowling fiercely, clothesline trailing behind me with the porch as a backdrop. Stunning, unthinkable defeat.

It's true to say that tying me to the porch was a good idea, saving as it did my mother's sanity and very likely, my life. It's just as true to say that this picture became a metaphor of my first forty years: a gypsy on a clothesline with a driveway as her world.

As an adult, when I was cleaning house and suddenly reached the limit of the vacuum cleaner cord, I'd react with instantaneous fury. In the aftermath, I couldn't understand my disproportionate response. Even obvious metaphors take time to see when you're buried deep inside them.

There was, however, a place in Spring Valley where I was free: 85 West Street, the house that my paternal grandfather had built from a 1916 Sears and Roebuck kit. It was just half a mile from our home, but for me, it was another country—another reality. Just inside the front door of this enormous two-storied home, with its sloping roof and protruding cupolas, three things always greeted me. The first was the steady ticking heart of the grandfather clock in the front hall—a gift from the Entenmann family for whom grandfather had worked, selling their baked goods from a horse-drawn wagon. The second, which merged seamlessly with the first, was the smell of fresh-baked cookies, a product of my grandmother's magic kitchen where the table was always piled with my favorite sweets. The third was my grandmother, Martha, with her quiet, approving smile. My three young aunts, Hilda, Harriet, and Lois, added to my delight with their pampering and playfulness. At 85 West Street, I felt free and cherished. Long before there was such a place, this was my Disneyland.

HOUSE TWO

Cottage at Groveville Park Campgrounds, Beacon New York

My maternal grandmother, Mary, died when I was two-and-a-half, leaving me as the household guardian of her mutinous legacy. Shortly after her death, my grandfather, John, received a new pastoral assignment to start a church in Beacon, a small city on the Hudson River, sixty miles north of New York City. He owned a cottage at Groveville Park, a church-owned campground, just outside Beacon. And so, until suitable housing could be found, we made our home in his cottage.

The campgrounds themselves must have spoken to my spirit: spaciousness, endless trees, cottages that dotted the periphery of the camp, suggesting the thrill of every gypsy: transience. Better yet, my grandfather's cottage was set back on a dirt road, removed from the main area. This was a summer only residence with two bedrooms, living quarters and an outhouse. Rustic and unfinished, the cottage was built on a slope with seven steps up to the door.

The scent of pine and freedom must have gone to my head one Sunday morning. In the midst of my grandfather's sermon, I broke from my parents and ran up the aisle, mounted the steps, and then ran back and forth behind my preaching grandfather, laughing. A fresh wave of freedom had arisen within me, and now I had a sibling as an ally. My sister Rhea was born in the heart of that summer, providing me with a great gift: my mother's distraction. Every morning when she bathed the baby, I took my dazzling opportunity to leave the cottage, plunging headlong over the front lawn and down the road before she could catch me. The heavy-handed price I paid didn't keep me from attempting my escape the very next day.

"I'm going to Spring Valley," I had told her matter-of-factly when she asked, "*Where* do you think you're going?" But Spring Valley, of course, was not my true goal. The specific destination I had in mind was 85 West Street—the ticking, cookie-scented safety of my grandmother's smile.

By now, my mother must have been feeling ruefully inept as a mother, failing as she was in her attempts to keep me under control. And for a woman such as herself, this was unacceptable. Elizabeth Caldwell Blauvelt was a large, sturdy woman with long, dark brown hair. Any softness or grace that such tresses might have lent to her appearance was ruled out by a hairnet that not only plastered her hair to her head, but contained a tight and tidy bun at the nape of her neck. The scriptures by which she so rigidly lived her life stated that a woman's hair is her glory. And thus her hair gave witness to her definition of "glory." Snapping Irish eyes and lips that frequently pursed with disapproval were her only signs of liveliness. Her large frame was firmly corset-bound, its long laces securing a wide binding that flattened her breasts. As rigid and unbending as the metal stays in that corset, she set upon controlling herself and others through her fanatical religious beliefs. I never once heard her laugh out loud.

One memorable Sunday, we had come back to the cottage from church and evidently when dinner was ready, I was not. Preferring instead my artistic pursuits, I ignored my mother's order to pick up my crayons, and further exercising my two-and-a-half- year- old prerogative, told her "No". She repeated her demand and I clarified my position. From my mother's point of view, I had threatened her authority, and she had no alternative but to "break my will," as she would describe it over the years. Accepting the challenge with vigor, she set dinner on the back burner, and silently declared war. After repeating her demand to no avail, she spanked me, and repeated it again. I refused to bow. This alarmingly primitive exchange went on until, exhausted by the fray, she put me to bed for a nap. The rest only seemed to freshen my reserves. Full of renewed vitality, I was ready for the next round. I held out for hours, but unrelenting punishment and a lack of food eventually brought me to my senses. I picked up my crayons.

My mother had won. Or so it seemed. While a devastating blow was delivered to my psyche that day, in the end I don't think my mother was as victorious as she felt. Yes, I got the message about the limitations of my power and the cost of disobedience to those in authority; and yes, its effects ricocheted down the corridors of my life for years to come.

But underneath, my will still breathed: the will to be free.

HOUSE THREE

Washington Avenue, Beacon New York

I turned three in our house on Washington Avenue, a home I would live in three times. But I would have remembered this place if I'd only spent one certain night in it—the night three visitors appeared at my bedside.

At the end of the summer, my parents rented this house since the cottage, besides being too small for three generations, was not winter worthy in the New York clime. It had no heat, running water, or indoor plumbing. By contrast, this large two-storied home had a sunny, open kitchen, and adjoining dining and living rooms. The sloping roof gave coziness to the three upstairs bedrooms, a reward for the long climb that began in the entrance hall. Since my sister was still a newborn, I had a room of my own. It sat at the top of the stairs and had a high, square window I could see from the end of my crib.

Under this roof, I continued my flamboyant ways. I talked so much to our dinner guests at the age of three-and-a-half that my mother had to remove me so the adults could converse. *Seen but not heard* was evidently an injunction I didn't take literally. Undaunted by my early exit, I announced to her as she prepared me for bed, "Well, I guess I can entertain anywhere."

My antics continued in church as well, where for some reason,

I felt safe enough to be daring. Or perhaps I just couldn't resist an audience. Instead of delivering my memorized Christmas piece and making my parents proud, I boarded the platform and loudly proclaimed, "Ho, ho, ho, ho!" No doubt it won me a few laughs, which evidently were more valuable to me than my mother's approval.

Even the neighbor who lived behind us once alluded to the presence of a pending schism between my flagrant self and my family—no doubt having my mother in mind. I remember her remark, tossed casually to another neighbor in my presence: "Well, they're not going to keep *this one* down on the farm."

In the years just ahead, my mother would grow harsher and increasingly unreasonable in her control. With few exceptions, she would disallow all pleasure and all personal expression. Her religion-based rules would cast blight across our home and seep into the marrow of our family's bones. But in these years, she was still capable of tenderness now and then: allowing me to have a little picnic by myself with raisins and graham crackers while my baby sister napped and comforting me when my puppy Jetty (a rare gift from my father) was killed as he crossed the street in answer to my call. These stand out in my mind as moments when her love crossed the line into visibility—where for a brief moment, she could allow human pleasure and pain to be acceptable.

In this house, the anteroom between my mother's tolerance and her abject domination, I had a fleeting visit from three extraordinary guests—mere seconds that would alter everything. Alone in my crib that night, my face turned to the wall, I was unable to sleep. Perhaps in an effort to get more comfortable, or perhaps responding to the palpable presence in my room, I rolled to my other side. Three angels stood by my crib! I can still feel the surge of surprise that welled up in my body. But only that. I had no fear. And before I could do more than glimpse their silent, radiant beauty, they were off—swooping up and away through the small, high window, trailing white.

The next morning I told my mother what had happened. And because it was of a religious nature, she neither chastised nor challenged, but merely said, "Go tell your grandfather." I didn't tell him though, and don't remember telling anyone for years. And yet, the experience itself stayed crystalline within me. Whenever I thought of it, regardless of how long it had been, it was fresh and untouched by time—as real and immediate to me as the night it occurred.

Beyond the heavy rails of my crib, behind the heavy veil of my mother's growing rigidity, behind the walls of a religion I had yet to fully encounter, I'd touched another world.

HOUSE FOUR

9 Davis Street, Beacon, New York

The house at 9 Davis Street was an elegant, Victorian lady enrobed in a coat of dark maroon trimmed in green. Wisteria vines hung like a glorious, living scarf above her wrap-around porch, and large bay windows projected out on either side of her. Detailed ironwork crowned the roofline, adorning her with dignity. I was only five when my parents bought her, and I would turn twelve before I had to leave her refined embrace. From this exquisite lady, my love of old, charming houses arose and never left.

Inside the entry hall was a large archway that opened to the front parlor. Heavy brocade drapes, known as portieres, were drawn back on either side of the arch, revealing a formal room used for entertaining only. Looking in, one could see weighty track doors on the side wall, separating the parlor from the rest of the downstairs: the living room, dining room and kitchen. A winding walnut banister framed the staircase, leading to three large bedrooms and a bath.

At the top of the stairs was my room, shared now, of course, with my little sister, Rhea. Down the hall and to the left, was the largest room, occupied by my parents and a black, handmade trunk that sat at the end of the bed. Across from their room was my grandfather's sunny corner space: his study and his bedroom.

I remember Goo Goo most vividly for one single, satisfying reason: the lowly lemon drop. He kept them in a round black tin with a gold dragon on it. My sister and I would frequently go into his room and stand there until he asked, "Would you girls like a lemon drop?" It was a rhetorical question. "Help yourselves," he would say, and we would pull the tin out of the top drawer of his washstand, take our allotted drop and recite our thanks. Then we would close the door behind us and sit at the top of the winding staircase, seeing which of us could make the sour treat last the longest.

But no description of this house and its memories could compare with this: it was here that the angels began to reveal themselves. In the midst of a growing darkness, they began to shine. And for that reason, 9 Davis Street is not just the true home of my childhood, but the dwelling place of my earliest gratitude.

Our home, though privately owned, functioned as the parsonage of the church—not only because my grandfather lived in it, but because my mother had continued in her role as the surrogate minister's wife. And so the house operated entirely around one thing: the life of the church. There was a constant stream of phone calls, people dropping by, and visits from church dignitaries—all of which gave the impression that we were at the hub of something highly important. Yet, by contrast, the residing atmosphere of the house was dismal, teeming with one vehement "No" after another. Everything was measured as "bad" or "wrong" without any mention of what could possibly be good or beautiful. Judgment lived in every corner, waiting to pounce. Happiness itself seemed to be a sin. I clearly remember one morning when a high official from our denomination held me on his lap after breakfast and told me a story, drawing stick figures to illustrate. I recall that passing gesture of kindness because it was foreign to me in my own home: to be seen, to be held, to be given special attention.

My strategy for dealing with the environment of my home was an old and trusty one: any opportunity to escape. Kindergarten, therefore, was a boon, affording me a few hours away from home five days a week. Plus, I had clearly entered another terrain, which thrilled me even more. My teacher wore a beige coat with a billowy fur collar. Her bright rouged cheeks had imprinted themselves on either side of the collar, making it appear that the collar too, was smiling. I knew she couldn't be a Christian all made up like that. Yet I pictured a day when I, too, would wear rouged cheeks and a matching fur collar.

It took me less than a week to figure out how I could make a good thing better. I informed my mother one morning that I didn't want her to meet me afterward—that I could get home by myself. Uncharacteristic of her protective ways, she agreed. Even more surprising is that she hadn't learned to mistrust the wily ways of her ever-wandering firstborn. I didn't come home from school that day, but instead, went directly to the house of a classmate. My mother's warning that evening must not have scored high enough on the intimidation scale, as I did it again the next day. But this time the punishment of a whipping and a supper of milk and bread in my room was enough to deter me.

I did, however, start inventing more subtle ways to break free of restriction. I experimented with rules that had been well supported by warnings of severe consequences. "If you eat pickles with milk, you'll get very sick," my father had told me repeatedly. One evening the linen-dressed table was set for company, and a cut-glass dish of pickles sat on one corner. Knowing that I would soon be drinking milk with my dinner, and given that my mother was distracted in the kitchen, I helped myself to a pickle. Not only didn't I get sick, but loved the taste of my own little secret—delicious defiance. This successful challenge of authority emboldened me, and soon I tried dropping my boots over the neighbor's fence on the way to school—despite my mother's insistence that if I didn't wear them, I would catch "my death of cold." I waited, but no cold descended, so I made a habit of it.

"Just remember, when I'm not there, God is watching you," my mother would tell me repeatedly with a scold in her voice. But she didn't trust Him with that responsibility too often. And clearly, neither did she trust me or she wouldn't have needed to make God the bully in her absence.

When church wasn't coming to our house, we were going to it. We went to church at least three times a week. Twice on the Sabbath: Sunday school and worship service in the morning, and back again for service that evening. And just in case you might lag in your faith before seven days were up, there was Wednesday night prayer meeting to see you through to the finish line. Long hours on an unforgiving pew were torment for me, designed as the services were for adult minds who worshipped an adult God. My spirit and body languished on the hard wood in a field of hard words. And I could no longer get by with the antics of my younger years, when I was excused because I was cute and too young to know better. Now there was nowhere to run. Perched on the third pew with my parents at my side, dressed in heavy, fussy clothes, my behavior was on display and under tight control.

Sunday afternoons, which might have been a reprieve between services, were not much relief. Because it was the Sabbath, my sister and I could only hold our dolls, but couldn't play with them unless we played church—the place from which we had just come and to which we would soon be returning. No other toys were allowed. Especially in the summer when both the boredom and the humidity were stifling, the hours passed like old tortoises in no particular hurry. The adults napped after the big noon meal, and insisted we do the same, yet that was nothing but another dread for me: staring at the ceiling until it was time to get dressed to go back to church.

The height of Christian celebration is Easter, but in our

house an exception was made. Christ had apparently risen from the dead, but even that good news was proclaimed more with vehemence than joy—and came with its own restrictions. There were no eggs to be dyed and hunted, no baskets, or candy. Nor could we wear anything that might be considered "new." All this constituted worldliness in my mother's mind, and thus desecrated the meaning of this holy day.

One Easter, our church offered a prize to the person or family that brought the most visitors to Sunday School. When it was announced that my sister and I had won, the superintendent raised a large basket in our direction. My mother gave my Dad "the look." He stood and said, "They can't have it." We were crushed and deeply confused. *Why was a gift offered by the church itself forbidden to us?* This was the bizarre reality that was my mother's: standards that exceeded even those of the church to which she was as devoted as a nun.

I don't recall if that's the year one of the neighbors took matters into her own hands, but I like to think so. She saw me in the yard and called me over to her back door. "Do you have a chocolate Easter bunny, Adelaide?" she asked. I shook my head. And with that, she broke off the head off of a large, solid chocolate rabbit, and handed it to me. I found a place behind a tree and ate the whole thing. I didn't tell anyone and remarkably, didn't feel guilty.

The Easter basket incident is an incisive commentary on the dynamics of our household, and reveals what was clear, I'm sure, to everyone: sometimes my father, too, was my mother's obedient child. Public denial of a gift that my sister and I had earned would not have been the inclination of this tender, sensitive man.

Throughout my childhood, my father raised many kinds of small animals, but canaries were his specialty. Cages of these sun-yellow carolers brightened the corners of our downstairs rooms, some of them babies he had bred himself. In addition, there was always an enormous aquarium of colorful, fanciful fish in the kitchen. My father's love of nature extended to plants and flowers as well—anything that needed tending seemed to appeal to him. I wasn't invited into my father's private world. He never asked me to help him feed the canaries or plant the red salvias that he adored. Those realms were his own, places of refuge perhaps too fragile to be shared.

But this man, who nurtured so many small, dependent beings, could not bring himself to be an advocate for Rhea and me in the face of my mother's radical ideas and harsh discipline. Only once did I see him even try. One summer vacation in Vermont, we were staying in a cottage over Sunday. My mother had prepared sandwiches for us to eat after church. But because she had prepared them on Saturday night, so as not to break the Sabbath, the bread had turned moldy in the high humidity by lunch time. There was nothing else to eat. My Dad entreated her to let him go buy two apples for my sister and me. She refused. It was a sin to buy anything on Sunday. Had he taken action anyway, she would have punished him by pouting for days. We spent the long afternoon and evening hot and hungry. If he could not prevail against her when the hunger of her children was the issue, why would he even attempt lesser matters?

Motherless at three months old, Richard Wallace Blauvelt was raised by his cruel grandmother of fairytale proportions. He fled at the age of fifteen, selling cottage cheese from door-to-door, and living sporadically with a variety of family members. No wonder then that he was drawn to, and at the same time, overwhelmed by the presence of a strong, angry woman. And so in place of what he could not do, he offered what he could: his pursuit of hobbies, which gave our home some beauty and interest (in spite of my mother's disapproval), his personal kindness to us, and his openness to new ideas. But above all, he gave his presence. For while he never verbally opposed my mother, neither do I recall her ever beating us in his presence. That much power he did have.

As a distributor for Ehler's Coffee House of New York, my Dad's work took him into surrounding towns as well as into the city itself. In his drives across the countryside, he sometimes spotted boarded-up churches—a sight that deeply disturbed him. More than once, he'd take on the mission of rallying the community to clean, paint, and open the church for services, which he would lead himself as a self-ordained lay minister. He even bought an old hearse from the funeral parlor and used it to ferry people from our church out to the Sunday afternoon services.

Occasionally, I would go along with him too. I remember watching my deeply quiet father show another side: busily lighting the pot-bellied stove, putting hymnals on the seats, and welcoming his adopted parishioners into the fold of their own community.

Wednesday night prayer meetings were not as exciting. Here I was subjected to the same sincere recitations of testimonies delivered by the same folks who had held forth on the same pews for as long as I could remember.

"God has promised that he chastens those He loves," Mrs. Tomlin would say, her voice breaking with emotion. "So He must love me a lot because I've been going through some terrible things lately, and need all of your prayers to see me through."

Mrs. LaDue always had just the same request. "I just pray that somehow I can do some little thing for someone." (One time when my mother was ill, Mrs. LaDue called the house to ask if she liked apple pie. My father crossed town to pick it up and returned with a small single piece of pie. Her prayer had been answered—she had done some *little* thing for someone. But her testimony never changed.)

Dear Mr. Laird, a gentle soul in person, came to life each week, proclaiming, "He's the King! He's the King! It's a wonder we can be so quiet. He's the King!" Others were not so mercifully short.

On a good night, I fell asleep in the pew and awakened gratefully to the final strains of the closing hymn. But one evening, possibly out of desperation, I broke the monotony for all. When my mother stood to give her usual testimony, I stacked several hymnals on the pew behind her as she spoke. "I give God the glory for seeing fit to save a sinner like me, and purpose to serve Him with all my might until the end of my days." As usual, she *sat* with all of her might as well—but this time, landed a foot above the rest of the congregation.

My biggest act of insurgence, however, was the foiled candy incident. The price of milk was suddenly reduced at school one week, and so I found myself with the irresistible opportunity to conduct business at the candy store on the way home. I had several pennies to spend and in those days, that's all it took to buy a bag of candy. I was enjoying my brown paper binge when I saw my mother coming to meet me a long way off. I became generous in a hurry, giving away as much candy as I could to the kids along my route, all the while stuffing my own face in between the hand-outs. Miraculously, I didn't get caught. The taste of daring, however fleeting, was as sweet as the candy itself.

My small victories were not the only insulation against a life of stricture and captivity. There were gifts that arrived all by themselves, some looking ordinary to the untrained eye, but to me, all were extraordinary. One of those gifts was Betty and Helen. These two ladies from our congregation—one widowed and one single—

would occasionally invite me for Sunday lunch at their house. It was like being rescued from the clutches of the great, slumbering beast called Sunday Afternoon. The two of them called me "Sarah" after Sarah Berhardt, the French actress turned-movie-star, who had frizzy red hair and a fiery personality. My mother would have been mortified by such a worldly comparison, as theatre and movies were strictly forbidden in our religion. Betty and

Helen, however, didn't seem at the affect of such rules within their own walls. I loved their nickname, for without understanding all its implications, I knew that they were associating me with someone exciting, beautiful, and glamorous. As their little Sarah, I dined on delicious foods, a welcome contrast to my mother's culinary tragedies. (Time and time again, my father would bring home a luscious steak with a gleam in his eye. And just as often was crestfallen when it was served. The cow had been sacrificed not once, but twice.) Beyond the tasty meals, I relished the ease of being with these two. By simply being myself, I seemed to brighten their day. The long, dreaded afternoon magically melted away on this side of the universe.

The people who contributed most to my young life in those years were not from our church—or any church. They were our next door neighbors, Mr. and Mrs. Starkey. This middle-aged couple had no children of their own, but surely must have wanted them, for their love toward Rhea and me overflowed the banks of our lives. Perhaps two little red-headed girls were an answer to their seemingly unanswered prayers for children. And there is no doubt that they were an answer to our unspoken longing for affection. Another world was now just one door away, and that door was always open.

Since the Starkeys were not believers, it remains a mystery that my mother let us spend time with them, though I don't know that anything could have kept us away. Rhea and I showed them every new thing we got. Even our plain cotton underwear had to have their approval. Mr. Starkey used to tease us about our red hair, and thus we gave him the nickname, "Bricky" –something we would never have dared to do with any other adult. In contrast to my mother's angry rigidity and my father's withdrawal into his own world, the Starkeys were a safe haven: the sheltering tree of our childhood.

Every summer, Mr. Starkey's brother and his wife came to visit. Since Rhea's birthday was in mid-July, the four of them always threw a big party for both of us. There were lots of cheerfully-wrapped gifts, a big birthday cake, and the thrill of high festivity. Since our parents treated our birthdays like any other day of the year, that thrill was electric. My mother evidently didn't want to be bothered, or perhaps thought such self-focus only created vanity in a child. What must she have thought when we came home from the Starkeys with beautiful gifts and leftover cake, faces glowing like jewels? In her enigmatic way, there were no protests, and nothing was taken away—which given her threat of "the outside world," was the best birthday gift she could have given us.

When I was seven my father's uncle bequeathed an outlandish gift to him: an island treasure. He inherited a cottage off the coast of Maine. Basket Island was just big enough for seven houses and ours was on one end facing the sea. The two-room cottage had a fireplace and a ceiling that climbed all the way to the roof. Its two picture windows gave us a grand view of the ocean, and seemed to open up the vastness of the world from our living room. The houses shared a common lawn and a common well of fresh water that sat in the middle of the island. Reminiscent of our life in Groveville Park, there was no electricity or plumbing. But there was the sea! And for me, the escape from the confinement of Beacon. The travel alone was an elixir for my gypsy's sad heart.

For a few memorable summers, this was our vacation spot, which meant a two-day journey by car, meals in little towns along the way, and an overnight stay in a tourist home. Oh the wonder of handmade quilts, enormous breakfasts, and the splashing life of fresh flowers on the thick, linen tablecloth! My heart rejoiced in every unfamiliar pleasure. From the tourist home, we continued on the two-lane roads all the way to the little town of Biddeford Pool, each time impatient to catch that first glimpse of our cottage. "There it is! There it is!" we'd exclaim, as if we hadn't been certain that our fantasy was really true.

Because the island was a mile from the mainland, my father always studied the tide tables carefully in preparation for our arrival. Every twenty-four hours there was a window of time when we could transport ourselves and our supplies across the sand bar. Loading everything onto a horse-drawn flatbed that my father had hired, we crossed from shore to shore. Rhea and I sat side-by-side, swinging our legs over the wooden edge while the tide bowed low for our grand entry.

Those magical two weeks out of the year were not unblemished by my mother's irrational mandates: wearing long, cotton stockings, leaving the island each Sunday for a lengthy and tiring trip to the closest camp meeting, and refusing the beach pajamas that my aunt Harriet brought us when she came to visit. The full-legged jump-suits were after all still "pants," my mother pointed out. But for once, even the disappointment of those things was eclipsed by the great light of our life on the sea. We dug for clams. We fished for flounder from my father's dory. We climbed over rocks, bathed in the ocean, played on the beach, and built sand houses everywhere.

Every other day, when the tide was out, Rhea and I walked across the sand bar to pick up the mail and buy milk. An ice cream cone was included in the ritual. Other days, my father took us in his dory to Biddeford Pool for supplies, and sometimes to another island, where we picked up salted driftwood that burned bright colors in our fireplace. But no day on the island was more memorable than the one when we spotted our dear Starkeys coming across the sand, their arms loaded with goodies and toys. They had driven all that way just to spend the day with us.

For those two weeks each year, I was as free as I had ever been. My wanderer was on the loose. Free to roam, to leap and jump, to twirl in the sparkling beauty of the sea, and to sleep at night with the howl of the wind reminding me that it would all be there in the morning. In this wondrous place, I could go from world to world: the rocks, the sand, the sky, the ocean, the dory, the mainland—and back again.

The island added a dimension to my life that far exceeded its calendar time. The experience, like the waves themselves, carried me out into a larger sense of life—something more real than the little hill town of Beacon and the dreary cycle of our church. I always left with the island thrumming inside me like a melody of my own, magically remembered after a long drought of forgetfulness. But of course, it was not merely the island that sang inside me, but the angels themselves. Here, without my realizing it, they had forever opened my child heart to God through the power of His creation.

In contrast to the life-affirming joys of Basket Island, our time at Davis Street brought our family both close to death's door as well ushering us across its threshold. One of those experiences on the brink between worlds was mine. I was eight years old when scarlet fever and the measles simultaneously conspired to overtake my body. The house was quarantined and for the first time, the portieres were pulled across the archway to create my sick room. Only my mother and the doctor who came every day were allowed to enter. One of my mother's true abilities was physical caretaking. Nothing went undone with regard to my care, and it is certain that I owe my survival to her diligence. Even then, however, there was no physical tenderness. No kiss to the forehead. No touch on my arm or words of sympathy. Yet even at that young age, and in my compromised condition, I could feel her deep concern for my well-being—and behind that, her terrible fear of loss.

The comings and goings from that room, all intent upon my recovery, were the background for another memory, one that stood out brilliantly against the backdrop of deep illness. Out of the haze, I saw my Dad and sister appear in the porch window, eagerly holding up a big fruit basket that had been sent over from the church. Their faces were wide with smiles and hope. If they had known what that moment did for my spirit—not the basket, but their presence—they would have come every day.

I wasn't the only person in the household whose life was endangered in those days. My grandfather had been diagnosed with stomach cancer some months before, and while he had given up his ministry, he was still able to walk up and down the stairs. And so once I began to recuperate, a lemon drop would come sailing from between the draperies and land on my bed.

When the day of my release came, my mother washed all the toys, furniture, and curtains in Lysol, freeing the house of contagion. My family of teddy bears didn't fare as well. They had to be burned—the cost of my re-entry into life. The new preacher's son relieved us of the Quarantine sign on our front door, attached it to his bicycle and wheeled off with the evidence of my happy fate.

I was indeed alive, but something had changed. In the months following that crucial event, I began to respond to "the things of the world" in a new way: with fear. One day, visiting in Spring Valley, I went with my aunt Harriet to her friend's house. They put music on and playfully danced around the living room. I reacted with panic, running from the room and out into the hall where I stood feeling sick to my stomach. I was frantic to escape the influence of such evil. Back home in Beacon, I was now old enough to walk through our little town by myself, and began to habitually cross to the other side of the street when I approached the movie theatre—afraid that passing directly by its doors might taint me.

As that year progressed, my grandfather grew weaker, no longer able to leave his room. Yet even in the latter stages of the illness that would take him, he would ask to be helped to the dictionary to look up a word; and my mother, so long his companion in life and in work, would escort him there. But one sad day, the parlor was transformed again—this time into a place of mourning, with my grandfather lying in an open casket. People milled about, speaking softly in the twilight mood of death. My Goo Goo, who had quietly graced every house I'd lived in for the nine years of my life, was gone.

The following Christmas, it was my sister who was gravely ill. Christmas was the one holiday, for some incomprehensible reason, that my mother celebrated with generosity. Evidently a tree, presents, and special treats did not constitute sacrilege in her inscrutable book of rules. Each year, she and my father would trim the tree and transform the whole living room after we went to bed on Christmas Eve. The one truly magical moment in my parents' home each year was coming down the stairs on Christmas morning to a shimmering world of gifts and lights.

But on this particular Christmas, the festivities were minimal. I had been allowed to open a few gifts, one of which was roller skates from my aunt Hilda. Upstairs my parents and the doctor kept watch over a child they feared would not live 'til morning. Downstairs, I skated back and forth for hours in front of the Christmas tree. Unaware of the severity of my family's crisis, I rolled along on skates and a free-floating sense of happiness. I liked this feeling of no one watching, no one correcting, and no one interrupting. Without realizing it, a great gift had come unwrapped inside me: I enjoyed being alone.

My sister did recover, but within weeks an announcement came that could have been the most devastating blow this side of death. The Starkeys were moving! But the rest of the story came swiftly, relieving our anguish: they were building a new house right across the street from ours! We watched it go up with eager eyes, imagining it as our own. And once it was finished, it held new Starkey magic: a wide, railed porch to sit on in the afternoon and a radio to gather around by evening. Every night at seven o'clock Rhea and I joined our neighbors in their living room to listen to Amos and Andy. My mother wouldn't allow a radio in our home, but for some reason, she let us listen to it at the Starkeys' house. Perhaps her ongoing permissiveness with them had to do with taking pity on the "childless," or perhaps it had to do with wanting us out of her hair. Or maybe it had to do with keeping the supply of gently used coats coming from Mrs. Starkey—my mother's best resource for making us new coats each year. Whatever the reason, her leniency with the Starkeys sweetened my life in ways she herself was not capable of. It sweetened the tapioca pudding served over orange slices at their new dining room table; sweetened the pancakes served in their bright, cheerful kitchen; sweetened the thrill of racing Rhea around the block for money. Bricky gave the winner a dime. Second place garnered two nickels. Two of my angels had taken form now and lived across the street . The third one must have kept company with my mother. What else could explain this mystery? She allowed me be the Starkeys' beloved child.

The next summer, when the Starkeys' relatives came to town, another fabulous party was thrown in our honor. There were several gifts, but among them was one that nearly stopped my heart: a little silver ring of double hearts. As always, Rhea got an identical one. A piece of real jewelry! All such adornment was forbidden in our church as it represented being "of the world." Many married women did not even wear wedding rings. I knew this, and yet when I opened that little box, all I felt was ecstasy. I had reacted to the theatre and to my aunt's dancing out of conditioning, but the ring evoked my own response: rejoicing. I must have been too far over the moon to help myself because I went home and showed my mother. She informed me, of course, that I could not wear it and with that, I crashed-landed from my glorious sky.

But neither did she take it away.

I could have hidden it, kept it safe lest she change her mind. But instead, in keeping with my fiery spirit, I did just the opposite. I not only wore it, but wore it to camp meeting—the citadel of radical religious fervor. I sat on the wooden bench, my one bare hand carefully concealing the ring on the other. Risky business. As always, the sermon was harsh and condemning, but this time, I had something to feel convicted of. And so when the altar call came, with its compelling plea to repent of any sin toward God, my ten-year-old heart pounded with fear and guilt. I went forward to ask forgiveness. At the altar, I handed the shiny pair of hearts to my mother, who in turn, handed them off to the evangelist while I sobbed. While waiting for everyone else to complete their penance, I looked up to see the evangelist smirking as he showed it to another preacher. Despite my age and my mother's protestations to the contrary, I knew what I was seeing: the mockery of my treasure.

In a world where even the most ordinary thing was forbidden, I felt like a misfit every day. Even clear nail polish brought the punishment of washing the dishes daily until it wore off. Add to that the unpopular distinction of flaming red hair. And so, when Bricky teased me about taking me to his hat factory and dying my hair black, I jumped at the offer. Thinking he would remedy the situation he'd haplessly created, he said, "Tell you what, Adelaide. Be at my back door at six o'clock in the morning, and I'll take you to work with me." He was dumbfounded when I was there at dawn, ready to go have my hair dyed black. He sent me back home hoping, I'm sure, that my parents had not yet awakened to my absence, and in turn, would not hear my tale of a promised dye job at the hat factory.

That spring the circus was in town, and the Great Opening Parade was scheduled to come down Main Street en route to the big tent on the edge of town. Animals in cages! Monkeys on leashes! Jugglers and clowns! My mother had said we couldn't go down the hill to watch the parade because the circus was sinful. So I stationed my little sister at the top of the street to scout for her, and tumbled madly down the hill to see what I could see. Red hair flying, I was propelled as if by a last gust of the old impulse to be free.

As I approached twelve, it began to dawn on me that my mother's world was also mine. Yes, there were marvelous forays outside the boundaries, but always, there was the coming back—the return to that which was as narrow as it was inevitable. Nothing outside truly seemed within my reach. And so, at some indefinable level, I began to look for myself in the world I had. Instead of being an outsider in the world I loved, I could be an insider in one I knew. The answer came to me without effort and with great, relieving passion: I would learn to play the piano! I had watched beautifully dressed pastors' wives at camp meeting sweep the keys with style and vibrancy, one with the music. I would be like them! It would be my big place in this little world.

My mother agreed to pay for lessons, but those only lasted about six weeks. My teacher, Mrs. Nordeen, was always finishing up some household task when I arrived at her home. She would then go upstairs to change her clothes while I waited, legs swinging, on the piano bench. Well into the allotted time, she would appear at the bottom of the stairs arrayed in her finery, ready to give me the briefest of lessons. My mother was incensed by such irresponsibility and quickly ended the tutelage with no attempt to find a more suitable teacher. But this time I didn't protest my deprivation. I had already discovered what I needed to know: each key on the keyboard represents a musical note on the scale; the black keys going up are sharp, the black keys going down flat. From that, I was able to learn to read music on my own. My father was superintendent of the Sunday School, and so I prevailed upon him to let me play piano for the opening exercises. He was quite a musician himself—playing an old German violin as well as the piano. His lean, wiry frame seated on the piano bench, he would chord *Red River Valley* while accompanying himself on the harmonica which was held in place by a wire contraption strapped around his head. Perhaps recognizing the same musical inclination in me, he obliged my request.

"Choose a song, and practice it," he told me. "So when Mrs. Carey is unable to attend church, you'll be ready to fill in." I practiced and practiced. I waited and waited. Attendance might be low due to a flu epidemic or inclimate weather, but Mrs. Carey was always promptly in her place on the piano bench. At long last, she told my father that she wouldn't be at church the next week. Gleefully, I made my debut the following Sunday with "I Gave My Life for Thee" in the key of C, page 32. It was a somber, lumbering song, unsuited to the atmosphere of Sunday School, but had been carefully chosen for its absence of sharps or flats. It was my humble beginning from which other opportunities to play would come, each one offering me the scarce and blessed balm of feeling part of my own realm. In the midst of that which had brought me so much unhappiness, a great love had begun to flower.

The Davis Street years posed a great paradox. At the end of them, I had seemingly surrendered to the forces at hand, and accepted my lot in life. But underneath, a greater story reigned: a larger force had penetrated that life, inexplicably altering its course. Through Betty and Helen, the Starkeys, and the discovery of solitude; through the healing of my body, and the paradise of Basket Island; through the remarkable ease of playing the piano—the angels were weaving a thread. It was the thread that would ultimately dispel the darkness I had mistaken for my life.

HOUSE FIVE

Return to Washington Avenue, Beacon, New York

The depression of the thirties was a Grim Reaper. In its grip, we had to sacrifice our cottage in Maine, as my father could no longer afford the annual fifty dollar tax—or the outlay of money it cost to finance our island vacations. My father had lost his job, and though he found a new one almost immediately, he felt our lifestyle could not be maintained in the sinking economy. Against my mother's wishes, he sold the house on 9 Davis Street as well, a painful sacrifice for her. Her father had made it possible to acquire the home by providing most of the down payment. Now she would have neither him nor this tangible link to him. But she had no say in the matter. She prevailed over my father when it came to my sister and me; but in financial matters, he made unmitigating decisions. He had decided to sell the house and return to the rental house on Washington Avenue, and that was that.

I don't recall feeling deprived or upset myself, but I was aware of my mother's pervasive unhappiness—a great, dark blanket that blocked the little light we had inside our home. Of course, greater than the loss of the house for me was moving away from the Starkeys. Though we pledged to keep in touch, I knew it would never be the same.

And so it was that just before I turned thirteen, I returned to the site of the angels' visitation. The room was now my father's office, which meant I walked past it many times a day, but rarely went inside. In the face of accepting my fate in this small world into which I was born, the memory of that night, while still bright after ten years, didn't seem to make a difference anymore. I had given up on being part of another world. But perhaps the move back into this house was the angels' way of reminding me that they had not.

I made the transition without great angst because a greater passage was consuming my attention. That fall, I entered Beacon High School as a seventh grader. This was my greatest venture so far outside the world of the church, mingling with others of different faiths and socio-economic systems. It was not what I had hoped for. As soon as other kids found out where I went to church, I became the target of "holy roller" teasing. This was actually a term that referred to the Pentecostal church, where there was supposedly a good deal of shouting, running of the aisles, and presumably, some literal rolling down them. Our church was more like "holy boulders"—staunch and rigid. I don't think anyone at the Pentecostal church was standing up at testimony time and saying, "It's a wonder we can be so quiet!" But of course, none of this mattered to my accusers, who had already pegged me as weird because of my red hair, my long cotton stockings, and the name of my church. It didn't help my reputation that I had to sit on the bench during P.E. because my mother feared I would learn to dance.

In my mind, all this continued to build the case that I didn't belong in the outer world. To say the least. I was spared, however, from the great stigma of being a loner. A girl named Gloria lived just a few houses down from us on Washington Avenue, and seemed happy to be my friend. We made the long walk back and forth to school together, and for those hours, Gloria was my willing companion between two difficult worlds.

At church, I continued to embrace the piano as my means of belonging. I practiced continually at home, and began developing my ability to play by ear, discovering that I could sometimes pick out the notes of a song just from hearing it played at church. And I was always at the ready for any mishap that might befall Mrs. Carey. In the meantime, I was allowed to play for the youth services on Sunday evening before church. My burgeoning abilities began to amuse my father, and he invented a game for the two of us to play. "See if you can pick this up," he would say, before launching into song. Within a few phrases, I would join him, able to hear the key and allow the melody to come through my fingers in tune with my father. "Where did you learn to do *that*?" he would say with delight.

Soon he started inviting me to sit with him on Saturday nights and listen to The Grand Ole Opry. It wasn't music that I loved, but my Dad did, and sharing it with him was all that mattered. My mother didn't approve of this music, and contrived a way to interrupt our time together by calling out from the top of the stairs, "Richard, you are breaking the Sabbath on Saturday night!" He would ignore her until she commanded me to bed, and then shuttled me on my way.

Most things in our household remained as they had always been, with my mother commandeering our lives and my father excusing himself to take up residence in his own world. But some things increased in their severity—particularly my mother's abuse of my little sister. For some reason she picked on Rhea, a shy, compliant child who always followed my mother's rules with much less protest than I did. She found reason to punish her almost every day, her large body bent over my sister's frail one, thrashing her mercilessly. On the day that I couldn't take the pain of my sister's undeserved punishment one more time, I lashed out—beating my mother with my fist. Of course, she immediately turned her attention to me, which was better than watching my sister suffer, but proved to be a one-time solution. I had my music, and through it, a bit of my father, but Rhea had nothing. Except me.

By the time I was fourteen, I had already passed (and was in danger of going irretrievably beyond) "the age of accountability"—a term denoting the age at which a child is old enough to know good from evil, and must therefore make a conscious choice on behalf of her soul. In our denomination, this meant going to the altar as a public act of a private decision to be saved; that is, to give your life to Christ and be forgiven of your sins. I had heard testimonies from many an old-timer declaring, "I remember the time. I remember the place," while waving a Bible in which the date of his or her conversion was recorded. Our doctrine, like some others, also called for a second experience, known as "sanctification." This was an "eradication of the root of sin" and was evidence of "Christian Perfection" after which the recipient never sinned again.

I had watched for years as people went to the altar, crying and agonizing, while others gathered around to help "pray them through." They would testify afterward, often visibly transformed, sometimes radiant, but many would return again and again, caught in a fresh storm of fire and brimstone.

Not only was all of this confusing, but deep inside a thought kept coming to me that I wouldn't have dared breath to a soul: *something is wrong with this.* I knew these folks. They were sincere and committed to service. They loved God. Why were they so tormented about their relationship with Him? Why didn't their earnest seeking after Him seem to work as promised? Alongside this heretical line of inquiry was a mounting pressure: it was my turn. I, too, was expected to walk the aisle, profess a deep inner transformation, and record the event in my Bible.

I did it cold. My own relief was my only motivation: to get it over with so that my mother would cease her looks, her hints, her sanctimonious quoting of scripture. I went through the motions but felt nothing while everyone else rejoiced. My mother was exultant, exclaiming dramatically to the minister's wife, "It's done! The great transaction's done!" *What transaction?* I couldn't think of any sin except putting my boots over the fence or running down the hill to see the circus. For in those and other matters, I had deceived my mother. But she was carrying on as if I'd been delivered from the clutches of the devil, when in fact I didn't feel guilty for anything. Her words, resounding through the church felt false to me. As false as my salvation.

A few weeks later, I made a second obligatory trip to the altar to procure sanctification. My mother was right down there with me. "I'm willing to go to China, Lord," she kept repeating in her high-pitched, crying voice, as if to plant the words in my mouth. I didn't respond. I wanted to travel, yes. And I would gladly have gone to China to get away from her, but not in the way she intended. Not as a missionary. The thing I was at the altar to obtain didn't even make sense to me. Christian Perfection? What could that mean given that I lived with a punitive mother who also, supposedly, was sanctified and was therefore perfect? Just weeks before, my sister had requested a cake to celebrate her dog's birthday. My mother had set a little frosted cake before her, and encouraged her to take a bite. My sister did so, and immediately ran for the sink, retching, while my mother snorted with laughter. It was made of dog food.

Nonetheless, I duly recorded my sanctification in my Bible.

Though I didn't know it, I was in a dangerous place now. Having determined that this world was the only one I had—or would ever have—here I was, in conscious mistrust of its core. And on the other hand, it had been confirmed that the outside world, the one that I had been trying to escape into since I could walk, was not my home either. I was a misfit in both places. The only true home I had was inside the notes of music, inside the all-consuming world of white ivory keys and their black flat and sharp companions. Gloria, who had an amazing soprano voice, loved music too, and began to invite me to come to her house on Tuesday nights to listen to the Andre' Kostelantz' orchestra on the radio. Each week, I would sit with her, mesmerized by the unfamiliar strains of this rapturous music and wrapped in a private joy that no one could take from me. These melodies were not from the hymnal, which had been the whole of my musical reference; and yet, these grand and lilting sounds stirred me, opened me, and made me wish that every day was Tuesday.

I would carry the melodies within me all week, inspired to practice piano from a different place, with a new kind of imagination—wanting to feel moved, rather than just playing correctly. Without this newly budding passion, I might have caved in on myself and lost touch with anything that was beautiful or real. But instead, at this precarious crossroads, my decision to play the piano became something much more to me: a bridge to my own emotions. And in this, I had indeed been saved by the grace of God.

Across the next few years, I began to closely watch the pianists at camp meetings and district gatherings. I had been inspired by them as a child, but now I was their imagined understudy. Their exhilarating style—replete with dramatic key changes and thrilling runs up and down the octaves became my focus. My favorite was Mary Del Harding. She always had a handkerchief that matched her elegant outfit, and just before she started to play, she would get it out and place it at the end of the keyboard. There was something so thrilling about that gesture to me, the dramatic stroke of distinction. Mary Del had hands that looked like they were ready to play the piano at a moment's notice. Even when she was off the platform and talking with someone, her hands remained poised to play. What I saw in her was a style that reflected supreme confidence. Was it possible I could feel that kind of confidence? Exude that kind of charisma? After watching her, I would go home and hammer out the same songs, figuring out the chords and the finger work, experimenting with the runs. I had been emboldened, not just to play, but to play with finesse, with power and grace. Gradually, my own style began to emerge, moving through me like an underground river.

My growing confidence prompted me to embark on some new ventures. When an oratory contest was announced at school, I entered. The evening event drew students, parents and faculty—all gathered in the auditorium to hear twelve contestants deliver original oratories about the great historical figures of our country. My topic was George Washington, and at the end of the evening, I was awarded the medal for first place.

The real prize, however, was the chance to go on to the county competition and then, possibly to the state contest. For me, it was like a window that had appeared where there had been none, allowing me to look out on the vista of that larger world with fresh hope. But it was only a glimpse. My mother's only response to my victory was to immediately refuse my going any further in the competition. I can only surmise that she was threatened for the same reason I was hopeful: the possibility of my exposure to a place she didn't know anything about and couldn't control. No doubt it was the same reason she hadn't allowed me to join the Girl Scouts when I was younger. Always chalked up to "worldliness," I now began to see that such decisions were driven by *her fear* of the world—and specifically, her fear that she would lose me to it. My disappointment was more easily assuaged now because of my own resignation, and also because I had the medal to remind me what I'd known at three: I could entertain anywhere! My stint on the stage may have been brief, but I made my exit knowing that I could excel at public speaking.

When I was sixteen, there were only two young men in our church, and though a young man named Clarence was from a family my parents considered to be "low class," he interested me. The other one didn't. Clarence was good-looking and a few years older than me. He also possessed two other valuable attributes: a beautiful voice and a *car*.

At Clarence's prompting, I played hooky from school one day, imitating my mother's large, cumbersome handwriting on the written excuse. The impetus for this high-risk choice was worthy: to go to Poughkeepsie to see, of all things, a parade. Running away *out of town* for a day with *a boy* to see *a parade* and *lying about it* to my mother *and* the school truly qualified as sin. And yet because it was with "a boy from church," I was, in my own mind, exonerated.

Was it the mesmerizing lure of Clarence's beautiful voice or the irresistible feeling of being pursued that led to the next big risk? Something made me step outside my comfort zone, and violate a vow I'd made to myself as a seven-year-old. As much as I loved music, I didn't sing. As a child, I'd been given a solo in one of the children's programs, and under great duress had performed in a state of terror. As dreadful as it was, what followed was more so. After the program, old Mr. Elsner walked up to me, shook his finger and said, "You need singing lessons, young lady." My embarrassment turned to shame. Sitting in the car, waiting for my Dad to come, I told my mother what had happened. "Well, is he going to pay for those lessons?" she retorted. So distorted was my view of parental support, I felt like she had taken my side. Even so, I made a vow never to sing in public again.

But now, there was a big contest across the Hudson River in Newburgh. It was a try-out for the Ed Sullivan radio show. Clarence wanted us to enter as a duet, accompanied by my piano playing. But I had held so fast to my vow all these years that even when I was in the choir, I would barely move my lips, despite my mother's repeated admonishments to do so. But Clarence's faith in me, his great, splashing enthusiasm bolstered my confidence.

And of course, *he* would be singing with me. I said yes.

On the appointed day, we took the ferry across the Hudson River, and in a little studio, sang *I'd Rather Have Jesus.* My alto voice intertwined with Clarence's tenor like vines on a trellis. The winners would be determined by call-in votes from around the state and announced in a few days. We got a call just before it hit the paper. We had won! A big write-up followed, as did, predictably, my mother's refusal for me to go on. Surely I'd known that, regardless of the fact that we were singing a hymn, she would not allow me to go sixty miles away to New York City and perform on a secular radio show. Still, it was deeply disappointing—though more so for Clarence, who was not used to my mother's unreasonable ways. Yet like the oratory contest, I had still won something: my voice. I had gained it back from the perhaps well-intentioned, yet mean-spirited clutches of Mr. Elsner's opinion. The people of New York State begged to differ with him.

Running off seemed to be a theme with Clarence and me. To Poughkeepsie. To Newbergh. He and I came into church late one Sunday evening and sat in the back with his ill-esteemed parents. Before I knew it, my father was coming down the aisle with his gaze set upon me. He stopped at the pew's edge and motioned for me to come with him. I followed him out of the church where he informed me that he was taking me home. My mother would have put the ride to good use, delivering a masterful discourse on the shamefulness of my wanton ways, and how I had disgraced her by coming in late and sitting with the Bedels. My father employed his own brand of torture: thick silence.

Once home, I went directly to my room where I brooded until I heard a faint sound, a pebble on the window pane. Once, and then again. I opened the curtain to see Clarence standing below, extending the offer I'd been waiting for all my life. "Let's run away!" For one moment, the old desire welled up, as if cut loose from its proverbial clothesline. I nodded vigorously, afraid to raise my voice lest my Dad would hear. Since I couldn't leave through the house with my father in it, and since the ladder was too short to reach my window, Clarence suggested we wait until my Dad returned for my mother. Then our getaway! He hid out in the bushes watching for my father's departure. But we were foiled by my parents' own plans: someone brought her home from church. Truth was, I was relieved. I'd been losing interest in Clarence lately and as thrilling as a runaway might be, I didn't want to do it with him.

As my high school years progressed, I grew more confident in my relationships. I acquired a number of friends, despite the fact that I couldn't go to dances or even attend plays performed during school hours. I seemed to have transcended the label of being weird; yet inwardly, I still felt inferior to other people and distinctly different from them. I was uncharacteristically shy with anyone outside my close circle of friends. I did, however, take a job at the local dry cleaner's during my senior year, and enjoyed the perfunctory rituals and minimal socializing. One night, the "other" boy from our church, Jimmie Williams, came by right before closing time and offered to take me home. It was only five minutes until closing and the streets were deserted. "Go ahead and close up," he said. "No one's coming in at this hour." I didn't really like Jimmie, but he said he'd told my folks he'd bring me home, and so I closed the shop and went with him. His idea of "taking me home" turned out to be little more than an opportunity to "get fresh with me" in the vernacular of the day. When he headed toward Fishkill, a town about ten miles away, I threatened to tell my mother. For once her reputation served me well, as Jimmie took the first opportunity to turn around. The next day, however, the guilt about closing the shop early plagued me. I wrote a letter to my employer and told him what I'd done. In return for my honesty, I was fired. It may have worked for George Washington, but it backfired on me.

House Five

Mid-way through my senior year, a prolonged, silent conflict was apparent in our home, signaled by my mother's trademark pouting and my father's increased withdrawal. This occurred at intervals throughout our childhood and we rarely knew what the issue was. But in this case, I would find out years later that the struggle had to do with me. Through a relative I found out that my mother was insistent that I should go to our church college in Massachusetts, but my father was set against it, believing it was both foolish to send a girl to college and was beyond our means. My mother's jurisdiction over "the children" and my father's fiscal sovereignty, were at odds. At the time, I simply knew of my mother's intentions and for me, it was a grand prospect. College would afford me an environment where I would still feel at home, yet be offered release from the anxiety I'd been feeling about my future. Working at the local dime store and living with my parents was unthinkable. And by now, I'd exhausted all the male prospects at church.

I had long admired the college quartets that visited our church. And I'd taken note that these handsome, winsome young men were sometimes accompanied by a competent female pianist. Oh, the fantasies! I could be one of those young pianists who traveled with four college men, perhaps even dating one of them. It was the most romantic thing I could imagine, and it actually seemed within my reach. This was worthy of prayer.

My mother prevailed. Unwilling to back down from her position this time, she found a way to quell my father's monetary protests. She was already working, doing alterations for Schoonmakers, the department store downtown, but her earnings weren't enough to finance her objective. So she made arrangements (who knows if she asked my father) to take in a little girl to board. And as Rhea was not attending school due to poor health, she assigned her with the task of caring for the child. The six dollars a week that my sister earned was exactly the cost of my room and board.

And so, in the fall of 1939, I left home in search of the one thing that I believed could permanently free me from Beacon, from my mother, and from my pain: a dashing young man.

This time, the angels had worked a miracle almost too good to believe. And they had done it through the one person who seemed to stand in the way of hope for another life. But then, that's what angels do.

HOUSE SIX

College, Boston, Massachusetts

By the time I reached college that fall, I had raised my sights. And they were not scholastic. Dating a young man in a collegiate quartet had morphed into a higher goal: marrying a minister. Given my feelings toward the church, this might seem to be the worst, if not the most absurd, of all choices. Why not aim for someone studying business, or science, or literature--someone with great entrepreneurial or professorial intent? *Anything* other than a man bound for the ministry and looking for a piano-playing wife who by taking marriage vows would be taking another vow: to commit her heart and soul to the church. But as always, there was a force beneath the surface of things that ran by its own logic, and it was this: minister's wives were recognized; they had a built-in audience; they had guaranteed importance. And more than anything, they were candidates for being lavishly loved.

I had seen this for myself. Always there were certain pastors' wives around whom people flocked, and about whom they spoke with warmth and admiration. These women literally seemed to sparkle with grace and appeal. I could still remember, as a very young child, watching Mrs. Cook who was sitting in the second right hand pew near the center aisle. Her beautiful silver hair was gathered into a bun at the nape of her neck, and an immaculate white linen handkerchief was crushed between her black kid gloves. I watched in awe as she looked up at her minister husband with rapt attention, a living statue of adoration. A handful of these women, a chosen few, were celebrities in their own world, and I knew in a place so deep I couldn't even name it, that I could be one of them. I would have admiration, appreciation, and applause. All the things I'd never had, except for the love light in the Starkeys' eyes, I would have for the rest of my life simply for being myself. This was a heaven I could believe in!

With this as my agenda, I only had one obstacle: the unappealing challenge of a college education. In my senior year of high school, my art teacher had stopped by my desk, studied my work, and said, "Adelaide, you should be going to New York City to study art." The classroom stood as still as a snapshot, but when it came to life again, I was reeling. *New York City? Art school?* The very fact that someone believed that I was capable of that was thrilling. But I never mentioned it to my parents. I knew the response it would elicit. Why have that moment scarred for life when I could cherish it unblemished for years? But, here, in this little liberal arts college, I wouldn't be studying *art*, unless that happened to be the name of a dashing young man headed for life in the pulpit. No, I was here fulfilling the freshman year requirements that I thought of as a distraction from my one and only goal.

From September to Christmas break, I only dated one man: Tondra Border. He was a nice enough fellow, who went to the effort to buy me a lovely gift set of Bond Street Lavender for Christmas. The powder, soap, and perfume were housed in a sturdy box of subtle geometric design, and detailed with ribbons that held the lid up when it was open. The box not only outlasted the trio of products and their enticing scent, but the relationship itself. Just before leaving to go back to school after the holiday, I got a letter from Tondra, breaking up with me. I wasn't that disappointed. After all, he didn't meet my number one criteria: a ministerial student he was not.

I didn't date the rest of the year, and that was disappointing. With my talent as a pianist, I had imagined having the avid interest of many a ministerial student. Instead I spent my time in the company of my roommate Eleanor, a sweet, quiet girl who reminded me of the roommate I'd grown up with. Our friends Ann and Doris lived across the hall. The three of them became my resident audience and I their prime source of entertainment. They howled at my funny faces, especially my imitation of a monkey. Sometimes I would knock on Ann and Doris' door and they would open it to a "drunk" neighbor, slurring my words as I staggered into their room. Since drinking was strictly forbidden in our way of life and I had never personally encountered an inebriated person, I have no idea what possessed me—other than a need to make them laugh. They loved my antics, but not as much as I loved the freedom to do it.

The man I really wanted to date was Doris' brother, Ken who was tall, slim, and handsome. Doris and I sang in a trio with another girl, and Ken happily ferried us to various churches in the area to sing. I had such a crush on him, and kept hoping that regular exposure would elicit a mutual interest, but it never did.

And so I returned home for the summer devoid of prospects, but packing plenty of anxiety. My plan had failed and the portent of getting stuck in Beacon loomed large. I took a job in the National Biscuit Company for the summer, which didn't make anything as appealing as biscuits. Just boxes and labels. I assembled and stacked all summer, giving me long days to solidify my goal. My mother had made it clear on a number of occasions that without a man, I would be expected to live at home. After all, she reminded me, *she* didn't desert *her* parents—even after she'd married. And neither was I happy about the prospect of three more years in college. Most women who got engaged either dropped out and took a job to put their fiancées through school, or in the best of scenarios, moved directly into their new lives as homemakers. Those were the ones I eyed with a longing that stopped just short of envy.

But at the beginning of my sophomore year, the fall of 1940, the script I'd written for myself came magically to life. A good-looking junior—a good-looking *ministerial student* junior—began to pursue me. He was blond, nearly six feet tall, and had an air of authority about him. Nicknamed "Woody," he was a popular, well-respected student. Yet the first two times he asked me out, I turned him down. He was a farm boy from rural New York and looked it. I might have continued to turn him down had he continued to pursue, but his roommate, Dick, intervened.

"The guy's smitten with you, Adelaide. He really feels bad that you're refusing him. Why won't you go out with him?"

I hesitated, but told the truth.

"He's a farm boy, and he still looks like he's got hayseed behind his ears."

Dick was equally honest. "You're making a mistake," he told me. "Arnold is an exceptional man. You should really give him a chance."

Affected by his friend's sincere admiration, I agreed I would accept if he asked again. "But not on a monthly per," I told him. "Just a Sunday afternoon date." Monthly per, the one chance to leave campus for several hours was too risky. I wouldn't be able to get away if things didn't go well.

And so, Arnold Woodcook, the boy from the farm, asked again and I said yes. There was little to do but walk the campus, and that raw New England day was bitter cold and dank. My nose ran continually and my bones ached with the cold. I was too miserable to tell if I liked him or not. We decided to seek refuge in the dorm parlor, which was predictably crowded with other half-frozen couples for whom the weather was no ally in the quest for romance. We had very little time together before a bell signaled the end of the dating hour. But it had been long enough. Not only had I thawed from the cold, but had warmed to the likes of Arnold Woodcook. It only embellished my attraction when, in parting, he said, "I've heard you should never leave a girl after the first date without asking her for another. How about going on the next monthly per with me?"

This time I didn't hesitate.

When our day off-campus arrived, I was impressed by Arnold's clearly thought-out plans. He had arranged for a ride on the tram, taking me into Boston for dinner. Afterward, instead of taking the tram back to campus for church, we walked to Tremont Temple Baptist Church for the evening service. We sat in the balcony of this ornate building, built in mid-1800's, and listened to a mixed quartet that had far more polish and sophistication than anything in our own church. Throughout the date, he was attentive and easily in charge. The farm boy image vanished—as did my interest in other men.

After that we dated regularly, and even though many of those dates were simply walks in the rain, we were alone under one umbrella, sharing a private world. It was on those walks that I learned who this man was that I had come so close to rejecting. When he was a small boy, someone had invited him to go to Sunday School. That decision had set the course of his life, as his parents followed him to church, converted to Christianity, and became pillars of the church. By the time he graduated from high school, he felt he had received a divine calling to the ministry. However, his parents were poor, trying to make ends meet for their five children in the midst of hard times, and thus it was understood that there was no money for college. Arnold had applied anyway, fully realizing that he may need to stay home and work for a year before that application could come to fruition. However, several weeks after classes had begun, he received a telegraph from the college, notifying him that he had received a scholarship and needed to come immediately. The family pooled every resource, including his sister's piggy bank, to pay for his bus fare from Owego, New York, to Boston. Once there, he not only met the challenge of catching up in his studies, but took on a job serving in the dining hall to pay for his room and board. This was an ambitious man, I realized, as well as a man of faith. His roommate had been right. I'd almost passed up a very good thing.

I soon became keenly aware of him throughout my days: in the dining hall where he served, part-way across campus, and from the platform where I sometimes played piano for chapel. Even in chapel, the boys sat on one side and the girls on the other. And so, we made the most of what we had: glances across the room, Sunday afternoons of endless walking, an occasional cup of coffee in the college coffee shack, and those all-too-sparse monthly pers. On a bench behind the chapel, in a rare moment of privacy, we kissed for the first time.

By the time spring arrived in New England, our relationship echoed its irresistible, bursting innocence. We were in love. On a bench in the local park, Arnold asked me to marry him. Passersby would have seen no more than a young college couple sitting on an ordinary park bench, enjoying the spring day. What they couldn't see was that in those moments, a deadly fear had been dispelled. A dream had come true. A future had opened wide. An invitation to my own life had just been extended to me. And I had said yes to all of it!

On the way back to the dorm, we stopped at the local diner and celebrated with the only thing we could afford: a shared hamburger. It didn't matter. The deepest hunger of my life had been fulfilled. Someone loved me enough to give me a place in the world. Now I knew who I was. The years of believing that someday things would be different had crossed the border into reality: I was going to be a minister's wife.

Several days later, love possessed us to go against our training in a grand salute to our hearts. On a controversial mission to Boston, we went to a jewelry shop where Arnold bought me a small diamond ring on credit for twenty-five dollars. With it on my finger, and with that hand in his, I could smile at the lost ring of my childhood. This time the double hearts were not of silver or gold, but were our own.

As the school year came to a close, we made some practical decisions. Now that I'd achieved my goal, I was happy to be released from my educational bondage and return home to work. And though this meant being apart for Arnold's senior year, it would allow me to pay off a small college debt, buy some furniture, and focus on our June wedding.

At last my mother's house would be the right place for me—as a backdrop for beginning my own life, as a dark foyer with a sunlit coach waiting just outside.

HOUSE SEVEN

Second Return to Washington Avenue, Beacon, New York

This time my return to Beacon was a triumphal entry. The dreariness of my mother's home and the burden of her omnipresence were of little consequence now. My real home was with Arnold. I felt confident and self-contained. I had always known that someday it would be different, and now it was. I had a fiancé and a future. I was, at last, an adult in my parents' home.

My mother was thrilled about my engagement to a minister and seemed to take easily to Arnold. Yet at church, I wasn't met with congratulations. The church folks weren't happy about my newly-acquired engagement ring. The diamond was far too small to knock anyone's eyes out—not that anyone asked to see it–but it had no trouble setting the tongues wagging. The preacher promptly spoke out against rings in his sermon, and most of my friends kept a disapproving distance. Even Betty and Helen did not congratulate me. My mother, however, joined neither the silent, censorious chorus nor the vocal one. So great was her joy that I was marrying an ambitious young minister, that she ignored without rancor this, my second ring.

But that was not the end of the large matter of the little ring. When I joined Arnold and his family that summer for their camp meeting, Arnold's father, whom I had just met, took us aside. "The two of you have made a foolish choice," he said. "I'm not sure what you were thinking, but for the sake of your ministry, you need to make it right. Return the ring, Arnold, and buy Adelaide a wristwatch. You'll regret it if you don't." We didn't bow. As I sat in the back of the tabernacle with Arnold, I remembered the time that I had surrendered my precious little ring to someone else's convictions. Once was enough. Guilt couldn't reach me now as I sat close to my courageous fiancé, but I did feel the pain of my future father-in-law's condemnation.

That fall I got a job in the hat factory, where I cut ribbons to specific lengths, and then stood at an ironing board, pressing them into half-moon shapes so they would contour nicely around the hats. Tedious work, but temporary—and allowing me the luxury of getting paid to daydream about my new life. With the help of the hat factory, I paid off my college debt, bought my going-away outfit, and made payments on a beautiful walnut bedroom set. The monotony of my weeks was occasionally broken by a visit from Arnold, who had to hitchhike the 200 miles from Boston to Beacon. He seemed to light up the whole house with his genial personality and exuberant passion for the ministry. My mother adored him. Never a disapproving word or trace of doubt crossed her lips where Arnold was concerned. In the bargain I had made with myself—to shape my life into something I wanted—I had finally done something to please her.

Weeks before the wedding, my chiffon dress hung in my room, keeping me company as I counted the days until the 20th of June—the day of my emancipation. I gazed at it long and frequently, studying its sweetheart neckline and neat column of tiny, covered buttons. The purchase had been a family event. The four of us had driven to Poughkeepsie, the very place to which I'd escaped with Clarence to see the parade just two years before. In a very small dress shop, with its limited selection of wedding dresses, the chiffon gown caught my eye. I'd always loved chiffon—so ephemeral, it looked as if it could have been spun in some other world and then transported to this one. I tried it on, and because it fit me and my father's budget perfectly, we purchased it and left. I would have loved more gaiety and ceremony, but I dearly loved my twenty-five dollar dress, and refused to keep it in the closet.

When Arnold's senior year finally came to an end, it was with a flourish. He'd been student body president that year, but now was crowned with two new titles: Who's Who in American Colleges and Universities, and because he'd already received a call to his first church, the title of Reverend Woodcook.

The day before the wedding, he and his family of seven descended on Beacon. Since the reception was to be held on the lawn of my parents' home, there was movement everywhere—the whirring pace of deliveries, setting up tables, kitchen mayhem, and getting ready for rehearsal. But there was one moment when the commotion slowed to a standstill. In an inexplicable error of judgment, I showed up at the wedding rehearsal with my hair bound up in curlers. It was the first time Arnold had seen me in this compromised state, and jested to his best man, Dick, that maybe he had made a mistake. I knew he was kidding. But I also knew I'd disappointed him, and his words stung like the bee you didn't see coming.

On our wedding day, the church my grandfather had built was filled to capacity. Our family friend, Mr. Eichorn, had built steps and a bridge up over the altar to the platform. There, an arch was adorned with a rose bush taken from his garden. Two enormous tubs of his garden flowers sat on either side of the steps. Another pair flanked the archway where we stood to exchange our vows.

I walked into the sanctuary on my father's arm in my fitted chiffon gown with an elbow-length veil cascading from a tiara of white chiffon rosebuds. This was a place I had dreaded coming to all my life, but now, it was transformed. The space that had been the ground for so much pain was now the bridge to my new life. Arnold stood at the end of the aisle, beaming at me as I walked toward him. It was more perfect than I could have imagined.

My friend, Gloria, who had introduced me to Andre Kostelantz all those years ago, came from Connecticut to sing, "I Love You Truly," and "Come, Come, I Love You Only." The new pastor, Rev. Wood, presided over the wedding, and when the vows had been completed, I received a simple, gold band— the wedding ring for which we had traded in my diamond. Besides the matter of money, we needed to be careful in our new role as minister and wife. Wedding rings were not typically worn by pastors' wives so even my gold band might cause a stir. After the final prayer, Gloria sang, "Savior, Like a Shepherd Lead Us." I was Mrs. Arnold Woodcook, ready to be led.

On this gorgeous summer day, card tables, borrowed from our worldly neighbors, were scattered across the shady lawn at Washington Avenue. In the year of waiting for my groom to come, I had started my first choir: junior high girls—all of whom were now gaily serving a lunch of homemade chicken salad made from Mrs. Ballard's chickens. The yard was alive with the sound of the girls' long, swishing voile dresses, and the best wishes of people I'd known all my life.

I left the house that evening in a going-away outfit chosen to reflect my new status: a two-piece navy blue dress with a small flowered print of kelly green, navy shoes and white gloves. A navy crocheted hat with a large kelly green bow on the side adorned my red hair.

We took the train ninety miles to Albany, New York where Arnold had made reservations at a hotel. By sacrificing throughout his senior year, he had saved enough to provide us with a short honeymoon. The first night alone with my new husband in a hotel should have been the pinnacle of my long-nurtured dream, but in fact, it was a low point. The hotel was dismal— old and worn; even the large lobby and its restaurant were oppressive. Once inside, there was no invitation to stay. After checking in, we were ushered to our room by way of narrow, dark halls which were adorned only with naked, dangling light bulbs. Still I had hope for the room, but it too disappointed. A bed and chair, a small dresser and lamp were the sum of its contents. In such a moment, even an avid runaway like me was not immune to a wave of melancholy. After unpacking we returned to the restaurant for dinner. We'd been too busy making the nuptial rounds at our reception to enjoy the food over which all our guests were raving. And so for my first meal as Mrs. Arnold Woodcook, I had a B.L.T.

Of course, the intimate dimension of married life that was now ours for the taking could have made the gloom of our surroundings inconsequential. But sex was not on the honeymoon agenda. In my premarital exam, my doctor had discovered a "pinhead" hymen—a condition that made it impossible for me to have intercourse without first having surgery. But because we couldn't afford the procedure, and didn't know when we would be able to, the consummation of our marriage was off-limits for the foreseeable future. We were two married virgins alone in a hotel room, allowed only to cuddle, kiss and sleep.

Thus my stunted and enigmatic sex education would have to wait to be tested. At the age of seven, I'd asked my mother, "Where do babies came from?" She'd hesitated, obviously unprepared for this moment and embarrassed to be part of it. Finally she'd managed, "God plants a little seed." We were standing by the bay window, looking out over the rows of corn in my grandfather's garden. All I could imagine was that if, at the right time of year, I peeled back the husks, I would find a miniature baby there, growing inside the protective shell. Of course, by the time I was engaged, I'd managed to learn where that little seed was planted, and that babies grow inside *other people*, but little more. As the wedding drew closer, my desperation to know what to expect mounted. I knew better than to ask my mother, with her fount of misinformation. And so I'd approached a young, spirited woman in our church, asking her to explain the mechanics of how it all worked. She mercifully told me, but the whole affair seemed highly unlikely to me.

And so we spent our two-day, two-night honeymoon just as we had spent most of our courtship: walking, talking, and going to church. However, as deeply indoctrinated as we were, we didn't go to church on our first morning as newly-weds. Somehow, we allowed ourselves to stay in bed the morning after our wedding and just go to the evening service. Albany is the capitol of New York, which at least afforded some decent sight-seeing, and despite the disappointments that plagued our first married days, we were happy to be together and aglow with love.

The highlight of our honeymoon was, ironically, the trip back to Beacon. Instead of returning by train, we took a day-liner down the Hudson. Sitting out on the deck chairs, sipping lemonade and basking in the sun, I almost felt adult, urbane—and almost married.

Yet once on shore, another disappointment awaited us. Part of our mission in Beacon was to pick up our wedding pictures, but when we arrived at our photographer's house, giddy with anticipation, his wife met us at the door. Not with a smile. Her husband had used a new camera for the wedding, she explained, and hadn't realized the shutter was closed the whole time. "He didn't have the courage to face you," she told us looking as grave as an undertaker. We were heartsick—no culminating reverie to the experience we'd lived, but hadn't seen with our own eyes. No professional pictures to adorn our first home and gaze upon with wonder. I comforted myself with the knowledge that my childhood, friend, Blanche, had taken lots of snapshots. There would at least be a record of my dream come true.

The next morning was almost as exciting as my wedding day. I was leaving the boundaries of Beacon, Washington Avenue, and my mother's roost for the last time. As we boarded the train for our new home in Bellmore, Long Island, my spirits lifted again. I would not be coming back.

HOUSE EIGHT

Bellmore, Long Island, New York

"Bellmore, Bellmore," the conductor sang out. Shivers ran through me as the commuter train slowed and lurched to a stop. For the length of the trip, Arnold and I had barely been able to contain our excitement. Held in the gentle sway of the train's rhythm, we'd gazed out the window, floating past bustling communities and summer fields. When flashing red lights held back traffic for our passage, it felt like our own special motorcade, with the world stopped for our grand entrance.

As the train came to a halt, I stood and reached for Arnold. We descended the steps like two eager children arriving at summer camp, hearts pounding with anticipation. Our luggage was quickly thrust onto the platform, and we turned to see the world we'd only imagined: Bellmore, Long Island— twenty-six miles east of New York City and an unfathomable distance from our past.

Earlier that morning I had donned my going away outfit for the second time. But this time, I had truly *gone away*. My husband was dressed for the occasion as well, in his dark suit and white shirt. There we stood— he checking the directions to our new home while I checked the seams in my first pair of nylons.

Together, suitcases in hand, we walked down Main Street, past the Bellmore market and Sam's butcher shop; past the ice cream parlor with its cool, creamy breeze; past the barbershop's revolving red-and-white pole, making our way to Wilson Avenue and turning left. Here a canopy of old- growth trees lined each side of the long street, their bright green leaves meeting overhead like outstretched arms. As we stepped under the protection of their shade, I felt like God himself had come to greet us. I don't know if anyone was watching our promenade, but since this little town resembled Mayberry, it's likely that some curtains were pulled aside and conversations stalled as the two of us eagerly scanned the landscape in search of our new home. On we walked, past big porches with their rockers and pots of early blooms, right to the middle of the block. Tucked between two houses, sat our church—a whiite A-frame clapboard with a row of long narrow windows down the side.

Our living quarters, we'd been told, were on the back of the church and so we headed there first, unable to contain our bursting curiosity. Stepping onto the porch and then through the door, we landed in our living room. Here was paradise! No matter that the rugs were worn and the donated furniture sparse. No matter that the windows were without a single curtain. This living room, this dining room, and this kitchen with their creamy yellow walls were ours! Already, the loom of my creativity was spinning. I would transform it all, making a home my husband would be proud of and our parishioners would admire. We clambered up the stairs to see the bedrooms, and there in the larger one, sat our modern waterfall bedroom set, its cascades of beveled wood shining in the light. It seemed a miracle to me— the set I'd paid four dollars a week for on layaway was sitting right here, waiting for us.

Scrambling back down the staircase like two unsupervised children, we opened the door that led from our living room into the sanctuary of the church. It was a large, bare space with rows of collapsible chairs. The edge of the platform was just a few yards away from our door and held a plain wooden pulpit. Behind it hung Solomon's "Head of Christ," the classic rendering of Jesus that had greeted me every Sunday of my life. In front of the pulpit, stood a simple wooden altar, and between the altar and the door to our quarters, sat the piano, angled to create the illusion of a hallway between church and parsonage. I looked at the humble piano bench adoringly. Here was my chosen place in the world. With Arnold at the pulpit, me at the piano— what could be more perfect?

I watched my husband as he walked silently around the sanctuary. As I had envisioned an attractive, appealing home just moments before, he was no doubt seeing velvet cushioned pews and an organ on the other side of the platform. When you're twenty-one and in love with each other and your calling, grand schemes are easy to come by.

Late that afternoon, there was a knock on the back door, and a young woman held out a casserole dish and a genuine smile. "I'm Gertrude Whurl," she announced. "Your next door neighbor and a member of your congregation." *Your congregation.* Somehow hearing her say it made it real. She came into the kitchen, put the dish on the table, and shook hands with both of us. "Welcome to Bellmore," she said. "Everyone's so excited to meet you."

On Sunday we once again donned our going away outfits, but this time we weren't outwardly going away—just walking through the looking-glass door into a new reality. "Everyone" turned out to be about thirty-five people. The congregation was billed at twenty-five, but of course, a new preacher pulls in the curious on his first Sunday. It had never occurred to us that we were terribly young for this kind of responsibility; but if these good folks were dismayed by the age of their new leaders, they didn't show it. In days to come, there would be incredulity from people on the outside: a door-to-door salesman who asked me if my father was home; a passerby who asked Arnold as he mowed the church lawn how he could contact the new pastor. But from the first day, our members embraced us as equals and treated us with respect.

So here we were, just as I had dreamed and dreamed and dreamed: my handsome minister husband in his pulpit, and me at the piano bench ready to entertain the crowd. I felt so lucky I could hardly breathe. Sunday, at long last, was a good day.

Having launched our ministerial career, Arnold and I turned to our new tasks. The first one for me was the project of creating a home out of the rooms of our house. On fifteen dollars a week, there wasn't much to work with, but our wedding gifts gave me a start. I placed our lovely glassware and serving plates in the glass-front cabinet in the dining room, and decked out our bedroom and bath with sheets and towels unblemished by use. I waxed and polished, cleaned and shined with a kind of vigorous joy I didn't know housekeeping could produce. And emboldened by the results, I decided to teach myself upholstering. The small remnant of wedding gift money bought me two yards of a striped beige and brown material to recover the seats of four dining room chairs and a side chair. Arnold helped me with the tricky process of lining up the stripes and getting them nailed without shifting. "I'm holding," I would say when I had the fabric where I wanted it. "I'm nailing," he would respond.

The bare windows were a source of bafflement until a woman from the congregation, who evidently felt that our exposure was undignified, showed up one day with two sets of white ruffled curtains— half of what I needed to cover the double set of windows in both living and dining rooms. So instead of placing both pairs of curtains on the two living room windows, I stretched my good fortune by treating each pair of windows as one, placing curtains only on the outside edges. Then did the same in the dining room.

I was busy on the other side of the wall as well. I played piano not only for congregational singing, but to accompany a women's sextet that I'd organized. In a congregation this size, it was the closest I could get to a choir. I also taught a class of junior high teen-agers, served on the church board, and frequently went calling on members and prospects alike with Arnold.

Cooking had never interested me, but now I was expected to entertain special speakers as well as visiting church officials. If my mother was able to do it with her innate culinary weaknesses, so, I assumed, could I. The hardest part was creating an impressive meal for guests without exhausting our meager food budget. When the dignitary stakes were high, Gertrude would come to my rescue. The first time the District Superintendent and his family came, not just for dinner, but to inspect the pastoral wares, she'd arrived at my back door three days before with a plan. In her capable hands were the makings for a full German meal: a marinated roast that I needed to turn every day for three days, sauerbraten, and potato dumplings called *Kartoffel Klobe*. I seemed to be Gertrude's personal project. Frequently she would take her day off to improve the quality of my life—teaching me to make pie crust with confidence and good results; removing the worn, dirty rugs off our floors and dragging them into the backyard for a cleaning they almost didn't survive; helping me wax the hardwood floors to an equally hard shine. In those days, Gertrude was the angel who'd been sent to do the work of three.

Just a few months into our ministry, I realized that I had hitched my wagon, not just to a star, but to a super nova. From the earliest days it was apparent to all that my husband was bound for success. He poured his young body into his work as if possessed. Early every morning he was in his "study," a space he shared with the furnace and the hot water heater just off our kitchen. By mid-morning he was off on foot to visit parishioners and prospects, logging many miles every week in his zealous jaunts around Bellmore. When a member was in the hospital, he took the bus to see them almost every day. I was so pleased with his obvious ambition and the prospect of where that ambition might take us! Surely beyond New York— perhaps even beyond the east coast. Young ministers like Arnold were both noticed and rewarded for their relentless pursuit of growing a church.

Therefore, when I began having intermittent periods of depression, I was mystified. *Wasn't this all I'd ever wanted?* I couldn't even imagine another life. *What could possibly be wrong?* The obvious and only conclusion was that it must be me. I must be doing something that God was displeased with. But since I had no idea what it could be, the only tool I had in my bag was to wait out these periods of a day or two until they passed. Each time I hoped I was free, but the intruder would return a week or so later. Then late summer it came to me! I hadn't been serious enough about my conversion as a child. I'd done it merely out of obligation and thus, it "didn't take." Now was the time to do it right. I decided to lie on the bedroom floor until I received whatever it was I was missing—preferably accompanied by lights or waves of ecstasy. But after an hour or so of intense and growing discomfort on the hardwood, my commitment waned. I got up and went to bed with the depression crawling in beside me.

With the next bout of depression, I decided that I must not be sanctified; otherwise, why would I be feeling this way? No one who had achieved true Christian perfection would be struggling with such feelings. I'd certainly never heard "the professed" talk about them. And while I didn't feel like I was *sinning*, neither did I have any assurance that the root of my sin had been eradicated. Surely such assurance would dispel depression forever, wouldn't it?

The summer was gone, and we still had no money for the surgery I needed. Though Arnold was burning up his energy elsewhere, I knew he must be troubled. I didn't know what to feel about our conjugal loss because I still didn't know what to expect. When my condition had been made known to my mother, she had given me her parting wisdom on sex— I suppose in an attempt to console me. "Well," she said with her trademark air of righteousness, "I can honestly say I never enjoyed it." I had no idea if I would enjoy *it* either, but knew whatever it was, we needed to get started.

In September, I got a call from my curmudgeonly Aunt Mae, my mother's wayward, unchurched sister. Just the person to address the issue that my mother couldn't address herself, but could easily pass off to her sister, the nurse._"Your mother's concerned about your predicament," she told me. "and I know a doctor here in Freeport who will do the procedure for free in his office." Previously, we had been told it would require a hospital stay, which had made the cost insurmountable. But evidently, some dear soul was willing to risk doing the procedure in the clinic for the sake of our plight. No doubt for Arnold, this was an answer to a fervent prayer. For me, it brought some trepidation, but I was relieved it was going to be taken care of without cost. Arnold had been so patient. He had earned the reward of a time-honored tradition that we were not aware of: not charging "men of the cloth" for medical services._

The following week, Arnold and I took the bus to my aunt's home in the neighboring town of Freeport, and she drove me to the doctor's office. She stayed with me while the doctor administered local anesthetic, performed the task, and then plied me with enough packing to make mere walking an effort. After a brief stay at my aunt's, Arnold and I boarded the bus back to Bellmore. However, toward the end of our ride, Arnold announced that the next stop was just blocks from the home of an ailing, elderly parishioner and he felt we should stop and call on her. And so we walked the three blocks and made the long climb up a steep stairway to her apartment. I was bleeding badly, afraid I was going to leak through my clothes as we visited, but hoped the dike would hold. I didn't say a word to Arnold, exemplifying the model of silence that went hand-in-hand with obedience to one's husband. Our parishioner distracted me, engaging me in conversation about music, and giving me books of songs I could use for my sextet. Afterward, we walked back to the bus stop, rode a couple of miles, and walked the five blocks home. I collapsed in bed without the wisp of a thought that anything should have been different.

Several months later that parishioner died, and I was shocked to hear that she had left me something in her will: a sewing machine encased in a beautiful walnut cabinet. We had evidently talked about sewing that day. In my state, I hadn't remembered. Thanks to this woman I'd only spent a few minutes of my life with—and that under dire circumstances—I could start making my own clothes again *and* had a new piece of furniture! Inspired by this gift, I tackled a project I'd wanted to take on since our arrival: making a slipcover for the worn and drab overstuffed chair in the living room. I found seven yards of Waverly fabric of bright orange, yellow, pink against a white background for only ten dollars. I left the store smiling to myself that I'd just bought a new chair for a song. I had no reason or experience to think I could pull this off, but plunged in with zest and, to my credit, persevered when the going got tough. There wasn't money for a zipper, so I used large safety pins in the back, angling the chair so they didn't show. The transformed chair transformed the room, making me wish for company. As overjoyed as I was with the results, it was the first and last time I would slipcover a chair. Some projects you only have enough youthful ingenuity to take on once.

Once I had healed from the surgery, the low-hanging cloud of *something missing* from married life had lifted. For the first three months or our life together, despite my trepidation about sex, I'd felt the incompleteness of our marriage and secretly segregated from other couples. The first time my husband and I came together sexually, my eyes filled with tears. It was the emotion of union, of completing what we had vowed to be. What affected me most at that initial stage of sex was the intimacy it ushered into our lives, the privacy it created, and the temporary cocoon inside which I had Arnold's complete attention. Because outside this envelope, the life of the church seemed to gobble up any remnant of our own lives. We didn't talk about our personal concerns with each other, or even go the few miles to the famous Jones Beach—even once—for an afternoon. Before the surgery, fierce noon-hour competitions of dining room table tennis had been our only shared enjoyment as a couple. That was, I reasoned, more than my own parents had. I had no memory of them laughing together, sharing a private joke, or talking casually over a cup of tea. And as for sex, my mother had made sure I knew that it was no source of enjoyment.

By the time we set up our first Christmas tree, meagerly decorated with tinsel and a few ornaments from home, our lives were moving like a rushing river. Through Arnold's unrelenting efforts and talent in the pulpit, our church was already starting to grow and he'd been rewarded with a five dollar raise. I was so proud of this handsome young pastor who was so quickly showing such promise, and I passionately wanted his success because *his* success was mine too. Everything I did was done with consideration to that end: what I wore, what he wore, what I said and didn't say, what I served our guests, how we *looked* to others. Impressing people became my reason for being, and since I seemed to be good at it, between short bouts of depression, I thrived.

Consciously, everything had changed. I was free of my mother's rabid convictions and the angst of not belonging anywhere. People in the church praised my piano playing. They called me "Mrs. Woodcook" with warmth and affection. They admired my support of my husband. But in another way, one I could not see, little had changed. I was still living in a small, confined world with the church as the hub of my reality. The parsonage, the sanctuary, the homes of our parishioners, comprised the whole of my life. Only the necessary marketing and shopping took me outside my sphere. So contained was I within this world that in the four years of our ministry in Bellmore, I spoke only once to the lady next door, and that was a mere *hello*. When I was invited to attend a local World Day of Prayer service and sit with pastors' wives from other denominations, I didn't even consider it. Because I wore no jewelry other than my wedding ring, and didn't wear make-up, I was embarrassed at the way I looked. I feared that they already thought we were strange, and didn't want to personally corroborate their suspicions.

With the next round of depression, I took a drastic measure. Fearing that my sin was the sin of pride, I decided that I needed to humble myself. Perhaps if I went forward to the altar the next Sunday evening when the invitation was given, I would demonstrate to God my humility in front of all our parishioners. The fact that I played the piano during altar calls, helping to create an environment conducive to surrender, made my move conspicuous. In the silence, I crossed to the altar and knelt. No one came to pray with me, as is the custom when someone goes forward to pray. Finally, the woman whose son had been the previous pastor and she the previous pianist knelt in front of me, scowling. We had heard that she was upset when we were given our raise, and it was understood throughout the church that she was displeased with her replacement at the piano. Now, she was all I had, and she seemed all too happy to have me at her mercy. She put her angry face next to mine, imploring me to repeat after her: "It's me, oh Lord. It's me that needs prayer!" I dutifully repeated it as quietly as I could, and made what I hoped was a graceful retreat to the safety of the piano bench. My attempt to relieve my depression had ended in a recurrence of my childhood—an angry woman trying to insert her own words into my mouth. I hoped that once home, Arnold would ask me about it, and I could pour out my angst to him, but he never did. My trip to the altar only left me deeper in despair. *What could God possibly want from me that I hadn't given?*

As my intermittent struggle ensued, the life of the church went on and I rolled, if not always merrily, with it. The congregation was continuing to grow, and yet, we were finding it increasingly difficult to make our salary cover our expenses—especially in winter when we had to reimburse the church for our heat each month. World War II was in progress, so times were hard for everyone. One week nothing but potatoes, string beans, and eggs were blessed in prayer at our table, but we never felt deprived. There were unlikely provisions too. An enterprising member of our church decided to tithe her canned goods, and thus one day we arrived home from an afternoon of calling to a kitchen floor literally covered with all kinds of home-canned food. And almost every Sunday night a treat no one would expect in this climate: a beautiful cake delivered by two young men who came from Brooklyn for the evening service.

Eventually, however, we had to act on our own behalf. Arnold was already working three jobs as minister, janitor and groundskeeper, so we decided I would go to work. That spring, I got a job at Dade Aircraft Company inspecting strips of wood that were used to make gliders for combat. The extra income was indeed a boost, but to my dismay, I noticed that the odor of the wood was making me nauseous. And then I missed my period.

I was pregnant.

Though it was completely unexpected, Arnold and I were both joyous about having a baby. I eagerly anticipated each new phase of my pregnancy, and kept waiting to grow enough to wear a maternity dress. That, I'd decided, would be the way we'd announce our good fortune to the church. Finally, at six months, with nothing to show, I couldn't wait any longer. I invited all the ladies to come upstairs with me after the morning service, and when they were gathered, I flipped open the lid of a large box, revealing the baby clothes that my overjoyed mother had sent. The women were utterly shocked, but seemed delighted. "It's been too many years since we've had a baby in the parsonage," one said. Everyone agreed.

The depression had lifted with pregnancy, with the surge of something new and unknown filling my life. And after my announcement, I felt a new sense of camaraderie with the women who made up my world. Feeling special seemed to make my spells of emptiness a distant memory, a passing phase.

On a bitter cold day, much like the wintery night of my own birth, our son, Dale, was born—though, thankfully, not in the parsonage this time. We were ecstatic! When the grinning and exhausted new father returned home from the hospital in the early hours of the morning, he was pleased to see a light on at the neighbor's house. Someone to tell! They were astonished by his break of dawn exuberance, and said if he hadn't been a minister, they would have assumed he was drunk. They had no idea I was pregnant.

The hospital maternity stint in the forties was a ten-day stay. Arnold came every day, sometimes twice, in the car we'd acquired with the church's help. He was so tired one afternoon that he laid his head down on the bed. I startled at the sight of bright red streaks of paint in his hair. *What was he up to? And would I have to pretend I loved whatever it was*? By the eighth day, I was allowed to sit on the edge of the bed. By the ninth, I could stand. This was the rigorous preparation for going home to care for an infant. On the tenth day, when Arnold came for me, we stopped on the way out to pay the bill of $125.00. "What a bargain!" he exclaimed to the clerk. I loved his unabashed joy over his firstborn—and for the red trim on our white kitchen dinette set.

I hadn't been a babysitter in my youth, and so, had taken a Red Cross class before Dale's birth. It was not much to go on in the face of gross inexperience. The women of the congregation, while they cooed over Dale at church, didn't come to my aid as I'd imagined they would, and I felt it inappropriate to ask. Even my mother, who was wild with happiness by the birth of a first grandchild, didn't come to help. A county nurse came by on a follow-up visit, listened to my anxious spill of questions and fears, and then countered them all by telling me to just relax. And so, I groped my way through the first days of our son's life, feeling inadequate and alone except for the assistance of Gertrude who gave me as much time as she could spare. The one who came to my aid every day, though, was Dale himself: an easy, uncomplaining baby with the face of an angel.

In the years that followed, the growth of our ministry broke all previous attendance records, and on the day we hit 100 in attendance, the church rejoiced as one. With more people to solicit from the audience without depleting it, I organized a choir and began directing cantatas for Easter and Christmas. With the rumblings of Arnold's success throughout the denomination came well-deserved attention, and in our third year the inevitable happened. We got a call to pastor a much larger church in Kingston, New York. It was an invitation that seemed ideal since the departing pastor and wife were not only friends from college, but a couple with whom we had continued a relationship. They were leaving Kingston to be missionaries in India. As success-driven as Arnold was, he also possessed a keen inner sense of guidance. He turned the offer down, feeling that his work in Bellmore wasn't finished yet.

The next year, my overworked husband started a new church about thirty miles away. He didn't serve as the minister, but under the auspices of the district, spent many hours getting the congregation organized, finding a suitable meeting place, and lining up available ministers and laymen to preach until a permanent pastor was found. "Adelaide, you'll never have to worry where your next meal is coming from," our district superintendent said to me with a chuckle one day. True enough, the thought had never crossed my mind.

In the midst of this overwhelming success, my own inner battle deepened. Outwardly, I was buoyant and bright, faithfully following in the tracks of my own image of a minister's wife. But inside, I was in trouble. The days of emptiness and foreboding were stretching out now, harder to emerge from, and compounded by profound confusion. I'd done everything I knew to do, but still, I carried the same guilt and sickening discontent that I'd felt as a little girl. *I should be happy. I should be happy. What's the matter with me?* In desperation, I pleaded with God again to show me what was wrong, begged Him to help me make things right.

One night as we approached our fourth anniversary in Bellmore, Arnold got a call after the evening service. This time it came from Cleveland, Ohio—and this time, he said "Yes."

Over the next month, we made our painful goodbyes. As I packed up our household, I turned to the spirit of spring bursting alive in all directions just outside my window. I stole from its hope. Maybe that awful, gut-wrenching despair wouldn't find me in the shining, new land of sight-unseen promise.

HOUSE NINE

114th Street, Cleveland, Ohio

"This is the parsonage here on the right," the driver said casually as we headed down the street to see our new church. Through the back seat car window, it was love at first glimpse. Even in the late stages of twilight, I could see what mattered: two stories, a large porch, and a huge picture window. The four of us (my mother had made the journey with us) were all bundled inside a parishioner's car, en route to see the main attraction: a long, narrow collapsible building complete with belfry. But my heart had stayed behind, waiting under the enormous oak that dominated the small front yard of our new home.

Compared to the church we'd just left, this one, though unquestionably modest, was an upgrade. Instead of folding chairs, 100 opera seats were fastened to the floor. Instead of a mere sanctuary, an extension room filled with the rubble of things "too good to throw away," offered potential. It would be, I knew, one of Arnold's first projects. And another virtue I didn't voice, but that secretly pleased me was that our house was no longer attached to the church.

The parsonage proved to be larger than I imagined—bigger, in fact, than the church itself. Its open, square spaces were like wall-to-wall possibilities. From the entry way, three choices met you at once. Straight ahead was a long climb to the second floor; to the right, a glass-paneled door to Arnold's study; and to the left, a large living room with a fireplace—and beyond that, a dining room with a window seat flanked by glass cabinets. To the right was a doorway that led to a big kitchen with an oval eating nook. In place of a refrigerator was an ice box that reminded me of the ice wagon of my childhood, from which Rhea and I had confiscated small slivers of ice as a treat. That memory was more pleasant than the reality of not having a refrigerator, but the disappointment was short-lived. Off the kitchen was a long sun porch with glass windows that looked over an enormous backyard.

Upstairs, another surprise: not a hall in sight, but instead, a big open space that served as the common area for two bedrooms and a bath. The largest room looked out on the street. The other bedroom was long and quite narrow and would be Dale's room. The bath had a claw-foot tub! How was I blessed not just with a big house, but a house with charm? This was the kind of home that mature parents lived in—not couples in their twenties.

In the light of day, I would see that our white house was drab and needed painting; that the carpet was badly worn and dingy, its pattern faded beyond recognition. But as I fell into our bed that some thoughtful parishioner had made up for us, I was living in my dream house. I wouldn't see it again for three days. In the night, I was taken hostage by the flu. My mother took care of Dale and of me while I drifted in and out of consciousness just long enough to remember where I was: in Cleveland, Ohio, in a house that reminded me of Davis Street, where once before, my mother had nursed me back to health.

I was well enough to make my appearance at our congregational debut, taking my advertised place at the piano bench. A minister's wife with talent at the keyboard was a benefit to him—which is why so many ministerial students gravitated toward young women whose ivory-pounding reputation preceded them. About sixty people gathered to hear their new pastor's inaugural sermon--a crucial moment for any congregation. They've hired, but not yet *heard*, and they assume that it isn't going to get any better than this. This sermon would be a bona fide sample of what they'd be listening to for many years unless they took the unpleasant measures to send the man on his way. Needless to say, therefore, it is also a crucial moment in the life of the pastor himself: a one-time opportunity to set the tone for his entire ministry. But no one thought to inform Arnold that he could expect an intruder. About half-way through his discourse, a rumble began. It started distant and deep, but built quickly to a thunderous roar, shaking the entire building. *A collapsible building at that.* No one in the congregation flinched, accustomed as they were to the 11:25 making its mid-sermon rounds. There was nothing for Arnold to do but stop, smile and wait. Not only that morning, but every Sunday thereafter.

The metropolitan locale of this new church was a great match for Arnold's spirit. Far from feeling daunted by it, he was motivated to do what he did best: plunge headlong into a foreign land and make it his own. Even as we were getting settled, he was busy getting the congregation unsettled from the familiar and acquainted with his vision of the future. The force that shook their little white church every Sunday at 11:25 came and went, but the runaway train they called "Pastor" was always on track. His energy was electric, contagious, and limitless. He was dreaming possibilities for them they didn't dare to dream for themselves.

I, too, was eager to take on the new challenge with its expanded opportunities for expressing my own talents. But not as eager as I was to make a home out of this charming old house. One could say I was "starting from scratch," but it was more like "starting from itch." We'd come to town with our walnut bedroom set, the poppy-upholstered chair (a donation from the Bellmore congregation),

Dale's bed, and the double set of sheer white curtains. But this time, the house we'd inherited was empty. Over the next few months, between three services a week, calling with Arnold, and attending church functions, I made our house my personal project. With the permission of the board, I painted the dark woodwork and fireplace white. Now the lovely beveled mirror above the mantel graciously welcomed, instead of hiding out in dark wood. Next, I wallpapered the living room, making the fireplace a striking centerpiece against the green and white stripes. And, as I suspected, my Bellmore curtains were put to good use—this time, sewn together and crisscrossed on the picture window. Our first furniture purchase was a rose-colored sofa, so lovely on the new beige carpeting with its clumps of soft roses scattered into the weave. Two side chairs, purchased from friends leaving for the mission field in Africa, completed the room. I could just barely believe it belonged to me. To my heart's dismay, the dining room stood empty. But late that summer, we came home from my parents' house toting the dining room set I had so reluctantly dusted as a child. Now I was only too happy to do the same thing.

Most churches in those days were fortunate enough to hire one person, but get two for the money. No one thought of it that way, but it was understood by all. Arnold's ministry was mine as well. And though I was now a mother, I took on far more than I had in Bellmore. As before, I played the piano and regularly called on members and prospects with Arnold. But now I taught the adult Sunday School class every week, a group that filled a quarter of the sanctuary. I also entertained at a whole new level. New and prospective members, visiting missionaries, special speakers, and evangelists gathered around the table at which my mother had served the same kind of guests. And in time, I would further my musical calling by directing Easter and Christmas cantatas every year. Not only didn't I complain, I didn't think to. Most of it I loved and the rest I accepted as part of my duty, part of being my husband's counterpart, his ally in success.

In the name of that success, I even branched out on my own. I had an idea, accompanied by enough courage, to ask the District Superintendent for permission to do it: start an annual Minister's Wives Convention. The first one was held in Akron, and fell far short of my vision. I'd imagined two days of inspiration and fun for the perennially weary and proper. But with one of the general superintendent's wives as a speaker—warm and insightful as she was—it was just more *church*. As opportunity would have it, however, I was elected president of the new enterprise, and thus, the following year, church was not in session. My committee members and I sent out invitations to attend an "All Girls' School," and the first night the five of us dressed accordingly as headmasters, feigning seriousness as we set forth ridiculous rules and unleashed general silliness. The next day, after the morning speaker gave her inspirational talk, the Sunday School rooms were turned into a craft bonanza, offering a wide variety of projects from which to choose. The rest of the day was dedicated to an oddity called "free time." We still prayed and nodded thoughtfully at the speaker, but that's not what everyone remembered. I left in high spirits, eager to create something even more fun the following year. But then, entertaining had always had that effect on me.

Youth, enthusiasm, and our drive to be successful propelled both Arnold and me to take on far more than was wise. For me, the excess translated as an inability to complete another pregnancy. I'd had one miscarriage shortly before we left Bellmore, and then another in Cleveland. But in March of 1947, I was pregnant again and crazy with hope. This time the pregnancy stabilized, and on the eve of my twenty-seventh birthday, I gave birth to a daughter, Maridel Lee. Maridel was a combination of my two names, Mary and Adelaide; but her middle name was a tribute to the Lees, our pastor friends from New York, now missionaries in India. As with Dale's birth, I was consumed with joy. I couldn't understand why the nurses weren't exclaiming over Maridel's beauty—after all, the doctor himself told me that she was the most beautiful baby he'd ever delivered. Arnold, too, was ecstatic. "I can tell this is your first baby!" one nurse said to him when he lingered so long at the nursery window. By now, the hospital stay had been mercifully shortened to five days, making it possible for me to be home for Christmas. My parents, Rhea, and four-year-old Dale welcomed me and our newborn back home.

In the midst of the unending demands of the life I'd longed for, the angels had not been forgotten, but rarely came to mind. Yet with the birth of my second child, they'd secretly begun to answer the agonizing prayers that began in Bellmore and were soon to reemerge in Cleveland. In fact, it was the birth itself, demanding cessation from my perpetual activity, that let me stop long enough to feel the anguish underneath. Up from the depths it arose—not post-baby depression, but that same, same familiar ache without a name. I hadn't outrun it after all—though God knows, I'd tried.

And so began the intermittent periods of private agony, of uncontrollable crying, of desperate, repeated asking for an answer to something I couldn't define—like a child who can't tell you where it hurts. When it stole over me, a shadow that no one else could see, I couldn't sleep, and walked the floors at night, alone. I even tried prayer and fasting, which I'd been taught could cut through Satan's power. But as a young mother of two, with manifold responsibilities outside the home, fasting only made me weak when I needed every ounce of strength I had. And if the prayer helped, I couldn't tell. Even when the depression abated, I was still left with the awful feeling that something crucial was missing in my supposedly golden life.

And then my depression started courting a sidekick: anger. When I wasn't depressed, I was susceptible to frightening bouts of this, the most forbidden of all emotions. *How could I be getting worse instead of better?* I worked to control my feelings, but one day, feeling sick with rage, and scissors conveniently in hand, I cut a two inch slit in the middle of my mother's crocheted table cloth. I immediately had it repaired so that no one else would ever notice, but for me, it was a secret scar of shame.

My yen to perform, and talent for it, was at long last serving me well. No one knew how unhappy I was, how depressed—how angry. Out among the people, fulfilling my roles, I was cheerful and smiling. If anyone ever suspected something else, they never inquired. And oddly, such a convincing performance only added to my pain.

One Sunday morning, gazing out over the crowd, I spotted a young woman sitting in the back row. She looked as if she'd wandered in out of sheer curiosity and might duck out the door at any moment. I eyed her warily from my perch on the piano bench. At the close of the service, Arnold and I walked down the aisle as we did every Sunday, taking our place at the door to shake hands with people as they left. The young woman was first in line, introducing herself as Jeanne Andrews. "I'd love to take your family to dinner after church next week. I'm a pediatric intern at St. Luke's hospital, so I won't always make it to church—or through church—if I'm on call. But next week I have off." Always eager to have Sunday dinner provided instead of *being* the provider, I accepted.

I watched, intrigued as she strode away. *A doctor? A woman doctor?*

Parishioners often invited us to Sunday dinner, but none took us out, as most believed it was wrong to purchase anything "unnecessary" on the Sabbath. But Jeanne was obviously not cut from that particular piece of religious cloth. Perhaps she would be more in line with my own sentiments on the matter. If Sunday was a "day of rest," wasn't it more restful to go out to eat the *necessary* food than spend hours in a kitchen cooking, serving and cleaning up?

When the next Sunday came, she took us to a beautiful restaurant in Shaker Heights, an exclusive area of Cleveland. There we learned that Jeanne had grown up in Wisconsin and in our denomination. But without hearing her say so, I never would have guessed it. She had a different air about her, casual and easy—less encumbered than anyone I had known. She had immense responsibilities as an intern at St. Luke's hospital yet her manner was so relaxed, so unassuming, I had to keep remembering I was talking with a doctor.

Arnold and I made it a practice to have new prospects over for Sunday dinner or after the evening service, thereby fostering a personal relationship with them in the hopes they would join the congregation. A few weeks later, we invited Jeanne. It would be an enormous boon to a small church to have a doctor in its midst, but for me, the motivation was personal. I wanted to know her better. Because of her schedule, she wasn't always at church, yet I'd found myself looking for her every Sunday. She was unlike anyone I'd ever met and something about her fascinated me. After her visit to our home, I started imagining a friendship, a connection that wasn't based solely on church activities. But there was an obstacle.

Just before leaving Beacon to enter the ministry, I'd been given a letter by my pastor's wife, the written version of a speech she'd heard at a ministerial convention. "The Pastor's Wife" was a two-page, single-spaced treatise of heartfelt advice that frequently crossed the line into hearty admonition:

"I have always said to myself, if my husband fails, it's my fault," the treatise stated. Other instructions followed: "Do not ask for new things because it is very important that your husband look nice." "It is better to let someone abuse you than to kick back and defend yourself." "You should at

all times have the respect of everyone." But no counsel was stronger than the one about making friends with parishioners. "Love everybody the same, at least outwardly," it said. "This is difficult because it is so easy to be very friendly with some and not others. So many times, a pastor gets in thick with one or two families and then his work is done. Don't confide in anyone but God and your husband. Some days you will long to talk with someone like you used to with your sister or girlfriend, but you must not pour out your troubles to anyone. Talk to Jesus about it and he will be a real friend to you."

As a brand new pastor's wife, this advice had seemed sound. Of course you had to be careful about playing favorites. But now, faced with a real person whose company I enjoyed, and who seemed to enjoy mine, what should I tell her? "I can't have any friends except Jesus?" And as far as confiding in my husband, I'd already tried. In one of my dark periods, I'd left him a note one evening when he was out, asking to talk to him. I thought if I made a private appointment with him, he would take my problem seriously. When he ignored it, I'd taken a bolder step. I'd approached him one night at bedtime, confessing that I didn't really know if I was sanctified, and asked him to pray with me. I'd knelt by the bed while he sat on it by me, yawning and patting my back as he half-heartedly petitioned God in my behalf.

Jeanne Andrews, I reasoned, wasn't a family with whom we were *getting thick*. And I wasn't planning on pouring out my troubles. Still I cautioned myself about crossing a line. But as it turned out, she crossed it for me—without even knowing it was there. One afternoon she simply showed up at my door with a grocery bag of simple foods: peanut butter, bread, apples—and made herself at home. Surprisingly, she needed a friend herself, someone to talk to outside the complicated, emotional world of the hospital. I decided that if I ever had to account for myself, I could always say I was counseling with her. But even the need for an excuse melted away in the easy flow of our friendship.

Though Jeanne confided in me about the challenges of her

work, mostly we just enjoyed great conversation—about her many friends around the world, her relationships at the hospital, her family in Wisconsin. I loved the exposure to different kinds of people and experiences, all of which transported me out of my cloistered life and into that ever-tantalizing larger world. But most of all, I loved being a witness to Jeanne's faith. She was the first person I'd known whose beliefs weren't run by fear or rules. She made no bones about the fact that she did sports on her Sundays off because recreation was a kind of rest to her—and wasn't Sunday called "the day of rest?" She also went to movies, which was strictly forbidden by our church. When I questioned her about it, she waved it off in that low-key way of hers, as if to say, "I make my own choices about those things." Now I knew why she'd looked different to me the moment I set eyes on her—even from platform to back pew.

If ever I needed a friend, it was now. Arnold was in complete overdrive. After two years in Cleveland, our church was packed to capacity almost every Sunday, including the extension room, which he'd cleared and made part of the sanctuary. With a demand for more Sunday School classrooms, Arnold engineered the project of digging out space in the basement of the church. It was an enormous project, and even with a crew of men from the church, adding it to his duties physically taxed him. But as always, he was undaunted. It was a temporary fix, but one that made obvious the pending need for a new church.

The following year, Arnold started graduate classes at Case Western University, aware that a Masters degree in Religion would enhance his ability to minister as well as improve his standing for advancement in the denomination. In addition to the evening classes, this added study time to his overflowing agenda. The children and I rarely saw him except at dinner, where he sat obviously preoccupied and ready to launch from his chair with the first ring of the phone or the last bite of his meal.

I'd found I could stave off the depression as long as I was grasping some new enterprise by its challenging horns: the next cantata, the next ministers' wives convention, the next project on the house. But often in the aftermath, when the routine of my life set in again, I was delivered once more into the morass. Sometimes it was weeks between bouts, sometimes months; but always, it returned to pummel me with its penetrating, enigmatic questions.

And because my desperation was growing with each round, I got bolder in seeking an answer. The next ministers' wives convention was held in Cleveland, and the speaker stayed at our house. She was knowledgeable and warm, and at the end of an inspiring day that had engendered great admiration on my part, I felt safe enough to broach the subject of my own spiritual struggle. I imagined her smiling with understanding, reaching for my hand and telling me that it was just part of Christian growth to keep wrestling with such feelings, and that in time, faith would overcome them all. She listened intently, and then looked at me with puzzlement. "Well," she began, "it sounds to me like your spiritual well has dried up. What you need to do, Adelaide, is pray and read your Bible more. God will reward your efforts with a deeper faith." I felt like a child who, having divulged some painful secret to a trusted adult, was told that the pain was all her fault, and that if she would just do *more* of what *wasn't working*, there would be no problem.

I was now bereft of all hope. And out of resources.

Help was actually on its way—in fact, already here. I just couldn't recognize it yet as an answer to my prayers. Help was here the presence of my friend, Jeanne, who spirited me away to a concert at Severen's Hall; who talked me into buying a black knit form-fitting dress that I would wear out with love; who showed up at my door when I most needed support in Arnold's absence;

who introduced me to classical music—Mozart, Beethoven and Brahms—a gift that would become one of the great, enduring loves of my life. And more than all this, she gave me a small port-hole out of which to view a larger sea of faith.

Help was also present in the questions themselves. Heart-rending as they were, they would prove to be my allies, pushing sprouts of consciousness up into my being, like scrawny flowers that against all odds, find air and life between the rocks. Even my pain, disruptive and seemingly destructive, was help of the first order, insisting that there was more to God than this version of religion into which I'd been born, and insisting that my searching, pilgrim heart wouldn't rest until I found it.

And there was help in the presence of a child, asleep at night in her crib while kittens tumbled and tangled in vast yards of yarn on her wallpaper. When my daughter was born, I'd looked at her brand-new body and wondered how anyone could believe that an infant created by a loving God could be born in sin. Perhaps it was that errant query that had sent me sliding back into depression, standing as it did between me and everything I supposedly believed. But one suffocating August afternoon when Maridel was three, she hinted that her birth, and the uncomfortable paradox it evoked, was just the beginning of her part in liberating me. As we sat on the porch swing, doing our best to create some faint breeze, she turned to me and said, "Mommy, there isn't really a Santa Claus, is there?"

Perhaps I did see it then—just for an instant: that this child, born on the eve of my birthday and given a name fashioned after mine, *was* me—the perceptive, questioning self that I wrestled with in the dark. And perhaps, just for an instant, while I twinkled with laughter at her ability to trust her own insights, I knew I'd given birth to my own.

The growth of the congregation had exploded into a vision

spearheaded by Arnold, but now embraced by all: a new church and parsonage in Garfield Heights, a burgeoning suburb just west of the city. The first step was to sell the outgrown facility, thereby raising enough money to buy land and begin building the new church. To stretch the funds, one of the men from our congregation was hired as the contractor, and his crew was made up of men willing to donate both their time and skills. Arnold worked his shifts alongside the men as they labored six days a week. On Sunday, we met in the bleak Elk's Lodge. As morbid as a morgue, even the 11:25 would have been a welcome relief from the gloom. Yet, as much as I dreaded going there three times each week, I soon realized that this unpleasant situation had its hand outstretched, offering me a boon. Without our own building, the social life of the church had diminished almost to extinction, leaving me room to breathe.

The building endeavor had been underway less than a year before it became apparent that more construction funds were needed. The plan had been to keep us in the parsonage until the new one was ready, but now our home would have to be sacrificed to finance the completion of the project. Nine days before Christmas, the day Maridel turned five, we moved from our two-story home into an apartment. Unlike my mother, who had lost her home to the depression, I was happy to let ours go. It would be a few years before our parsonage was ready, but I didn't mind. For me, the status quo, however appealing, never shone as brightly as the radiance of change.

HOUSE TEN

Apartment on Indiana Avenue, Cleveland, Ohio

In years past, the sight of an upstairs flat with a large porch had evoked a wistful longing in me. What would it be like to sit on a balcony in the cooling shelter of green? To look out upon the world from my own private tree house? I was about to find out.

The flat on Indiana Avenue was just five rooms, but all of them spacious and generously endowed with windows. It was beautiful even in its bare state: hardwood floors, freshly painted walls, diffused December light that invited you to linger. The dining room with its welcoming window seat, was central to the living area; and just beyond it, through an archway, was the living room. Its long double windows looked out on the wide porch, which ran the length of the front of the house. Green sang to me from every view.

Settling into this place was easy. No drapes to make or carpeting to replace. No painting or wallpapering to be done. And for once, we had plenty of furniture. Even Christmas that year didn't require the usual outlay, arriving as it did on the coattails of the move. But it wasn't until my children were off to school after the holidays, Maridel in Kindergarten and Dale in fourth grade, that I realized something I had missed entirely: I wasn't living in a parsonage. This monumental news dawned on me one morning as I sat in my bathrobe having a second cup of coffee at my kitchen table. This luxury, I suddenly saw, would be mine for as long as we lived here. Most parishioners didn't even know where we lived so no one was going to be stopping by with a problem or a pie. For the first time in almost ten years, I didn't have to make my house *or* myself presentable by eight o'clock in the morning.

My sea of obligations, already eased by the hiatus of the church's social life, was receding still further. Both of the children were now in school. Arnold was seldom home except to eat dinner, change clothes for the evening, and collapse into bed late into the night. In the absence of a proper parsonage, the church board had decreed that all evangelists, special speakers, and missionaries would be housed and fed by the parishioners.

With the realization of this release, a feeling slowly began to emerge that I would have cheerfully denied just weeks before: I was emotionally drained. The years of relentless responsibility and obligation had left me exhausted from within, leaving my cupboard of reserves bare. For someone like me, it was the kind of awareness that arrives in only one of two ways: either through physical collapse or in the sudden cessation of responsibility. Only then could I allow myself to know the truth of my condition. But there was more to that truth than my exhaustion. I was desperate for time alone, for quiet and some sense of inner peace.

But my respite was brief. When a long-distance call brought news that my mother had suffered a stroke, I boarded a train for New York as soon as I could—leaving the children in Arnold's care despite his lack of experience and impossible schedule. I needed to go see my mother; but more importantly, I needed to be there for Rhea who was now carrying the double burden of my mother's care and the running of the household. A hospital bed not only dominated the bedroom, but so did it dominate my sister's existence. Never strong, she looked frail after the strain of these few weeks. I was more worried about her than my mother, whose stroke had impaired her, but not completely debilitated her. Nor had it softened her temperament. I dreaded the prospect of leaving my sister standing on the porch beside my father, clinging to her for his own support.

As it turned out, my dread turned into a greater one. Before I could complete my visit, another crisis took away the consolation of returning to my own safe harbor. Arnold called me, crying uncontrollably. The polio epidemic had found its way into our family. Dale was in the hospital. Complaining of a headache on Sunday morning, he hadn't gone to church, and when Arnold had returned after the service, he was worse. "Jeanne got here as fast as she could," he told me, struggling to get the words out between sobs, "and when she put her hand behind his neck and lifted, his whole body came off the bed."

"I'll take the next train home," I told him.

"Addie, you'll have to fly."

Rhea and a friend took me to New York City, and within hours I was on a prop jet headed back to Cleveland. Unlike my husband, my initial response to trauma was calm. Even with the potential gravity of the situation, I felt some excitement about flying for the first time—and managed to appreciate the beautiful meal served in mid-air. In the years ahead, Arnold would often describe the composure with which I had walked off the plane and the ensuing strength that held him together. I did feel composed. And strong. But in hindsight, I also see how well I had mastered the art of hiding from my own pain.

Once home, I had Jeanne's support—as both friend and doctor. Dale's case, she assured me after seeing the results of the spinal tap, wasn't as severe as she'd feared. He was a good candidate for full recovery. Since we had a personal physician in Jeanne, and because the polio epidemic was taxing the hospital's available space, Dale was released within a couple of days. Bed rest and limited activity for several weeks brought him steadily back to the verve of his eight-year-old self.

Once Dale was back to school, my relative solitude returned. Other than playing the piano at the services and continuing to teach my Sunday School class, I did little else in my role as the minister's wife. Instead, I became a woman in her own home. I read, did the minimal housework required by the apartment, wrote letters to family and friends, and sat on the upstairs porch in my nightgown watching the moon through the trees. Miraculously, for lengths of time, I was once again the girl skating back and forth in front of the Christmas tree—with no one to answer to. And like the spaciousness of my apartment home, an opening began to grow in me, nameless and formless, but real. I felt far, far from the old depression, as if it were an old, haunting nightmare I could still recall, but that no longer affected me.

But within a few months, my quietude was disrupted again—this time by the thing we had prayed God would spare us. Maridel got polio. Jeanne rushed to the house when I called her with my suspicion, and then drove us to the hospital herself. The spinal tap revealed that Maridel had a lighter case than Dale's, having had two vaccinations to his one. The hospital was a grim place, crowded with ill children and overflowing with makeshift beds in the corridors. Never was I more grateful for the young woman who showed up on the back pew of our church than I was on that day. "We'll take her home," she told me. "I'll take care of her myself." We moved Maridel's bed out into the dining room to make her recovery more pleasant, and with Jeanne's constant care—despite her exhaustion from the demands of the epidemic—Maridel, as her brother before her, healed without complication or lasting effect. My gratitude was overwhelming.

The following August we made our annual trip by car back to New York. It was the only "vacation" we could afford, but it still didn't deserve the title. A week with Arnold's family consisted of his working almost around the clock. One year he helped his father jack up the corner of the sagging farmhouse; another he scraped the peeling paint from it in the stifling heat. I wasn't expected to help, but might have been better off. I sat in the kitchen, swatting flies away and fanning myself while sweat ran in little rivulets down my neck. Unaffected by the heat, the children fared the best, watching the cows being milked in the barn; learning to ride the old horse, Beauty; and taking her on trips to the general store for ice cream and candy.

The second supposedly rejuvenating week was spent in Beacon. My parents had left the house on Washington Avenue behind for the last time, and bought a bungalow set high on a hillside outside of town. Every year, we climbed the steep Mountain Drive to find my mother running from the porch, ready to pull the children from the car before it came to a full stop. Returning to my mother's home, even in this gorgeous surround, was punishing. Inside a day, she and I were sparring over the least of things, creating a tension that ebbed and flowed, but never went away. Yet we never spoke of our disharmony—as if acknowledging it would be unchristian. And each year, I was soon counting the days to departure. My sister, now in her late twenties, still lived at home. She had worked at IBM prior to my mother's stroke, but had given up her job to take over the household. The only respite of our stay there was the few half-evenings that Rhea and I would sit on the porch, reminiscing and laughing—often at my mother's expense. But mostly, we were occupied with my mother, the children, and the constant meal preparation for the seven of us. Witnessing my sister's life made Beacon a doubly painful place for me. I had escaped into my own life, whatever its pitfalls may be, but my sister hadn't moved at all. She was still the obedient daughter wilting under the hot sun of my mother's control.

This particular year, however, Rhea did side with our mother on one account. They had a good laugh together at what they deemed to be my folly: heirloom furniture rescued from the chicken coop. One day I'd wandered into the coop at the foot of my father's terraced flower garden and saw a something I'd seen many times before, but now with new eyes. Lying on its back was my grandfather's eight-foot secretary. Its elegance was veiled in almost every way, like an heiress who has lost her fortune and lives in disgrace and tatters. The glass was broken, the writing board was missing, and the brass pulls were badly tarnished. It wore so many coats of black varnish—the annual spring ritual in the 1800's—that any hint of the wood's original nature was vanquished. And as a final insult, its drawers were full of chicken feed and mouse droppings. My mind skipped back to the years I'd seen this massive piece of furniture relegated to the garages of our various homes. I'd thought nothing of it then—just some old furniture of my grandfather's that we didn't have room for in the house. Though now I did recall that my cousin, Ruth, had asked to have it once, and that my mother had declined her request.

But I was no longer a child and had been exposed in recent years to a wider interior horizon. I'd frequented parishioners' homes where beautiful antiques caught my eye; and from them, I'd learned about their history and their value. When my eyes adjusted to the darkness of the coop, I saw other pieces in the corner, and my heart picked up its pace. My grandfather's wash-stand! I felt as if I could pull out the top drawer, reach inside the black tin with the gold dragon, and help myself to a lemon drop. I ran my hand over the cool marble top, his kind face fluttering in my mind's eye. Next to the washstand sat his dresser, a larger version of this beloved piece. These, too, were covered with the sooty stain of varnish.

I ran from the coop to find Arnold, and breathless, took him to see my treasure, hoping he wouldn't scoff at me. "Look," I said, flinging open the door. "We need furniture for the new parsonage, right? How about this?!" By now I'd learned that Arnold was an enigmatic man. It was almost impossible to judge his responses to things, and just when I'd thought I could do so with confidence, he'd surprise me. But this time, he shocked me.

"Let's take them home," he said, after assessing them. "I'll help you refurbish them."

Before we left Beacon, we took a necessary first step: stripping away a patch of black varnish to see if the wood underneath would merit our considerable efforts. Arnold chose a small area, and worked his way through the layers as he did everything else in life—with impatient determination. At last, wiping away the final layer with a rag, we saw the wood: a walnut so rich, so beautiful that it made you want to turn back time and stop the hand that applied that first and fatal coat of varnish. The wood gleamed up at us and we grinned at each other.

But my sister and mother laughed. "Spending the money to haul those things back to Ohio?" they scoffed. "Who'd want to put that old junk in a brand new house, anyway?"

I did. Oh, I did!

Arriving home from our precarious journey, towing our abused treasure behind us, we unloaded everything into the garage. When the children were back in school and the heat tolerable again, we plunged in. True to his word, Arnold not only helped with the project, but took a personal interest in it. Even with his added responsibilities for building the church, he took responsibility for getting the tarnished pulls professionally dipped, took charge of replacing the glass, and of getting a new pull-out writing table made to specifications. And when we realized that the secretary would be too tall for the ceiling of the new parsonage, he borrowed the proper tools and carefully sawed off the top shelf of the cabinet.

Undaunted by the immensity of what we'd taken on, I relished this project. It gave shape and incentive to my life, as did my vision of these handsome pieces adorning our beautiful new home. I wasn't a fan of new houses, always preferring the charm of older ones; but these beauties, I told myself, would bring their own enchantment to the ten rooms that had never known laughter, tears, triumph or pain. The work was hard, but step-by-step rewarding. I was on a roll.

And then Maridel got ill again.

This time her illness was more life-threatening than polio. A combined case of pneumonia and strep throat put our six-year-old in the hospital and out of my hour-by-hour reach. Parents weren't permitted around the clock then, and even with Jeanne making access easier for me during the day, I had to go home at night.

I had always been stronger than Arnold in a crisis, serving as his strength in the midst of shared turmoil. I'd not only taken on this role with the children's polio, but also in a crisis with the building project the year before. While still living on 114th Street, a nightmare had catapulted Arnold out of bed one night. "The floor fell through!" he cried. "The floor fell through!" The day before, over the assurances of the contractor, Arnold had protested that the structure built to hold the wet cement for the floor of the sanctuary wasn't strong enough. He feared that it would give way and fall into the basement of the church. Early the next morning, he'd arrived at the building site to find that his nightmare of a basement full of wet cement was, in fact, a prophecy. Once he had the emergency crew in place, he came home, seeking refuge in my arms as he sobbed with exhaustion and heartache. I was the calm to his devastation, the rock to which he clung for his survival.

But on the night of our daughter's hospitalization, a night that could take her from us, I had no solace to offer. Jeanne had tried to hide her worry, but her eyes had betrayed her. Collapsing into our bed, I turned to my husband for refuge and he returned what he'd been given. Wrapping me in his arms, he cradled me while I cried, comforting me in the darkness that enveloped both of us. The next day, Maridel began to turn back toward us instead of drifting further away, yet Arnold's willingness to release me from my strength and be *my* rock, remained.

In the days that followed, as I watched over Maridel's progression back to health, I thought about my mother. I was once the daughter precariously balanced on the beam between living and dying. Now I was the mother, and for the first time, I felt a link with her through a mother's heart. While she couldn't express her love with touch or emotion, I saw now that it did not make her anguish less. Her steady, meticulous care-giving was simply her only way of showing that she cared deeply whether I lived or died.

On the blessed day when Maridel returned to school, I returned to my relative solitude. But of course, I was not the same. The imminent threat of losing a child changes you as nothing else can. And the grace of having that child restored changes you too. The sheer relief, the profound gratitude of that experience began to work in me—in a different way than the depression with its unanswered questions had. I felt myself longing for something deeper and truer than I'd ever known before, and a connection to God seemed to emerge—a connection that was both old and new. I recognized it as the feeling I'd had as a child on Basket Island—that abandonment to the living, untamed spirit of nature, to something bigger than the God of Sunday School. And suddenly one day, as I allowed that feeling to wash up on my own inner shores, I remembered an experience I'd had in that place where God seemed so obvious to me.

The summer I was ten, I'd spotted a little brown, fuzzy bird lying just under the edge of a bush. Overhead, a group of large sea gulls screeched and swirled in the air. My father was coming up the path from the ocean, and I'd called to him to look at what

I'd found. As I pointed at the bird, I moved toward it, and the screeching surged.

"Stay back!" my father warned. "The baby is probably wounded or sick and the gulls are protecting it. If you get too close, they'll swoop down and peck you on the head."

"But we need to help it," I protested.

"We can't. We have to leave that to the gulls. They know what to do."

The next morning after breakfast, I ran to the bush where the bird had rested, barely moving. It was gone. I looked upward to see the gulls once again lazily gliding the skies, unperturbed. Feeling safe, I looked deep beneath the bush, walked around it, and finally covered a wide circle in search of the bird. It was gone, and I felt sure was back in the fold.

I felt that way now. A force larger than myself, and infinitely wiser, had protected my child when I couldn't, and had brought her back into our circle once again. For long days afterward, I watched her when she didn't know I was looking, drinking in her beauty and praying she was here to stay.

After three years in the apartment on Indiana Avenue, we'd been in the new church for a year. Once we'd dreamed of having an organ and pews instead of folding chairs. Now we not only had a whole new church complete with organ, but a platform with a bona fide choir loft. I had room for a real choir at last! And Arnold had his first office at the church—a little attic that could only be reached by a small, circular staircase. The basement housed attractive and well- equipped classrooms of various sizes. Once the church had been dedicated, work on the parsonage had begun and at the end of the third year, our new home was almost ready. I was packing again.

Early one evening, shortly before we abandoned our upstairs home, the downstairs doorbell rang. It startled me. It was the first time in all these years that someone had shown up unannounced.

I made my way down the steep enclosed staircase, and opened the front door to find an elderly parishioner, dear Mr. Huston, standing before me. His wife's large hurricane lamp was cradled in his arms.

"She would want you to have it, Mrs. Woodcook," he said, unable to say his deceased wife's name aloud.

"Oh, are you sure, Mr. Huston?" I said, earnestly.

"She knew how much you loved it," he said, and with that, placed this glorious gift in my hands. I had openly admired this double-globed lamp of variegated green with soft, pink dahlias that glowed against its opaque finish. But I had never once thought about inheriting it.

"My goodness!" I said, feeling that rush of deep pleasure that an unexpected, but much-loved gift evokes. "Thank you so much for thinking of me. I'll cherish it always."

I hugged the lamp to my body as I climbed the long staircase with great care. How perfect this piece would be with our newly refurbished antiques! But sometimes gifts are more than just the beauty of themselves. I set the lamp on the sideboard in the dining room, plugged it in, and stepped back. Soft, radiating light—just what this place had been to me. Despite facing some of my worst fears here, one thing had kept its distance. The specter of depression hadn't stalked me in these hallowed walls.

HOUSE ELEVEN

Turney Road, Garfield Heights, Ohio

The house on Turney Road was not a dream come true. It was the *un*dreamed coming true. As a minister's wife I had never imagined having such a grand home. No one does. In this calling, one is prepared only for modest housing and the grace to accept whatever is given without complaint. Actually, I hadn't needed grace so far. Every house had seemed to suit us perfectly. But if I *had* imagined a new house, it would not have been this one: a brick manor with two stories and five bedrooms, one of which included a living area for guests. No visitor—lauded or lowly—would be housed anywhere but here now. We had moved not just into a parsonage, but into a bed and breakfast, luncheonette, and diner.

Our house was seamlessly connected to the church, their basements joined by a short tunnel. Perfect for the pastor's wife on rainy Sunday mornings, but the *real* reason was ingenious: expanding the parameters of the church by using the would-be "basement of the parsonage" as a fellowship hall. With the house on 114th Street, our home had been once removed. In the apartment, it was uncharacteristically remote. But this was more like Bellmore—joined by a door.

I was leaving my semi-secluded life among the trees, but I

was ready. Three years out of the full-time spotlight had restored me, and new projects waited. One was already underway. A few months after the church was dedicated, I'd set about creating my first real choir. There was something invigorating for me in taking on a project for which I had little training or experience. I'd done it my whole life: piano playing, upholstering, sewing, directing cantatas, furniture refinishing and now, choir directing—which meant finding music for every service, holding Wednesday night rehearsals, and directing the choir twice on Sunday. Fortunately, we were blessed in this congregation with Gladys, a highly-talented pianist to accompany the choir. Her husband was someone I had known long ago and far away: college sweetheart Tondra Border of the Bond Lavender gift set.

I relished this new work, though never thought of it as such. Music had never been a discipline for me—only joy. The clock stopped as I searched for choir songs and familiarized myself with all four parts of the harmony. Rehearsals were a pleasure for me, and hence, for everyone else. I joshed the tenors along when they struggled with a complex sequence of notes, and praised the sopranos when, after several tries, they didn't fall the least bit flat on the high notes. And when the harmony came together, when the crescendos built like a rising wave, or the quiet phrases felt like a collective whisper, I was as proud as a mother. Sometimes in rehearsal I would whoop with satisfaction. I couldn't help it. Prayer meeting still didn't lift me up. But choir practice did.

My second project was musical too. No new self-respecting sanctuary would be without an organ, which is why a beautiful walnut Hammond was purchased despite the fact that the congregation lacked one essential ingredient: an organist. Of course with Gladys Border on the piano, I became the obvious candidate. After all, except for when I was directing the choir, I *was* just sitting there. And besides, I'm sure the reasoning went, if one can play the piano, they can play the organ too. Well, almost. Unlike the piano, learning to play the organ involved two keyboards to amuse the fingers and two rows of foot pedals—for bass and volume—to entertain the feet. But if you wanted to play with expertise, you needed to maneuver the row of "special effect" stops above the keyboards. *Wouldn't a bit of trumpet sound nice on second chorus? How about a touch of drums on the interlude?* I never mastered the organ, but I did learn to play; and like anything associated with music, it was another chapter in a long romance.

My biggest challenge sat under the roof next door. Nine rooms to furnish with furniture that had fit perfectly into a two-bedroom apartment. Ah, plus antiques! The secretary, restored to its former splendor, sat as the focal point of the large living room, with bookshelves made from leftover bricks flanking either side. The marble-topped dresser and washstand found a home in the master bedroom, making the waterfall bedroom available for the guest room. We did make one major purchase: a round, drop-leaf maple table and chairs for the eating area at the end of the kitchen, along with a matching hutch. The white Bellmore sheers, after a rest of their own, were called into service once again. I was happy to have them back, gracing the dining room window like the presence of a friend who "knew you when."

Next up: the immense picture window that faced the street. I found a fabric that I loved so much I was actually glad I had to make drapes. It was a brown, white, and teal blue pattern overlaid with another pattern of metallic gold. Cottage style drapes didn't sound like something that would suit a big, contemporary house, but they were perfect with our blend of modern and antique. The lower tier provided privacy with style, attached by large gold rings to a matching rod. The upper tier was drawstring and opened to provide light. Once up, I found reasons to take admiring strolls by my creation. My handiwork of the past, the large peony-covered chair from Bellmore, didn't fit the emerging look of our home, so we splurged to have it recovered to match the drapes. That was one challenge I wasn't willing to take on again—especially since it would involve a zipper bigger than my courage.

For the first time in almost ten years, I wasn't really satisfied with the results of my decorating. What was there was beautiful. But all the rooms except the kitchen were sparse, advertising the obvious: we didn't have the means to furnish this new home. I was so grateful for the antiques, but bewildered as to how we could make this home as comfortable and complete as the others had been.

As my life had continued to expand, my sister's had grown smaller. Her hope for a return to her work and the possibility of her own home only diminished with time. Even though my mother could now manage the household with the help of my retired father, she wouldn't hear of Rhea moving out. When my sister called me one night, still sounding like a trapped, beaten child, I hatched a plan.

"I'm going to get you out," I told her.

"You can't Addie. No one can. It's just my lot."

"Give me a little time. I'm going to do it."

I hung up the phone and called my friend, Jeanne—the only person in the world to whom I felt close enough to ask for this kind of help. Well aware of my sister's plight, she readily agreed to help me rescue her. But Rhea would have to step up to the opportunity too. After living in Beacon and in my mother's house all her life, she would not only have to find somewhere to go, but do the unthinkable: start a new life behind our mother's back.

With help from her closest friend, Margie (whose husband happened to be a District Superintendent), a job interview was set up in Kansas City, Missouri, at our denomination's publishing house. Jeanne and I drove to Beacon, and under the ruse of taking a vacation together, the three of us left in two cars the next day. My mother seemed to accept the idea that we had to take two cars so that Jeanne and I wouldn't have to drive all the way back to New York after the trip. What she didn't know, of course, was that Rhea's car had been secretly packed to make her getaway permanent.

By the time Jeanne and I left Kansas City for Cleveland, my sister had a job. We'd helped to settle her into her temporary home—a big, old house that the company provided for single women new to the area. Leaving her there alone was hard, but not as wrenching as leaving her standing on the porch in Beacon, waving goodbye in sync with my mother. I comforted myself with the knowledge that despite her shyness, Rhea had always made good and lasting friendships. Unlike her experience with our mother, she had always seemed to find people who easily loved and accepted her.

As our tenth anniversary in Cleveland approached and plans were made for a celebration, inspiration struck. The popular television show, "This Is Your Life," would make a perfect format to give tribute to Arnold's ten years of ministry. Since it would involve transporting and housing a number of people from out of town, I knew I'd have to get the board's permission—which proved to be easy.

Unknown to Arnold, I started working steadily across the weeks, making phone calls and writing letters, preparing a script for my mock TV show—and keeping all of the evidence hidden between our mattress and box springs. I was also careful to tuck my brimming enthusiasm away with the script. One little slip and the surprise would vanish.

On the appointed day, Arnold stepped to the slide projector to narrate a pictorial of our ten years in Cleveland. After a few slides, the screen filled with these words: "This Is Your Life, Pastor Woodcook!" Ushered to the stage, one of the laymen took over the microphone and began to narrate his life story.

The "secretly housed" guests were all sequestered in a room off the platform, and at the appropriate time, each announced his or her presence over a microphone before stepping onstage to greet him. As the story unfolded, all of them emerged: his parents, Earl and Rena Woodcook; his brothers, Bud and Geren; our dear Gertrude Whurl from Bellmore; Donald and Jimmie Shelp, a couple that had gone into seminary as a result of Arnold's ministry. In their arms they carried their new baby, Arnold, named after their mentor; and of course, Dale, Maridel, and me. Never one to hide his feelings, he cried through most of it.

Few things are more exciting than a well-kept secret. Once my debut as a script writer, director, and producer had passed, and everyone had flown or driven away, I basked in the glowing embers of success. I'd felt energized as long as I had the next big thing to focus on: the house, my sister's rescue, the surprise presentation. Now only endless weeks of services stretched ahead of me with the church bulletin as my calendar. Members could pick and choose from the entrees on that menu, but every one of them was on my sizeable plate.

Soon I was heavy again, inwardly dispirited though outwardly smiling—sincere, but also back to the business of hiding my pain. Even Jeanne had very little awareness of my struggle. In those early years, I didn't feel free to talk to her about it. Then, for such a long period, it seemed to have evaporated. Now we were closer than ever, and though she regularly shared her own challenges with me, I didn't reciprocate. She was the closest friend I'd ever had, yet she didn't really know me because I'd protected her from the haunting darkness of my life. Our friendship, as blessed as it was, was limited by my inability to step outside my role and share my pain.

And my pain kept surfacing.

Maridel called me one day while on an outing with friend.

They had walked a few blocks down the street to spend their allowances.

"Where are you calling from?" I asked quickly, afraid something had happened.

"I'm in a phone booth at the strip mall."

"What is it, honey?" I said, knowing she wouldn't have spent a precious dime for no reason.

"There's this little ring at the dime store. It's so pretty and it's only fifty cents." The longing in her voice lingered in the pause. "Can I get it?"

"I don't see why not," I heard myself say.

Because the truth was, I didn't. Maybe Arnold would be bothered by it; but then again, he might not even notice. People in the church might frown, but I really didn't care anymore. The only thing I did care about was the excitement in my daughter's voice when I'd said "Yes." And the light in her eyes when she proudly showed me her dime store ring.

I couldn't impart my own memories, my own ordeal, to her then, but perhaps someday I would. She was the same age I'd been when I lost my cherished gift of a ring to ignorance and guilt. I could feel the ache even now—not just of that incident itself—but of all the shame and pain it was attached to. Yet giving her permission to buy and wear that ring felt sweet, as if against all odds I was becoming the mother I'd needed.

We had been in our new home a year when Arnold received and accepted a call to a prominent pastorate in Muncie, Indiana. The Sunday night that he tearfully announced his resignation, many wiped away their own tears. In ten-and-a-half years he had taken this little congregation by the railroad track to a thriving suburban church with a facility that enhanced the surrounding community. Under his ministry, the congregation had quadrupled in size.

Over and over again in the following weeks, I was asked the same question: "Isn't it hard to leave your beautiful new parsonage?" My outward answer varied, but my inward answer was always the same: *not at all.*

As soon as Arnold had told me of his final decision to move, the heaviness had vanished. I was sad to be leaving the people I'd come to love so dearly, but underneath that sadness another feeling reigned: excitement. As always, I felt saved by movement and expansion, carrying as they did the hope for a different kind of life—one where this gut wrenching feeling would cease and the peace we sang about in church would be mine.

HOUSE TWELVE

Hackley Street, Muncie, Indiana

Christmas lights reflected brightly on the wet windows and streets of Muncie, Indiana, offering cheer and comfort to our family's otherwise cold, dreary entry into this new city.

Arnold's hasty trip there prior to our move had confirmed what the chairman of the board had told us: The church needed a new parsonage. Upon his return, Arnold had given a disheartening report of high, small windows, lots of dark wood and a dated kitchen. I assumed that my "need for grace" was about to catch up with me on my fifteen-year tour of ministerial lodging. But sometimes to be prepared for the worst is a grace all its own.

At first glance, the large, shabby home lived up to its word-of mouth reputation. But an inside tour of the first floor was heartening. Yes, it needed work; but more importantly, it had potential! Antique leaded-glass cabinets stood on either side of the arch that separated the large, rectangular living room from the dining room. An L-shaped stairway with a look-out, a fireplace and a small sunroom off the living room immediately redeemed 218 Hackley Street in my eyes. Effortlessly, I envisioned a cozy, comfortable setting worthy of the pages of Good Housekeeping magazine. The reward of having made my own drapes in Cleveland was that they had moved with us, and would be perfect for the living room windows. And those ruffled sheers from Bellmore? Once again they would go through surgery: separated to suit the single windows in our upstairs bedroom. And a sun room! Who could be unhappy in a house with a sunroom? I knew that once our new round, maple table was ensconced in the kitchen's breakfast nook, I'd feel right at home.

As for the "small high windows," Arnold had described, they were in fact a set of square windows above a built-in credenza of drawers. To me they were classic, a decorator's pleasure.

Upstairs, one of the women from the congregation was making up our beds. "I just *knowed* you was the right people to be our pastors," she said with a grin. Her grammar startled me. *Did everyone in Indiana talk like that?* I sincerely hoped not, yet her genuine warmth made me feel that even if they did, it would somehow be all right.

From the parsonage, the four of us were escorted to another area of town to see the church. It was an impressive contrast to the parsonage: a high, rectangular building that housed a sanctuary and an impressive balcony. Through doors on either side of the choir loft, we entered a two-story educational unit and two offices: one for the pastor and one for the church secretary. Across the back alley from the church sat another amenity with its obvious implications: the assistant minister's house. Arnold and I were thirty-five years old. His hard-working zeal had delivered us to a church that would usually be reserved for older, more experienced clergy. Yet here we were.

As if he had always been at the helm of such large operations, Arnold took command—rearranging the use of space, delegating responsibilities to church leaders and inspiring the entire congregation to share in his ever-present vision of growth. In keeping with his style, Arnold wasn't the type to gracefully inherit a predecessor's assistant minister. Within a few months, and without knowing who the new associate would be, he let the existing one go. Doing the work of two people was hardly a deterrent to him. Besides, he reminded me, he needed the support of a full-time secretary now.

Within weeks, I too, had slipped into my well-established roles: adult Sunday School teacher, choir director—and as needed, pianist. Outside the church walls, my prescribed, if unwritten, duties continued as well: entertainment of missionaries and evangelists; attendance at showers, potlucks and picnics; hospital calls with Arnold. It was as if one stream had merged with a larger one and was carrying me along faster than ever.

But I'd acquired a new function in Muncie too. Evidently I was now mature and experienced enough to be seen in a different light: as a model for the women of the church. When we'd arrived, very few of the women in the congregation wore wedding rings. But across our first year, they started to show up on the ladies' hands, arriving as anniversary gifts, birthday presents, and Christmas surprises. It seemed my own modest band of gold had silently given them permission to have something they'd wanted too, but were afraid to have. My more stylish dress replete with scarves, jeweled pins, and fabric flowers were also openly admired by many of the women in this land of plain, and some followed suit in this as well.

Perhaps that boost of seeing myself differently gave me the confidence to make a crucial suggestion to my typically independent husband. "You're going to need an assistant soon," I told him. "We aren't by the railroad tracks in Cleveland anymore. You can't do this one alone." I knew where I was headed with this, and thus when he admitted he had no one in mind, I gently made my pitch.

"You know, Irving just graduated from Seminary. I think you might take a look at bringing him and Beverly here." Irving was the only child of dear Mr. Laird—the man who had repeatedly livened up the church in Beacon with his exhortations: "He's the

King! He's the King!" I was only ten when Irving's carriage was wheeled into church for the first time, but by the time he could walk, it was evident to the whole congregation that he should remain an only child. Irving had enough energy for any and all siblings that theoretically might have followed. And as an adult, he still pursued life with that same brand of abandon and zest. Arnold knew Irving from visiting Beacon over the years and had often commented on his remarkable zeal.

There was much more to my suggestion than the personal pleasure of having Irving as part of my life. It was apparent to me, even if it wasn't to anyone else, that Arnold wasn't exactly a team player. He was a strong personality with forceful ideas and opinions. He was used to running the whole show, being in charge of everything right down to the last insignificant detail. Few could keep up with him. Few could match him. Few would last for long. But I knew for a fact, that if anyone could, it was Irving. Not just because of his energy and drive, but because Arnold respected him.

I didn't know if my suggestion had taken root or withered in the vast fields of Arnold's mind. But a few weeks later, as I prepared to visit Rhea in Kansas City, he said to me, "Why don't you go meet Beverly while you're there and see what you think of her?" It was understood in this line of work that a pastor's wife could make or break his ministry. Presumably, an associate could do the same—as well as *his* wife. Once in Kansas City, I crossed my inner fingers even as I dialed to make the arrangements to visit Beverly. Arnold was trusting my opinion in this matter. As much as I wanted Irving to join us, I would have to be honest about my impressions of his wife.

Back in Muncie, my report filed, Arnold made his own phone call to the Laird household. I could picture the phone ringing in the humble little basement apartment where I'd sat with Beverly. Some women are unassuming and naturally sweet, but lack strength and presence. Beverly Laird was the most intriguing mix of both that I had ever met. She was like a shawl placed around one's shoulders before the realization of chill had set in. I knew this woman could calm an inner storm and stand firm in an outer one, embodying as she did that old phase "still waters run deep." Irving had chosen well—not just for his excitable, driven personality, but for all of us.

The arrival of the Lairds was nothing short of a godsend for us. For one thing we now had a couple we could be close to without the concern of "getting in thick" with parishioners. And with Jeanne now a long-distance friend, I had Beverly to fill the void of female companionship. With her, I could be more open about the frustrations of the pastorate and the liabilities of being married to a fiery, ambitious man.

The biggest benefit was that Irving immediately took some of the pressure off Arnold. I was temporarily relieved until I realized that full-time assistance had just ramped up his goals and widened his vision. He was more possessed than ever and it was beginning to show in our relationship. He was frequently abrupt and abrasive with me, as well as with Dale and Maridel. Even when I needed to talk with him about household decisions, money, or scheduling a school event, he couldn't stop his whirring mind long enough to absorb what I was saying. The children saw him very little except at church and at dinner, where his body was present but his attention was clearly elsewhere.

As I watched the church flourish—the congregation steadily grow and the choir loft filled to capacity—I began to feel another round of the old heaviness, but it was different this time. My own love for God, my own faith in His goodness and love for me, had deepened with life and time. However, it was as if that experience lived in a different room from the church and its doctrine—the two separated by a long, narrow hallway. It was the same with scripture. Some verses were meaningful to me and a source of true comfort. But when I heard them quoted as pat answers or in Sunday School debates, they fell flat inside me, barely recognizable. *How to bridge this schism within me?* This became the new question. It was a welcome relief from its predecessor "*What in the world is wrong with me?*"

Of course, this separation of church and state-of-heart was more than a private one. I taught an adult Sunday School class every Sunday of the year. I stood in front of people as one who has the right to be there and who has the doctrinal knowledge to be guiding them. I was also aware that the official lessons provided by the general church were to be presented as written—with the teacher as mouthpiece for the material. I had always enjoyed adding anecdotes and examples to make the typically arid material more palatable. But now I had a new dilemma. I began to feel that it was wrong to mandate that the material couldn't be altered, signaling as it did that people shouldn't think for themselves. I tried to stay as close to the script as possible, but couldn't always bring myself to deliver the prescribed message intact. I began to tinker—to leave out and add in, always careful not to cross the boundaries of the doctrine. It felt like I was breathing life into a flat balloon that needed my spirit to rise and float. More and more, I drew on books rather than just the lesson material alone. And as long as the authors were still from within the denomination, I felt free to offer and embellish those things that rang true for me and leave the rest aside. As long as people were nodding and smiling on Sunday morning, I felt I was safe. But no one knew that underneath my public delivery, I harbored and treasured a secret place of my own.

We had been in Muncie for a little over a year when Arnold finally relented to a long overdue physical. Continual neck pain and intermittent Monday morning migraines ultimately spoke more convincingly than my pleas.

"Your blood pressure is very high—especially for a man your age," the doctor told him. And with that, he exhorted him to find some diversions from the church. "You need regular recreation, Arnold, or you're going to burn yourself out."

The doctor was even more frank with me about Arnold's condition. A few weeks later at my own appointment, he spared no words. "I don't want to scare you, Mrs. Woodcook, but at the rate your husband's going, he'll never make old bones. You'd be wise to prepare yourself for that."

I understood the reason for his forthrightness. He saw a dependent woman coming into her middle-age with two young children to raise and a "heart-attack in the making" as their sole support. He was warning me to make plans for what he saw as the inevitable. Arnold ignored what this caring, insightful doctor had told him, but I didn't take his caution lightly. Suddenly, my mind was overtaken by a thought that had never occurred to me: *What would I do without Arnold?* And with that thought, I was catapulted back to the panic of my youth. Then the fear had been based on the unimaginable possibility of an endless life with my mother. Now, I realized with swift and searing certainty, I was no better prepared to avoid that same fate. If something happened to Arnold, I would have nowhere else to go but back to Beacon. At the age of thirty-seven, I still had no skills to make my own way in the world. The piano would no longer be my escape into another life.

Now every time there was a crisis in the church—a split on the board over a financial decision; an evangelist who went too far mixing politics and preaching or stepping on members' toes; or an angry mother who thought her son wasn't played enough on the church softball team (which Arnold coached), I worried. It was getting easier and easier to read the alarming rise of my husband's thermometer in the midst of such conflicts, each one adding a spike to his already high pitch. And thus when the biggest tidal wave of our ministry came crashing into our lives, I literally feared for Arnold's.

It started out as a happy occasion. One of the couples in the church made an appointment with Arnold to set the date for their wedding. They wanted a Sunday afternoon ceremony, which he tried to discourage. For one thing, it was hard on him to officiate a wedding with services sandwiched on either side of it. In addition, and more importantly to him, Sunday evening attendance always slumped significantly on these triple-header events. On top of all the usual reasons, *this* request was for the closing Sunday of a revival. Arnold wouldn't hear of it. They would have to find another date. The couple was obliging, but as so often happens with the young, they had a parent who *wasn't.* The bride's father, Jess, was affronted and challenged his pastor's call, insisting on their right to keep the chosen date. But Arnold wouldn't budge. The wedding, he reasoned, could be rescheduled. The revival could not. And thus a vendetta was launched and for Jess the timing was perfect. The pastor's recall vote was coming up.

Recall was by its very nature humbling: the church members voted whether to keep their pastor—and for how long—or whether to let him go. We had been brought to the church on a two-year unanimous call, but our tenure was up. The recall could be for anywhere from one to four years. I'm sure that few, if any, people in the congregation thought about the pressure this arrangement put on a pastor and his family. Even when there was every reason to believe it would be a good vote, it was still the whole experience of *being voted on* that was difficult. Always one to smooth ruffled feathers—especially those Arnold had ruffled—I was especially aware of any lingering tension when recall was in the air.

On most church membership rolls, there are scores of people who no longer attend the church. Some ministers liked this way of padding their roster, but Arnold was just the opposite. He liked paring the list down when he went to a new church, thereby giving a more accurate picture of the financial base and accurate projections for growth. He'd done that when we came to Muncie, but perhaps not as thoroughly as was necessary. The father of the wedding family not only started campaigning within the congregation to oust Arnold, but got access to the rolls and started calling people who hadn't attended in the years of our ministry. We got wind of the campaign, but there was nothing we could do—and thus the tension in our household built like a pressure cooker with a stopped-up release valve.

For the first time, Arnold seemed drained of his vitality—except for outbursts of impatience and irritability. I didn't know from minute to minute whether to expect sullen silence or disruption. My strategy was to stay as even as possible—something I was good at in a crisis. Even in the turmoil, my heart ached for him. Everything he'd built was on the line.

On recall Sunday, our family exited the sanctuary after the service so the vote could be taken. In the shroud of silence that pervaded our car, we drove home to wait for the results. The results of this vote could cost Arnold his ministry or at least the trajectory it was on. Pastors don't recover from a failed recall in a high profile church. This could also cost me my husband, as I didn't really know if he could withstand the rejection and the loss of something he had poured his body and soul into. And this could surely cost Arnold what was left of his health. No doubt I was holding back my own deep emotion that morning, but cut off from myself as I was, I was unaware of it—determined to remain strong.

When the phone rang that afternoon, like the shrill blast of the warden's whistle, the news was not jubilant. But neither was it fatal. The vote itself wasn't as bad as we'd feared. The biggest blow was that our call had only been extended for two years rather than the four we had hoped for. It would be up to Arnold to decide whether to stay or go. Sometimes ministers did choose to leave under such conditions, feeling that the pressure of continuing in a divisive climate would be too much.

When we told the children, Dale bolted from the room and ran upstairs, slamming his door behind him. Arnold sat unmoving on the couch, staring into some other world none of us could share. Rejection is always hard to take, even when you know circumstances behind it are false. But somehow, the heart responds the same way: as if *every* person you'd touched and loved for two years had said *no* to a full vote of confidence. And this leaves room for the mind to play its own hideous games, obsessing about who had been influenced and which of our members were still in full support and which were not.

When Arnold had collected himself, he went upstairs to talk to Dale. "Don't the people in this church *want* us?" he'd cried out to his father. It was the question echoing in all of our minds and ricocheting off our pain.

Worst of all, we had to go back to church for the evening service.

There had never been a question about Irving Laird's worth: it unquestionably topped his weight in gold. He and Beverly had put as much enthusiasm, heart, and talent into the work as we had, contributing greatly to the church's success. But when our spirits faltered on this critical edge seventeen years into the ministry, Irving stood gallantly by us. He was both our cheerleader and our voice of reason. "Don't let them win, A.E.," he coached Arnold, using the affectionate nickname he had coined. "This will pass and we'll go on. Don't let the people who believe in you down." He took Arnold golfing the next day as a way to stay close to him, as well as to encourage the release of his pastor's frustration. But even Irving admitted to me that Dale's anguished face broke his heart.

Disgrace—real or imagined—is difficult soil in which to

deepen one's roots, but with Irving's help and the solidarity of our foursome, Arnold did just that, accepting the two-year call. Jess and his family were absent from the congregation for a couple of weeks, but then returned. As a whole, the church rallied around us. The next Wednesday night, one of the elders of the church rose to her feet at the close of the service. "Sister Glore," Arnold said, "Do you have something to share?"

"Pastor, we'd like to have your wife come join you up there in the front of the church. Those of us here tonight want to let you and your family know how much we appreciate your ministry and how much we love you." By the time I reached Arnold's side, everyone was standing. They then lined up, all carrying bags of groceries, and after placing their gift in front of the altar, personally shook our hands. It was an old-fashiononed "food pounding," but this time it was more like a healing—something to ease the pain of the pounding we'd taken. There were testimonies afterward, with people sharing their gratitude for all we had done for the church. It was a beautiful gesture on the part of our people—broken only by Jess's obvious need to maintain his grudge. He talked solely about all the starving people in the world who needed food.

As relieved as I was to have the ordeal behind us, and as heartened as I was by the outpouring of support—not just in food, but in the condolences of many people, I was left deeply disturbed. This rift brought up a memory of another church division in my history. When I was young, my parents were part of a group that boycotted the Sunday evening service one week, meeting in our living room instead. I didn't know what might have caused such an odd departure from ritual, but only that my parents were upset about something that was going on in the church. Years later, when I was away at college, my father had dropped out of church entirely due to a dispute that revolved around him. Some years before, he'd petitioned the church for a bus to help bring youngsters in for Sunday School. Black children were not exactly what the board had in mind when they granted the funds, but since the children were in the basement singing "Jesus loves the little children … red and yellow, black and white, they are precious in His sight …" it was hard to openly protest. Besides, the pastor approved. With the arrival of a new minister, however, the tide turned. My father was denied the use of the bus to transport the children. The church members were divided over this issue, but not my father. Since withdrawal was something he knew how to do well, he made it his statement of displeasure. On Sunday, he faithfully ferried my mother to services, then drove away in silent protest, reappearing to pick her up two hours later. After a couple of years, he went back on Sunday mornings, but never fully participated again. Now I had been at the heart of another such division. Disillusionment took the form of nausea.

How could this be? If as Christians, we can't sit down and *reason together,* to use a scriptural phrase, what did all our talk about being "sanctified" and "living in grace" mean? Was this the demonstration of faith that we offered to "a needy world"—that we couldn't even get along with each other?" I was part of a system that purported one thing, but often lived another. Jesus talked about being *in* the world, but not of it. I felt that way about the church—inescapably in it, but not of it. *Wasn't anybody else asking these questions*? I didn't dare ask.

I did less calling with Arnold now than I had in previous years, but still accompanied him to the hospital whenever I could. The one we visited most frequently required us to drive through the campus of Ball State Teacher's College. Each time we made that passage, I felt a longing to return to school. The brick and ivy administration building beckoned to me. I felt its summoning presence but always responded with my impressive list of obstacles: my age, the cost, my church obligations, my children, the certain disapproval of some members and most of all, the vision of Arnold's protestations. Even the general church, I was sure, would frown on a minister's wife compromising her husband's calling with her own ambition. But no matter how reasonable my litany, the strength of the longing did not diminish. Instead, it became like a thumb in my back, unwilling to be ignored.

Even so, I felt unable to broach the subject with Arnold—until a weekend away from home made it impossible *not* to. The church had paid for me to attend a music conference at Winona Lake. I was thrilled at the prospects of meeting other choir directors and musicians, as well as learning how to improve my own skills. In the registration line, another woman and I were getting acquainted while we slowly shuffled ahead. As soon she heard I was from Muncie, she pointed to a lady in the line across from us and said, "That's Bea. She just graduated from Ball State Teacher's College." I eyed Bea with an admiration that wasn't free of envy. My mental list of well-rehearsed defenses followed. But once upstairs, at the door of my assigned room, I was eye-to-eye with Bea. We were roommates.

"I heard you just graduated from Ball State," I said. "I'd love to do that, but my husband is the minister of a large church and I have so many responsibilities that it would just be impossible to …"

"If I can do it, you can do it," she replied, not waiting to hear my roll call of objections. "I run a bed and breakfast, serve as the church organist, am on the board, and care for my aging mother. *And* I drove forty miles each way to class."

I don't remember what the conference at Winona Lake did for me as a choir director, but I've always been clear why the Spirit led me there: to meet Bea Thomas and allow her challenge to take me past my excuses and into the heart of my dilemma. The truth is that I was fearful I would fail, felt guilty for wanting something for myself, and didn't think I could thrive outside the church. Now that the door to the cage was open, would the canary fly out?

Presenting my desire to Arnold was the next step. I told him my dream of returning to school to become a school teacher, fully expecting my own excuses to come pouring out of his mouth and hoping I could counter them. But when I'd finished, he simply said, "That's the best insurance policy I could buy for you. I'll pay the expenses."

I immediately sent for my eighteen-year-old transcript, and at almost forty, entered the imposing administration building and signed up for three classes. Twenty years ago, when I'd gone to college to escape the torment of my mother and find myself a husband, classes were just an inconvenient means to an end. Now, I was here for myself, and because the "thumb in my back" was God's, I knew I couldn't *back down* on this enterprise. It was fortunate that I had such a commitment in place. The first day of class when the professor called my name, I looked around to see who it was that shared the unusual name, "Woodcook." When no one responded and the name was repeated, I realized he was calling my name. In my life I'd been "Adelaide Blauvelt", "Adelaide Woodcook" and "Mrs. Woodcook," but never "*Mary* Woodcook," my legal name—and therefore, the one I'd used to register for school. It was shocking not to have the familiarity of my own name in this brave new world. Later I would warm to the symbolism of it: Mary was the name of my "pastor's wife" grandmother who lived not for the church, but for herself.

A few days into classes, still adjusting to my new alias, I awoke with a severe case of strep throat and was in bed a week—not only nursing my body, but I'm sure, my rising anxiety. Losing that first week cost me, but didn't defeat me. I was happy to get three C's at the end of the term.

The church was bulging at its mortar seams now, classes crowded and space insufficient. We desperately needed a new facility and fortunately, Arnold's uncanny intuition knew just where to begin. Our church was on a corner, but a house and its good-sized piece of property sat on the other side. Never mind that it wasn't for sale. Arnold knocked on the door one morning, introduced himself and simply asked, "Have you ever thought of selling your home?" The owner stepped back as he spoke. "How did you know?"

With one question, Arnold had launched the building project and located our next home. It was the house we would call "the parsonage" until it was time to tear it down.

HOUSE THIRTEEN

Jefferson Street, Muncie, Indiana

Moving into a home purchased for demolition purposes is a strange feeling—a bit like living with someone who's unaware they'll soon be dishonorably discharged. It was an "as is" enterprise for sure. There would be no improvements made unless they posed threats to health or safety. But because it *was* temporary, I could forgive the old house's many flaws—one of which was that it put us back to being the church's closest neighbor. But even that had its conveniences. The children and I could come and go from services without having to arrive an hour early and stay an hour late. Sick children, forgotten items, hot casseroles and mandatory meetings were all just a few steps away. And the thought occurred that the three of us might even see more of our husband and father.

The glaring reality was, however, that this house was just not parsonage material. There was no guest room; the master bedroom was directly off the living room and visible via glass-paned doors; the dining room less than ideal, vying as it did with the television and its corresponding couch. There were rolling floors and a badly out-of-date kitchen with a sink that dominated the only countertop. The stairway to the second story was steep enough to make you think at least twice about the act of ascension, and thus all things heading north collected on the bottom steps—though a staircase door that opened awkwardly out into the living room did hide the unsightly piles. Upstairs, two large bedrooms pleased the children, but their rooms were unfortunately joined by a warehouse-sized, bright scarlet bathroom. The commode sat almost dead center in the room, either a flaw of measurement or character.

The house did, of course, have its redeeming qualities. The glass-paned doors between the living room and bedroom were French in style, adding a bit of charm to both sides. My favorite feature was a sun room that served as a large entry area with windows on all three sides. I couldn't resist this one decorating urge and had cottage curtains made of a red, Early American design that I adored. Calling on the grace of acceptance was not required because its great favor was that it asked very little of me. We were just passing through after all, and no one expected it to fit the image of a parsonage. So other than purchasing a braided rug for the living room from one of the members (to camouflage the wavy floors), and arranging the furniture as artfully as I could, I was free to turn my energies elsewhere.

And elsewhere was *every*where. Adding college to my roster of duties was just that: adding. In order to avoid the criticism that my studies were interfering with my church responsibilities, nothing could be eliminated or even cut back. I don't know if this concern existed only in my mind or was an actual issue for our parishioners, but it hardly mattered. I didn't believe I had a choice. Therefore many were the evenings when I chatted at showers, took my famous meat loaf to potlucks, or attended tedious committee meetings, knowing that I'd be up half the night finishing a paper or studying for an exam. Fortunately, it wasn't just the midnight oil that was burning. I, too, was aglow, lit up by learning and spurred on by my academic success. Even when that success required visiting the children's section of the local library to tutor myself in chemistry, I was an eager student. I had never expected to love learning so much and was constantly spurred on by the thought of having a place in the world outside the church—a teacher with her own classroom and her own paycheck.

This dream kept me going through mid-terms, finals and the times when revival required me to be at church every night for two weeks. Occasionally the dream grew dim and I was tempted to trade it in for the remaining balance of my tuition. One cold, rainy winter morning I came very close to that. Waking in the dark facing a math test I didn't feel prepared for, I had the strongest impulse to go directly to the business office and use the proceeds to buy a new dress. I'd arranged a ride with a fellow student that day as Arnold needed the car. She suggested that I go ahead and take the test and then decide. "What do you have to lose?" she asked. It turned out that if I had put down answers I thought were wrong (and thus left blank), I would have gotten an "A." Even so, I was exultant to get a "B" and inspired to stay in school.

I was deep in study one afternoon, cramming for an exam, when my sister called. My mother had died. The heart that had held its own for the five years since her stroke had suddenly given out. Fortunately, Arnold was close by at the youth center. I ran down the street to tell him, and across the next few whirlwind hours—sending Dale to fetch Maridel from her drama lessons, notifying the school of my absence, cancelling plans and packing everyone up—I felt nothing except shock. Arnold packed the car, making beds for the kids in the back while I packed food for the trip. Then off we went into the night that would turn to morning before we arrived.

We'd only been en route a few hours when Maridel's voice broke the silence. "I don't know if this is a good time to say this," she said. "But I really love you guys." The sweetness of her words pierced my mind, breaking through the chaotic buzz of thoughts and straight into my heart. *Oh, yes … my mother is dead.* It was suddenly real. "It's the perfect time, honey," I told her. "The perfect time."

I didn't shed a tear in New York. Not when I saw her body. Not at her funeral. Not even when I heard my father crying in his bed every night after her burial. I didn't shed a tear because I felt nothing.

Arnold left with the children the day after the funeral and I stayed on with Rhea to sort things out and help my father through the transition. She and I were sitting in my father's car in the cemetery a few days later, just having made arrangements for my mother's headstone when she offered a startling thought.

"I hope she made it," she said.

"Made what, *heaven*?"

"I'm afraid she might not have."

"I'm sure she did, Ree. She did the best she could. I think that's all God asks."

My own words felt odd to me. Like I was reassuring a child that the bogey man didn't exist. My mother had *lived* for the church and for God. How could she possibly be turned away from heaven? But I knew what Rhea was saying. My mother wasn't a loving person. The infliction of her extreme convictions upon us was one thing, but she had physically beaten my sister without cause almost daily. She had pouted for days when she was upset with my father, making our household miserable. She had judged people in the church for their lack of commitment. Even if it was the best she could do, who would ever call it Christian behavior? Let alone Christian perfection?

It was a puzzle without all its pieces—pieces of a picture I didn't even want hanging in my mind. If I allowed these questions to find a foothold there, they would only compound the haunting questions of the recall debacle. And if I started a collection of such inquiries, others would follow—like my husband's increasing abruptness with people and his neglect of our children in the name of God's work.

I was glad to get back to school where the questions, no matter how tricky or taxing, had definable, understandable answers.

We'd been in our temporary quarters for a year when three graduations culminated in our household. Maridel graduated from junior high, Dale from high school, and me from Ball State Teacher's College. I'd not only made it through three years and two summers of tending the conjoined twins of church and school, but had also survived an abusive student teaching experience.

The school I'd been assigned to was just up the street from the parsonage, and the assigned teacher was the daughter of one of our members. It seemed like a propitious beginning, and due to the support of the principal, would, in fact, come to a grand finale. But every day in between was wretched—and not because of the children. The teacher herself was my self-appointed adversary. I was never sure what motivated this woman to treat me so badly: the fact that I represented a religion she had rejected, perhaps? Jealousy of my skills or of the kids' responsiveness to me? My age? Whatever it was, I was helpless in the face of it. She grabbed pictures out of my hand in the middle of a lesson, ripped the children's work off a board I had designed for that purpose, and criticized me in front of the class. The final blow was her belittling of my final project. It was a whole line of cardboard store-fronts where the students learned to do business and make change. They loved it, but for her it was merely fuel for the poor evaluation she gave me at the end of my term.

I felt I had no choice except to go to the principal with my painful predicament as her evaluation would directly affect my ability to get a teaching job. Fortunately, having observed my work himself, he was equally disturbed, and alluding to previous problems of this nature, overrode her evaluation with his glowing one.

When the grand, triple-graduation weekend came, Arnold took our picture in front of the church, enrobed in our black, purple and blue garbs. *Why not in front of the house?* I wondered years later when looking back on the photos. Yet the reflection was true. No matter how personal the achievement or the passage, the church was our backdrop, our context for every occasion.

That fall, Dale departed the transient nest of Jefferson Street and headed to our church college in Illinois. I entered my own new world as well. Going back to school had been an awakening. Outside the boundaries of the church for the first time, I had met people who were just themselves: warm, friendly, fascinating people who didn't even know I was a minister's wife. And because of that, I became one of them. No one had expected anything special of me or even called me by the familiar name associated with my prior life. That experience alone had been worth the price of admission. But now, that awakening was the corridor to another. What might be possible now that I was a teacher?

The schools inside Muncie proper were looking for "younger" teachers than my seasoned self, but one principal was kind enough to direct me to the outlying areas. Presumably these were places that either preferred maturity to youth or simply couldn't afford to be choosy. Whatever the reason, it was a stroke of fortune for me to be hired in the little town of Alexandria, fifteen miles from Muncie, to teach third grade. Here, I had the first-year fantasy that people envision when they choose this profession. Actual first years, by contrast, are often a boot camp of pain and perseverance. But what met me in Alexandria was a well-kept, modern school; a supportive, *older* woman principal; a host of exceedingly co-operative parents; and a large classroom with windows across one side. I was allotted full creative reign and took ecstatic advantage of it. The room was soon a feast for young senses: eye-catching bulletin boards of the solar system; a terrarium that housed a tarantula named George; paneled closet doors that progressively displayed the supernatural origins of Hawaii; and in winter, pots of geraniums along the window ledge. I'd dug them up from my yard, not only to add life and color against the backdrop of winter's gloom, but to provide the children with the mystical experience of watering something and watching it grow.

At Christmas, I brought in a small electric organ I'd acquired, and transformed it into a "pipe organ" with empty gift wrap spools. Covered in gold foil, the spools made an impressive looking instrument and the fact that their teacher could play it was even more impressive to my students. The children had gathered the spools from their mothers and then gathered around me to sing carols. Except for the duet I'd sung with Clarence when I was sixteen, it was the first time I'd used my musical talent outside the church.

I learned two of my most valuable teaching lessons that year. The first came when I awoke one morning with laryngitis, a recurring visitor to my throat. "Whispering in sick" might have been the best of all choices on that day, but the one I made had a greater impact on me. I went to school and proceeded to write, point, and whisper my way through the day. To my shock, within an hour or so, the children were all whispering too, and I had the quietest classroom on the planet—with no coercion whatsoever. Shock turned to revelation: children will speak more quietly if I do. Children will talk more loudly if I do. I modulated my voice in the classroom from that day forward, and passed my discovery on.

The second lesson arrived via a cocoon. A student brought it in housed in a small aquarium.

"Mrs. Woodcook, could we keep this in the classroom and watch a butterfly come out?"

"Of course, of course, Danny." *What an easy science lesson* I thought to myself. *Ready made.*

What I didn't know is that all sticks don't come bearing butterflies inside their tightly-wrapped houses. Some come bearing fleas. Whole classrooms full of them. I learned to do some investigating before granting a child's request to bring something into my classroom.

That first year was liberating for reasons that were both obvious and obscure. Yes, I had a paycheck—my own money for the first time in my marriage. Yes, I could let go of the soul-depleting question of what I would do if Arnold pushed himself into oblivion. Yes, I had an identity of my own that wasn't connected to the umbilical chord of my husband's ministry. But more than that, and hidden from view was this: I had created a new world for myself by simply listening to an inner urge and having the guts to follow it.

And now it was time to move on.

HOUSE FOURTEEN

Wayne Street, Muncie, Indiana

"That's when I moved out!" I quipped, creating a burst of laughter in the room. The picture on the screen was of a wrecking ball in full swing. The target was the parsonage on Jefferson Street. It had been a memorable day watching our home of two years destroyed before our eyes. No tears though. The building fund had finally reached the top of the big paper thermometer that kept visual track of its progress. And the ingenious plans for a contemporary new sanctuary would rise off the blueprint and replace the old house. New would be joined seamlessly to old.

And as for a new parsonage, we had been given the very best. Evidently the church, after promising us a new parsonage early in the scheme of things, and then moving us into a "save-the-space" lesser model, thought they should compensate us. And as a bonus, for the first time in our lives, we had a say in the matter. We were asked to find a group of houses that we liked for the board's consideration.

Wayne Street was at the top of our list, but our hopes weren't high. The neighborhood was manicured and mature with spacious lots; the house was perfect for entertaining inside and out; and even the price was right. But one obstacle could foil it all:

there was a swimming pool in the backyard. Ordinarily of course, this would be a plus, but "public bathing" was one of the injunctions still listed in our church's manual. Not that there weren't a few members with swimming pools by now; but of course, this was *the parsonage.* I passionately wanted this home, as did Arnold and Maridel. Even Dale, though away at school, would be home for the summer and was buoyant at the thought of a swimming pool. But the final decision wouldn't be ours.

The board was invited to view the property and after touring the house, sat poolside for their debriefing. "Well," one member said after discussion had come to a halt. "I don't see why we should turn down the perfect house just because it has a pool." And that seemed to settle the matter.

The house on Wayne Street appeared to be a single story home from the street, with its traditional brick front, healthy shrubs and tree-studded yard. Yet it was like a person who at first comes across as stately and reserved, but who with a bit of time, reveals true quirkiness and charm. Once inside the door, the entry level had a surprise for you: it was the top floor. In the midst of its four-bedroom, living room graciousness was a descending wrought iron staircase that took you into another persona. Here an enormous open room sprawled across the whole back of the house: family room, dining area and a kitchen with space for its own table. Now you actually *were* on the ground, and what you saw through the wall of oversized windows was not just a pool complete with diving board, but spacious garden-like grounds complete with a cabana. The upstairs was a parsonage. The downstairs was a casual, sensual place to be oneself.

From the residence on Wayne Street, I ventured forth for my second year of teaching in Alexandria. The mood was different for me this year, however. As happy as I was to return to my classroom, and as much as I enjoyed teaching, I knew it wasn't permanent for me. I could feel that there was something else in the wind, and by mid-year I knew what it was. The thumb was back, urging me to get my master's degree.

By now, the building project was off and running and so was Arnold. Maridel and I saw less and less of him as the mission began to take him over like a drug for which there was no antidote. Even when he was home, it was merely his body that was present. He sat at dinner with his body turned away from the table, ready to spring up at the ring of the phone or the end of the food—whichever came first. Maridel and I would discuss the day's events, occasionally trying to draw him into the conversation, but it was clear that it took too much energy for him to disconnect from his world and come into ours.

"Penny," Maridel said to him one evening, and she and I both laughed. Even Arnold cracked a smile at the recall of a game the kids had played in the car on long road trips. If either of them had spotted Arnold with his index finger in his mouth, chewing away as if it were Juicy Fruit, "Penny," would be called out and he'd owe one to the caller. But of course, the underlying agenda was never taxed a cent: with his finger in his mouth, Arnold was far, far away, returning only long enough to smile, say a few words, and drift off again.

There were also benefits to his obsession with projects. Early on, as the footing was being laid, he was overseeing the progress as usual and caught an error: the footing was a couple of feet off from the blueprint specifications. Had the project moved forward without correction, it would have been impossible to align the new sanctuary to the existing building as designed. The incident only served to crank up his vigilance.

At the end of my second year of teaching, I cleaned out my room, made my farewells, and headed back to Ball State—now a university—to begin my master's degree in elementary education. The campus was now within walking distance of our house and so began my first experience of exercise—although I didn't think of it that way. Something about stepping out onto the sidewalk with my books in tow, striding through the trees toward campus, made me feel young and strong. I found, to my surprise, that it energized me. And on the days when rain or snow forced me to hitch a ride, I missed it. What surprised me even more was my insatiable love of learning.

When I'd returned to college the *first* time, I'd been plagued with the thought that I might not have what it took intellectually—and that my lack would be exposed to the embarrassment of all. Even when I succeeded, my joy was compromised. *I must be getting by with something. Perhaps professors go easy on me because I'm older.* But as my undergraduate degree had progressed toward graduation, I come to realize that, in fact, I had a good brain—better than I'd known.

In the year of my master's work, that budding shift of perception began to flower into a small, flourishing patch of self-esteem. *Why me?* I would ask on the jaunt to school. *Why had I been singled out of all the ministers' wives I knew to find my own calling?* I honestly didn't know another pastor's wife who had carved out her own life inside the all-consuming labyrinth of the church. And though I continued to live with a foot in both worlds—staying as involved as ever in the activities of the church—my inner life was rearranging itself.

The people, ideas, and experiences outside the church were now mingled into the stew of my life, offering a nourishment I'd never known. And as I got stronger from sipping that broth, I was able to allow myself to know things that had been simmering for years. Though I loved them dearly, I was different from the people in my church world. I wasn't in harmony with the rigidity of the church, with many of its doctrines and rules. *And I had never been.* This realization was no different from the moment when a frantic search for the right key meets with the perfect match. It fit. Jesus had talked about being "in the world but not of it," a verse often quoted to explain the excessive rules of our denomination. But I was "in the church but not of it," and for the first time, I understood the origins of my recurring despair and emptiness.

The competence of scholastic success was a candle alongside the torch of this knowledge. I felt honest with myself. And with God. But there wasn't a soul I could tell.

My husband's star continued to rise. He had made a name for himself in our denomination, and was a popular speaker at rallies and conventions as far away as California and Canada. Everyone wanted to know the formula for his phenomenal success in church growth. I'm sure that whatever he delivered to those audiences was inspiring. But I knew the truth: Arnold was his own formula for success. He was innovative, motivating, and driven—*and* he was willing to sacrifice his health and his relationships to be successful. Even as he rose to prominence, our relationship was on life support. In the grip of the project that would allow his church to grow even more, he was barely available to me. It was both tiring and useless to try to talk to him. I did so only when necessity demanded it.

Even then I admired his genius. Other men may have been more polished and refined in the pulpit, but Arnold kept crowds coming because he delivered a twenty-minute sermon with three points, seasoned by anecdotes and crowned with a great illustration. He also held special "themed" services occasionally, getting people involved in transforming the platform into a ship or the sanctuary into a brush arbor. He was the originator of a change that was adopted by other churches over time: worship service first, then Sunday school. This was his answer to the problem of people coming into church late and disrupting the service—an occurrence he could never understand or accept. This reversal of order worked so beautifully in every way that even the initial resistors ended up endorsing it.

But never was I more impressed with the ingenious mind of my husband than the time he outwitted the new sanctuary's experienced contractor. He'd come to Arnold with bad news: some of the pipes for the air-conditioning would have to be exposed on a wall toward the back of the sanctuary. "I'm so sorry," he said, "but with the unusual design of the church, there's no other way to do it." Arnold wasn't convinced. Taking a folding chair into the hull of the unfinished sanctuary, he sat there until he figured it out. To the contractor's surprise and amazement, this pastor's alternate plan would work. Then the contractor came to him again. "Because the mezzanine is sloping," he explained, "there's no way to install partitions to create classroom space." "There's no way" wasn't a phrase in Arnold's repertoire. Again, he came up with a solution—one that the architect used on future designs.

I saw as never before that Arnold was brilliant beyond the scope of his world, and also, how incapable he was of living intimately within it.

Just as I was finishing the major body of course work for my master's, the new church was finished. In the process, the old sanctuary had been remodeled into two stories for a new educational unit. Now, instead of a set of steep stairs out in front of the church, a wide, elegant foyer greeted parishioners and served as the link to seamlessly join the two buildings. Off the foyer, double doors opened onto a breathtaking sanctuary, bathed in shades of blue and accompanied by dark wood, sloping floors, and subtle lighting. The space held an atmosphere of reverence even when it was empty.

The building was a triumph for both architect and builder, but even more so for the dear, hard-working people who had sacrificed to manifest it and for the man of vision behind it all. On dedication day that spring, with attending dignitaries and an overflowing crowd, Arnold's strength as a leader was apparent to all. Despite what it had cost him, what it had cost *us*, I was deeply proud of his accomplishment.

As if this immense project had put all other parts of our lives on hold, everything accelerated when it was complete. In June, Dale got married to Linda Hatton, a pastor's daughter from Illinois. Loving this young woman came easily to all of us. She was genuinely sweet, easy to talk to, and so obviously in love with our son. That fall, Maridel followed in her brother's footsteps, leaving for her freshman year at our college in Illinois. And I was once again in my own transition—back to the classroom and finishing up my master's coursework two evenings a week. My thesis was still ahead of me and my church involvement still surrounding me. Arnold and I barely saw each other except at church and the dinner table.

As our relationship grew more barren, I was giving birth to the richest of times. This time, I'd been hired by a school in Muncie, one that was looking for a *mature* teacher for one of the poorest areas of the city. It was a predominantly black school, and given my sheltered life, I might have shied away from such an assignment. But despite backgrounds that would have dictated prejudice, neither of my parents was. Not only did my Dad bring black children into a church discomforted by their presence, but one of my parents' closest friendships was with a black couple, the Carpenters. We went to their house and they came to ours. I thought nothing of the fact that we were different colors.

Still, my entry into George Washington Carver Elementary was a culture shock—though not in the ways one might imagine. The children were much more expressive and naturally inquisitive, and their parents were zealous of their progress in a way I had not seen in Alexandria. They seemed to be fueled by an underlying anxiety, by a driving desire to ensure a different future for their offspring. *How can I help*? They would ask. *What can I do*? They were desperately interested in their children and in my efforts to teach them. Fortunately, the class was smaller than my earlier ones, which allowed me to pay closer attention to the children and give more one-on-one help.

What these parents and students didn't know was how much they were enriching my life—exposing me to relationships and interactions that opened my awareness and let in the great light of diversity. I was awash in experiences that ratified my new admission of my own difference. After all, I was a secret minority in my world too.

A year after the dedication, Arnold received another of those life-shaping phone calls. I heard him answer the ringing phone, but his greeting was quickly followed by uncharacteristic silence. He was listening intently, saying little for several minutes. When he did speak, his tone was serious and his voice subdued. When he finally placed the receiver back in the cradle, he sat for a moment without saying a word. Then he broke the silence in a voice that was not his own.

"Dr. Williams has recommended me to the congregation of First Church in Nampa, Idaho."

"Nampa? Isn't that ..." I took a deep breath.

"The third largest church in the denomination."

"You've been recommended by a *General*?"

"I guess that's how it's done at that level. He said someone would be calling me to make arrangements to go meet with the board."

For a moment, we sat together in shocked silence. This was the kind of call we had dreamed of receiving ever since our Bellmore days—yet it seemed unfathomable now that it was here. In all my years of admiring other pastor's wives, none I knew had been privileged to receive this kind of opportunity. Yet I knew that rising higher would mean even greater internal conflict.

"That's great, honey!" I moved toward him, taking him in my arms. "You deserve it," I whispered. Of that I was sure.

The next week, Arnold flew to Idaho. The board responded favorably to the interview and voted to recommend him to the congregation. The vote was taken the Sunday he was there and when I met him at the airport, he was beaming. The congregation had extended a nearly unanimous call.

Now that Arnold was confirmed, the church generously invited us to fly out for a weekend. At the Boise airport, a large youth choir sang, "Up, Up with People," as we deplaned, and an enormous banner read, "Welcome Woodcooks!" I wore my favorite outfit: a beautiful grey tweed suit with a soft, fitted cut and black accessories. We were wined and dined—*sans* the wine—all weekend, starting with a steak dinner with the board and their spouses. The following day, as Arnold met with church officials, I was escorted to a Tea in my honor. The house was full of warm, welcoming strangers. I hoped I was making a good impression, but was more caught up in being impressed. I felt at last like my long-ago namesake, celebrity Sarah Bernhardt.

On Sunday, Arnold preached to our new congregation of eight hundred people. No pause was necessary for the 11:25. We weren't in Kansas—*or* Cleveland-- anymore. Afterward, we strode down the middle aisle and out into the foyer to greet the streams of people that poured out three double-doors.

I came home inspired to start packing up Wayne Street. It was the first parsonage I was reluctant to leave, but the church in Nampa was set to purchase a new one, which I was confident would be just as lovely as this one. With six weeks until our move, Arnold left to begin his ministry in Idaho. I stayed behind to finish out the school year at George Washington Carver and complete my thesis. In the final weeks of school, I packed at night and shared my venture with the children by day. My move to Idaho had sparked an interest in this faraway place. An enormous pull-down map of the states helped us trek the highways from Indiana to Idaho. My students were in awe to know someone who was moving so far away, and listened intently as I read to them about Idaho and its agricultural star: the lowly potato. As a finale, they drew pictures of this new land. To my amusement, most of them drew Indians and stagecoaches, but I had no time to correct their perceptions.

I was off and running—donning my cap and gown for a graduation under the blazing Midwest sun and hitting the road the very next day to pick up Arnold. He was flying into the city of Fort Wayne and from there, we would pick up Maridel in Illinois. The three of us would set out together on a trip across the country. I knew the way. My ~~third~~-grade class had already mapped the course.

I was elated the morning I headed out, flowing with the juice of accomplishment and adventure, and feeling ready for culture shock of new terrain. For even without the Indians and the stagecoaches, it did seem like the Wild, Wild West to me—a place where I might claim my own new territory. In my elevated state, with joy emanating like sparks, it's a wonder that I saw the two cars coming over the brow of a two-lane hill at high speed. In a heartbeat, I swerved to the right, across someone's lawn and into the narrow space between a ditch and a telephone pole—caught by a net of wire fencing. The drivers, white with shock, came running over to me.

"Are you alright, Lady?" they asked breathlessly. "Are you alright?"

In conditioned fashion, I assured them I was fine.

"Are you sure, Ma'am? You're okay?"

"Thank you, but I'm fine--*really*."

But I wasn't anything close to fine. I was badly shaken and should have asked for help in backing the car up onto the road. Yet it didn't occur to me. Instead, I sat in our Oldsmobile surveying the tangle of clothes on the floor under the dash and trying to get myself to stop shaking. My pounding heart simply refused to believe the danger was over.

When I finally maneuvered the car back out onto the highway, I was in a greatly altered mood. Of course, I was flooded with gratitude, aware that my angels had protected me. I'd had no time to make a conscious choice or enough skill to guide the speeding car down that narrow strip between two dangers. Now my goal was to get to my husband and pour out my story, hoping that his comfort would make me feel safe again. But Arnold had already given his soul to the Next Great Challenge, and barely responded to my tale of near collision and death. As I lay in the motel, with my husband breathing in sleep beside me, I felt more alone than I did in all our weeks of separation.

I promised myself that tomorrow my daughter's face would turn my world right side up again.

HOUSE FIFTEEN

Sherwood Drive, Nampa Idaho

Maridel was watching for us from her dormitory window and by the time we had pulled to a stop, she was flying out the doors and down the front steps. It was like greeting a long-lost image of myself. She'd inherited my slender frame and fair skin, though her hair was not flaming red, but auburn. More significantly, at 18 she was pursuing passions that paralleled my own: drama, speaking and writing. Gratefully, Arnold and I had given her far more rein in expressing her talents. While I'd been forbidden to even go to the school play, she had starred in her ninth grade performance—in fact, one that required her to *dance* in the final scene. Desperately wanting the part, she'd recruited me to ask her father, and I had done so with both trepidation and a strong personal recommendation. He'd consented—bravely, I felt—given that word of the minister's daughter dancing in a public performance could have raised more than eyebrows. The night of the performance, he saw her with new eyes—saw a piece of himself in her obvious talent. The following year, he coached her through four levels of competition in the Teen Talent contest of our district. Against competitors all older than she, Maridel won first place at the finals and Arnold's only wish was for more buttons to pop. She'd also been copy and headline editor for her high school's acclaimed yearbook, and written articles in the award-winning school paper as well as a column in the local paper. Through her, I had lived my unlived life.

We were all eager to set out on our cross-country tour, each of us spinning in our own little worlds. I was weary from the strain of packing, teaching, and finishing my thesis. Arnold was brimming with enthusiasm about the trip he'd mapped out. Maridel was relieved to be leaving this first year of college behind. After her dynamic high school years, college had been a disappointment. "The rules are suffocating," she'd written to us. "Chapel is five days a week in addition to church, and there are fines if you're late three times in a quarter. Not to mention the curfews!" She had languished in the grip of such restrictions. Arnold and I had never given her a curfew because she'd never needed one.

One of many reasons why Nampa, Idaho, was appealing to us was that another of our church colleges was located there—and from what we'd heard, a far less rule-bound one. Maridel had already decided to change schools for her sophomore year, so our move had been the perfect answer for her.

With her bright presence in the backseat of the car, the incident and hurt of the previous day receded into the shadows. Together we were a lively trio, refreshed by the rising winds of change. Golden stretches of wheat seemed to roll on for days as we traveled through the Midwest, but gradually the landscape transformed into rolling foothills, great rock formations, and finally to the grandeur of the Northwest mountains. Arnold had made sure that our route took us through Wyoming and into the heart of Yellowstone Park—the magnificence of which made my heart leap with possibility. At the Idaho border, we stopped for a photo shoot. My favorite was of my beaming daughter, leaning against the "Welcome to Idaho" sign, looking like one who has found her true home. Continuing south on winding mountain roads, we snaked our way into Nampa, Idaho—population

15,000. Located in Treasure Valley, the largest valley in the state, this little town was a hub of our denomination, boasting seven churches, large district offices, and a four-year college.

Arnold was anxious to show us the parsonage. Our first glimpse was impressive: a striking L-shaped brick home on the corner lot of a stately, well-groomed neighborhood. Big picture windows and a spacious yard brought a grin. A first walk-around was pleasing: the house followed the contours of the lot creating a private courtyard patio in the back. First look inside was crushing: mottled tan and brown carpeting was at war with pink and green oriental drapes, and the whole house seemed to be swallowed up in their feud.

Eventually, the rest of the house came swimming into view: an open, roundabout of a floor plan—expansive rooms that formed a circle of living, dining, family room, and kitchen—all linked by the hall and a laundry room. On one end of this area, a sliding glass door led to a step-down room that overlooked the courtyard. I'd run out of names. Den? Game room? Extra furniture room? Whatever it was, it served as a bridge between the main house and the garage. And on the other end, were the bedrooms—three of them, each large and sporting views of old-growth trees.

The next morning, I awoke early to sunlight and the caress of cool breezes. They carried with them astonishing delight! A summer day that didn't start with humidity and sticky skin? I'd never known anything else, but was willing to forget. I stepped outside to feel the air on my body, and there from my backyard, was a close view of the mountains! With the disappointing amenities of the parsonage at my back, their majesty infused me with awe, inviting me to look past the drapes and carpet—to behold a larger perspective. The interior could and would be changed, I knew. But no interior could ever fill my soul like the majesty in front of me.

I suddenly sensed that I was someone new here. Not just because I was 1,800 miles away from familiarity, but because of the self I had discovered in all of those places. The mountain breezes seemed to assure me that there was space here, and that in this place I would be freer than ever before. My sister's childhood nickname flashed in my mind. Only Rhea had called me "Addie." In our former pastorates, I'd primarily been "Mrs. Woodcook", with only a few younger women calling call me "Adelaide." Arnold had picked my nickname up from Rhea and used it occasionally over the years. But in this place, I wanted to *introduce* myself that way. The soft, warm sound of "Addie" now felt like my true name.

As far as the names of our members—that was another matter. As hundreds of people poured out of the doors of the sanctuary that first Sunday to shake hands, I felt completely daunted by the task of learning their names. So I decided to take action by spending time every day with the church pictorial directory, and attempting to make memorable associations. With a measure of confidence I cheerfully greeted Mr. and Mrs. Stone the following week. Mrs. Stone leaned closer and quietly informed me, "The name is Rock." I decided to stop trying so hard and let time and repetition be my teacher.

Even with five associate pastors—one for youth, one for music, one for children's ministries, one for elders, and one for adult education—Arnold's responsibilities as senior pastor were staggering. His health problems, particularly blood pressure, had increased over the years, but his drive only seemed to increase alongside them. His strategy was to take medication and just keep pushing. Some of the associates were inherited and not up to Arnold's exacting standards, which I knew was part of his stress. I was relieved, therefore, when the board gave him liberty to make adjustments to the existing roster of associates. After letting a couple of men go, his next step was to call Irving, who had taken on a pastorate of his own part way through our time in Muncie, and was now ready to join us again. With Irving as Arnold's reliable and efficient right-hand man, I could rest easier. He was the one person Arnold trusted completely and in who he could confide as a friend.

The solid, loving friendship of the Lairds would be a comfort in many ways. But one we couldn't foresee. Late one night, after just a few weeks in Nampa, our exhilarating venture in the great Northwest came to a heart-stopping halt. If we had been asleep in our own bed, perhaps the moment would not have been so memorable. But our new bedroom set had not yet arrived, and when the phone rang, we were dead asleep on a mattress in the living room. Startled by the shrill intrusion, Arnold had to haul himself up from ground level to stagger toward the sound. I sat up, following his journey to the kitchen. It seemed interminable. What you hope for, of course, is a wrong number—for which you'll feel both grateful and irritated. Instead it was a call that bolted the door to sleep's chamber. It was Dale. He had just received orders to go to Viet Nam.

One question hounded me as I staggered, sobbing, through the corridors of my sleepless night: how could I live thirteen months with my son in active combat? *How could I live*?

In the morning we placed a call to Linda. She'd been alone in her parent's home when Dale had called her. "I turned on every light in the house and waited for my folks to come home," she told us, crying. "I couldn't stand to be alone in the dark." I knew exactly how she felt.

In the intervening weeks before we made our journey to Camp Pendleton to see Dale off, I kept my body moving, but the light and the promise of that first glorious day was gone. The cool mountain breezes still came through my window, but I no longer felt their caresses. Though Maridel would be living in the dorm by fall, she was living with us for the summer, and I took all the solace I could from her presence. Once she was the child in imminent danger; but for her brother, the verdict was at the end of a much longer spool of living.

Despite the news hurtled into our home like a bomb, my responsibilities at church still called. They were actually a reprieve. The sanctuary choir, which seemed to be waiting for me at each pastorate like an orphaned child, let me slip into the comfortable old clothes of that role. The greater challenge was the vacancy left by the former pastor's wife. I'd rarely been without an audience on Sunday mornings, but this audience was a congregation in itself:300 college students. Daunting as the assignment was, it seemed like the perfect match for me. Who better than to test the waters of my growing awareness with than the young and often restless?

It's always unsettling to pack for a trip you don't want to take. But making a sojourn to spend a few hours with a son you might never see again isn't even a trip. It's torture with a map. On the way there, it felt as if it was taking all my energy just to keep my soul from unraveling. I wanted nothing more than to see the face of my first-born, to look into those water-blue eyes. But how would I crowd out the swinging pendulum inside my chest? The pending dread of our goodbye?

Dale was allowed to leave the base, but spent a fair amount of time showing us around and introducing us to his friends—trying to join his worlds through handshakes and humor. I managed to be cordial, using my best pastor's wife smile to belie the ache in my gut. We went off base to visit Disneyland for the afternoon—an atmosphere so incongruous to my inner state that years later, as I talked with Dale about that experience, I could find no shred of its memory. I didn't even remember leaving the base. All I could call up was walking those grounds with him, listening to him share his tales of boot camp, and wishing I could wake up on a mattress in my living room and sob with relief.

When the time came to say goodbye, Arnold and I each hugged our firstborn, our only son, close to us. When we were eye-to-eye again, he said calmly, "If anything happens to me, they'll let you know right away." We'd driven two days for this one day—a day that I wanted to end only because it would be one less until he was back home. But first, we had to walk away.

As we drove away from Dale, waving our goodbyes, my heart sank into my gut and took anchor. Arnold was crying so hard he pulled over and asked me to drive. I drove while he sobbed, filling the car with the sound of my pain. We tried, en route home, to enjoy our ride through Glacier National Park, but all I could think of was our recent visit to Yellowstone when outrageous beauty was still alive for me. We had dinner at a lovely restaurant where I ate without tasting, and afterward, slept in a motel where I wept without sleeping. I could not imagine what lay ahead for us. Time that had been speeding by just weeks before, I feared now would crawl so slowly I wouldn't be able to measure it. Linda had decided to spend the year with her parents, teaching school in Illinois. My heart ached for her, and even though I knew she was in the right place, I wished I could be close to her, reassuring her of the very things I prayed were true.

Once home, it occurred to me that there was only one way I was going to make it through the thirteen months that lay ahead: by nurturing my private and dissident faith. The experience of God that transcended my training would have to be my compass. Unless this were so, my prayers for Dale would be empty—drawing only on what I'd been taught rather than on my own growing relationship with Him.

As if that decision had been whispered directly into the ear of God, a response came quickly. One of my young Sunday school students recommended a book to me. It was the book I didn't know existed, but in my heart, had been looking for all these years. *The Psychology of Jesus and Mental Health* by Raymond Cramer came into my hands when I needed it most and became not a mere book, but a friend. Its pages were living validation of my private feelings. I devoured its contents, marking passages and making notes. In an act of sheer bravado, I set aside the Sunday school curriculum and developed a series of my own with Mr. Cramer's interpretations of the Beatitudes as its basis. But it was the tenet of this book that inspired me to be so bold: Spiritual and psychological health go hand-in-hand. Scriptures should be applied to practical living and be evident in our lives.

In a setting where loving one's self was considered selfish if not sinful, I began leaking my newfound message of self-acceptance and love to my students. Drawing upon my own insights from the book, the lessons seemed to prepare themselves. As the class grew, so did my courage. I was vitalized by the truth, and not only felt closer to God than ever before, but fortified to walk in the fields of landmines created by my fear.

Dale's life of active duty in Viet Nam was already claiming more than I had to give—like a tax extorted from the poor. I could barely sleep. The doctor prescribed a mild sleeping pill for the duration of Dale's tour of duty, and while I usually resisted the use of drugs, I took these with gratitude.

I lived for the sound of the mailman's truck. There was no rhyme or reason to the rhythm of Dale's letters. Two could arrive within a day of each other and weeks could go by without any. So every day, I pulled the mail greedily from the box, looking for the bold, round penmanship of my son. Everything else was just the cradle for his letters, which were already old, already not the truth—but all I had. Inside those envelopes, he was still safe. Still in this world.

My concerns about Arnold's health—compromised further by his anxiety over Dale—were still present as well. And so I was relieved when he found a recreational outlet that seemed to elicit true passion. Idaho was horse country. Horses had only meant one thing to my husband: big, plodding animals that plowed the fields of his parents' farm. But when one of our church members took Arnold riding, it was as if he'd been introduced to a radical new species. With a little coaching from Marv, he took to horseback riding. I watched, amazed, as he made time to go out to Marv's ranch a couple of times a week to ride. Soon he was hooked, and his interest burgeoned into a passion. He joined the Saddle Club at the church, began to ride in rodeo parades, and go horseback riding with various members. Soon, he had coaxed me into trying his new hobby, and though I didn't share his enthusiasm, I sometimes joined him. At a time when we desperately needed it, this unlikely sport gave us something to do together outside of church.

As with all things in life, Arnold didn't tread lightly or cautiously with his new hobby. Soon we owned an RV, and predictably, a beautiful pair of matched Saddlebred horses. I was grateful for the joy it was bringing him, and for the solace I sensed he garnered from being out in nature.

The church in Nampa was proving to be a different kind of challenge for Arnold. Already large and well-established as a top church in the denomination, the impetus was not toward record-breaking growth or new buildings, but toward keeping the constituency happy. Arnold's innovative ideas didn't have a breeding ground. His mantra of "Divide and Grow" wasn't seen as applicable. He was as busy as ever, but more restless—a king displaced. Idaho he loved. Horses, parades, and camping he loved. But the church to which he had risen seemed to carry more prestige than real satisfaction.

By contrast, this church was a great shifting tide for me. If Dale hadn't been in Viet Nam that year, that year would have clearly been one of my best. Being the "head pastor's wife" was a relieving pace or two behind being the *"the* pastor's wife." I still attended many social events, but now I had backup. If I didn't go, one of the appropriately younger or appropriately older ministers' wives would—and no one would think anything of my absence. I'd relaxed my style in other ways as well. When I didn't remember a name, I drew heavily upon what Arnold affectionately dubbed my "warm hello." "Well, *Hello* there!" I'd croon with a friendly touch on the arm. Its high effervescence made up for my lack of solid recall.

I still had enormous responsibilities, but my heart was in the challenges they offered. One was the sanctuary choir and its capacity to perform at levels beyond my previous experience. I thrilled at stepping into those higher heels. Music was, after all, the oldest love of my life. The other responsibility, my college Sunday School class, was more inspiration than work—giving me as it did an outlet for my own spiritual growth. At last I was teaching what I wanted to learn. In a religious system where the emotions of honesty, anger, jealousy and resentment were supposedly abolished by the experience of sanctification, Mr. Cramer was a heretic—and I his willing accomplice. Together we set forth the tenant that honesty and awareness are keys to a life of integrity, and that acknowledging in *ourselves* that which we judge in others is an opportunity for spiritual growth. I steadily steered my students toward awareness rather than denial; and all the while, I was listening intently to myself.

Maridel's life had opened wide in Idaho. In the more relaxed and less restricted atmosphere of this college, she flourished. Because the campus was within walking distance of the parsonage, she frequently and spontaneously appeared—to share what was going on at school, drop by for non-cafeteria food, or to study for an exam in peace and quiet. Her dual homes were a great boon for her; but for me, they were a tool in my thirteen-month survival kit. *How would I have managed Dale's precarious existence*, I wondered, *if she had been away at school as she'd been the year before? If we'd been linked only by letters and brief dormitory phone calls*? Even in the shadows of this valley, I was grateful. For Raymond Cramer's writings. For my own creative challenges. For horses. And for the proximity of my daughter's smile.

Linda and I were keeping in touch throughout the months. But the news was often painful: her letters spoke of sleeplessness, anxiety, and chronic stomach pain. Her heartbreaking attempts to be cheerful with us when we called often left me feeling low. It's not the way one envisions getting to know a daughter-in-law. But over the months, as we shared Dale's letters and counted the weeks turning slowly into months, I could feel a bond forming—like intertwining vines around the telephone lines that joined us.

In January, when Dale had been gone six months, that bond grew stronger. Our whole family flew with her in spirit as she traveled to Hawaii to share Dale's week of "R and R" with him. I'm not sure how much "Rest and Recuperation" one gets in seven days away from the holocaust of war, but as a family, it was the chance to send a representative to the front lines of our hope. At least one of us could touch and hold the man whose face came into view with every ring of the phone and every knock on the door. If Linda could touch him and report back, we could dare to believe we were halfway to a happy ending. He was missing from our daily lives but still "alive in action."

The months began to pass a bit more quickly after this midway mark, as if getting that far allowed us—and time—to breathe more easily. I knew that our son was just as likely to be wounded or killed in the last half of the tour as the first—but I welcomed this trick of the mind that made my heart feel better.

In June, two anniversaries merged into one. Arnold and I had been in Nampa for a year and together for twenty-five years. I could no longer fit into my twenty-five dollar wedding dress, but Maridel did—perfectly. At the church reception given in our honor, I watched my chiffon gown swish in and out of my vision like a phantom bride. In the midst of white cake, rosy punch, and punctuating congratulations, my daughter's presence was a sobering delight for me. There I was twenty-five years ago—young, wildly optimistic and in love. *Where is that girl now?* I wondered. We went home that day with a beautiful silver tea and coffee service, a stack of cards, and a mountain of leftover cake. Maridel took off the dress and returned to her unbridled self. But *Where is that girl now*? lingered.

By all outer standards, Arnold and I had every reason to celebrate a silver wedding anniversary. We had a lovely parsonage and an engaging life. We were successful and esteemed. We had two children we adored, and were closing in on the remainder of Dale's tour of duty. And we had our faith. Arnold's father, a prayer warrior of many years, had claimed God's promise to him that Dale would return "without a scratch." If that were so, we would have a reason to celebrate that transcended by far a twenty-fifth wedding anniversary.

But I knew where my lingering question was taking me: into the *inner* gauge of our twenty-five years. And by that measure, we were not doing well. Despite our love, or at least loving loyalty, the relationship was more shell than substance. "Adelaide" might have been content with the accoutrements of these twenty-five years of marriage, but Addie was not. In Muncie, I'd purposefully kept my fledging insights about myself and my beliefs private. I'd wanted to stir things up a bit in my Sunday school classes, but knew I couldn't risk injuring my husband's ministry. And so, I'd wrestled inside with my confusion about the doctrine of sanctification and with my growing discordance with the dogma that I stood for. So when the call came to Nampa—the call that Arnold had no doubt been dreaming of since he entered the ministry—I was glad I'd kept it all to myself. I was glad I hadn't done anything that might have robbed him of this deeply-deserved success.

I was still glad; and not just for him. This place, with its dawn and dusk breezes, its valiant mountains and open spaces, was my reward too. Not so much for my work in the ministry, but for continuing to wonder, continuing to seek. *That's where that girl is now*, I thought as I hung my celebratory dress in the closet. No longer young. No longer wildly optimistic. And truthfully, no longer in love. But continuing to seek.

A week before Dale was due to return home, the phone rang. Every ring coursed through my body now, a frequency that jump-started my heart into chaotic frenzy. Now that we'd weathered the grueling trail of his year in combat, and with his entire original platoon sacrificed, every ring was momentous.

This one most of all.

It was Dale. He was in Guam.

He was coming home.

Though my hands were shaking, my body trembling, and my heart soaring with joy, I managed to dial the number. It was the call I feared I would never get to make. "Honey," I said, voice cracking, "Dale called. He's coming home."

There are no words for a moment like this. It defies the power of the human vocabulary, however sophisticated. A moment like this explodes in your sky—a phenomenon that science can neither name or explain. Its brilliance washes over you like rainbow rain.

Our phone bill soared as we placed our jubilant calls all over the country. We didn't care. This euphoria reminded me of the night of Dale's birth when the neighbors questioned Arnold's sobriety. I'd never been drunk, but I thought this must be what it was like. And underneath the uproar of ecstasy, my heart kept beating out its unspeakable thanks for Dale's return. He was being born to us again.

We didn't know exactly how many days it would be until Dale

arrived in Boise, but we flew into eager preparation to be ready when the call came. Arrangements were made for Linda to fly to Idaho and wait with us while Dale completed his debriefing in Guam. Together we made a huge banner with his picture on it to go across the garage door: "Welcome Home, Dale." I went to the meat market and bought the best steaks I could find. Arnold procured a cottage on Cascade Lake, donated by one of our members, for Dale and Linda to have a private getaway.

When he called, we were ready.

Two days later, bursting with electric expectation, the four of us made our way from Nampa to Boise. Outside the airport, we huddled close in a crowd of families eager to have their prayers answered in the flesh. There was a steady hum of anticipation, a mood of restlessness punctuated by laughter. We were a waiting organism, bound together in this unforgettable moment made of anxious, radiant gratitude and abolished fear.

"That's it! That's the plane!" someone shouted at last. I lifted my face, shielding my eyes against the sun's glare. There it was, nothing more than a speck in the wide blue sky, but that speck held my child. My heart leapt inside me with a force too big to contain, and my whole body began to quiver. As the plane grew larger, a cheer went up from the crowd and as it hit the runway, another cheer—this one louder. I tried to join the chorus, but all of my energy was going into holding onto myself as the outrageous good news hit my body. Then the plane coasted to a stop and sat on the runway, silent. We waited, but nothing happened. My mind was spinning wildly with flashes of Dale running through my head like photographs all out of order. As the minutes passed, I could feel the tension building in the crowd, and inside me. *What if there was some kind of mistake?*

"Are they ever going to open the door?" a voice asked, echoing everyone's question. At last, the immense door was shoved open, revealing only a silent, cavern of black. Its creak hung in the air, and then fell silent too. A reverent hush fell over us now, as if collectively remembering that not all soldiers come home to joy. We waited in the sun and silence, my heart refusing to quiet, the memories continuing to flash.

At last, a young man emerged from the dark, and as the crowd roared, his arms stretched wide and began to crisscross in a fanning wave. "It's Dale!" I heard Arnold shout, and as he came down the stairs, Linda ran toward him and leapt into his arms. We stood back, giving them their moment, but when he reached out to me, I ran into his embrace with tears streaming down my face. With the reality of his homecoming still hard to take in, the reality of war was undeniable.

Dale was skeleton thin, his face as gaunt as the haunting visages of orphaned children in magazines. He was smiling, but inside his sunken eyes, a certain light was missing. He was not the man we had said goodbye to thirteen months before. In my joy and relief, in my understandable ignorance, I hadn't thought about his culture shock: his emergence from a world of survival, grief, and loss into a world of smiling people who looked the way he'd left them. A world with choice steaks and all the trimmings. Had I expected him to be like I'd remembered? I had. Of course I had.

Dale was restless throughout dinner, and halfway through excused himself. After a year of living on rations, real food was an offense to his system. Soon after our reunion meal, he and Linda left for the cabin, and I stood in a kitchen full of dirty dishes feeling strange and off-kilter. The gratitude that had swelled the banks of my being in the last few days was still there, but now its waters were tainted with fear. An enormous transition faced my son, faced all of us in the aftermath of this year. We'd walked on the continual edge of a nightmare, but he had lived inside it.

Within a few months, Dale and Linda made a decision to

come live in Nampa. She found a teaching job and he enrolled at the college where his sister was now a junior. I knew where to find both my children now, and very soon, they would know exactly where to find me. I was beginning to fully settle into a normal life in Nampa when another phone call shocked me. But this one was welcome. The head of the Education Department at the college was calling to invite me to a meeting with himself and the Dean. "We'd like to discuss a teaching assignment with you," he said. His voice was matter-of-fact. I cleared mine. *At the college?* I wanted to say, but caught myself in time to avoid embarrassing both of us. A week later, at the close of that meeting, I'd agreed to teach Elementary Education on a part-time basis with the possibility of graduating to full-time in the future.

I was stunned. And smiling.

It took a few days for another line of reasoning to poke its head through "cloud nine and a half." *What was I thinking? Teach college students to be teachers?* Maybe the Head of the Department hadn't really checked out my experience. Suddenly I imagined the good Dean calling, all apologies: "Mrs. Woodcook, we're so sorry, but we didn't realize you'd only taught school for three years. Our minimum requirement is ten." I felt pleased and nervous at the same time—as if I'd pulled something off and hoped no one found out.

Fall arrived and no one had called to awkwardly retract the offer, so off I went to claim my title as college professor. It was like slipping into the very best pair of old shoes you ever owned—the ones you wished you'd bought in three different colors. The only thing more satisfying to me than teaching, I came to see with haste, was teaching teachers. I had a passion for it. My lack of experience, as it turned out, was just my own phantom projected onto external authority. Once I was there, wielding hand-outs, creating exercises and illustrating my points, I saw that *all* my years of teaching went into this enterprise. I knew good teaching when I saw it, and I could see it in the faces of my students.

I don't know how far I was into the school year before the oddest bit of memory arrived, much like a postcard that's toured the country before it lands in the right mailbox. *Oh. I remember. I had wished once for this very thing.* In high school, I'd had this audacious thought that I would like to teach in one of our church colleges someday. In its brief life, before it was banished by another voice, it held such lofty, aspiring sweetness. It was a vision of me as someone else, someone I liked and respected. But it had been quickly replaced by a thought that seemed more real to me; namely, that it would never happen.

Now here I was—*living* that vision of a college professor. I chalked it up to happy coincidence without an inkling that it could be anything more.

With both my children around me again, and my relationship with my daughter-in-law growing, I felt as close to complete as I'd ever felt in my life. What I was doing in the church, I loved doing; and the rest of the week, I loved what I was doing even more. The fact that Arnold and I had little connection was becoming acceptable to me. Maybe that's just how it was when you'd been married a quarter of a century. Besides, I had my own identity now.

Even more importantly, I had something else—something I had once despaired of ever having: resolution of the episodic depression and private pain I'd endured for so many years. Now the origin of my emptiness was clear: it was the price I paid for fulfilling someone else's calling and believing it was my own. It was the cost of investing my whole self in a doctrine that had never made sense to me.

The next semester I taught child development as part of my methods classes. Studying this subject to pass a test in college was far different than articulating it with conviction. As I organized my lessons on the fundamental needs of children: individual attention, respect for their differences, support of their interests, and positive affirmation of their being, the bells were jangling so loudly in my head that it sometimes halted my preparation. *How had I not seen this before*? Almost everything I was about to stand in front of my class and proclaim as essential to a child's development had been either missing from my childhood or vigorously thwarted. My mother loved me of course. Why else would she turn Christmas into a gala of gifts? Or wear that mask of fear when Rhea and I were seriously ill? I understood now what passed for love in that generation: protection, provision and control. In wanting what they deemed "the best" for me, they had molded me after their own image without any ability to even wonder if the mold fit.

With this new found clarity, I had the impression that the past was now behind me. What I didn't know was that while it was indeed *behind* me, it was gaining on me every day.

The following year, my right shoulder started painfully misbehaving. It tightened up to the point that I couldn't raise my arm to my eyebrow, making it impossible to put on the mascara that I had started using—along with a bit of lipstick—since moving to Idaho. I went to the doctor, expecting him to give me an exercise or muscle relaxant and send me on my way. Instead, his prescription was a trip to the hospital for anesthetic and a procedure aimed at breaking up the logjam in my rotary cuff. Exercises at home followed—and failed.

"Well, this shoulder needs surgery, Mrs. Woodcook," he announced on the next visit.

"What could have caused this?" I asked, needing to explain the coming interruption to my lifestyle.

"You probably stretched too far to reach something on a top shelf."

Not the answer I'd been expecting. I instantly remembered

the incident: stretching on tippy-toes to reach a vase on the top shelf. But the doctor's answer held a deeper one. All the way home that day, these words kept repeating in my head: "stretched too far, stretched too far…"

I felt a connection between those words and my life. I'd never heard of a mind-body connection; but all of a sudden, I'd made one. For how many years had I been "stretched too far?" I loved my life now, but even so, it was as demanding as ever. I rarely stopped working and felt uneasy when I did. "Stretched too far" was all I'd ever known, my well-worn storyline. Now with a surgery scheduled and a projected six weeks of recovery, stopping was my only option.

The surgery went well, and the ten days in hospital, with full endorsement to do nothing but rest and recuperate, was acceptable to my mind. In fact, that sterile room became a place of solace all my own. Amidst the fragrant beauty of my flowers and happy to be served meals rather than serve them, I read several books and wrote lengthy passages in my journal. I'd had to come to a hospital to feel comfortable with taking time for myself.

Another building was brewing in Arnold's restless mind. A church of this size needed an appropriate fellowship hall in his estimation, and the old house across the street that served as one was not only inadequate, but a mismatch to the rest of the facilities. His proposed solution was sweeping: build a new sanctuary and remodel the existing one to include a fellowship hall, expanded offices, and more classrooms. The man who had once knocked on a neighbor's door and procured their property with a single question, went into action—presenting to the board and to the membership a vision that befit the status of this church. This time, however, it would mean negotiating for several houses—and in a feat that only his indomitable spirit could manage, the prevention of a proposed convenience mart was already in negotiations.

Although this mammoth undertaking put him back in his favorite ministerial saddle, the years of unrelenting drive were telling on him. Physically, he was suffering more migraines since coming to Nampa, and with them, his high blood pressure had taken another leap. Most people probably didn't notice, but Irving and I had a long history of observing Arnold, and it was clear to us that his pulpit ministry and general demeanor were suffering. *This project might give him new purpose*, I told myself. *Or might kill him*. I knew what the other building projects had demanded of him and this would demand far more. Nevertheless, an architect was hired and a drawing of the new facility made its home in the foyer. Arnold the builder was back in business.

As Maridel began her senior year, her involvement in drama and collegiate speech competition was paired with another love: a young man named Brad Bowes. She'd had her eye on him for a year, but could never get more than an earnest hello as he flew past her, trombone in one hand, briefcase in the other. But for the final event of her junior year, the Junior-Senior banquet, he had asked her to be his date. Soon after, they'd been elected President and Vice President of the senior class, which assured their proximity for the year ahead. After a few year-end dates, they went their separate summer ways, but to her delight, letters kept them linked, and by fall they were a couple.

I realized quickly that Arnold and I knew his father, Alpin Bowes. He had stayed in our home for a week at the Jefferson Street House, spearheading a study on church growth. When I reminded Maridel of this, she smiled at her memory of Alpin passing his wallet around our table one night, leaning forward to point out and name each of his three boys. "I was only in junior high, and I was looking at my … college boyfriend," she said dreamily. We both knew that she hoped one day to finish that sentence another way.

That year, I was asked to speak at the annual pastors'

retreat—not to the men, of course, but to their wives. With the invitation came memories of those early pastors' wives retreats I'd organized in Cleveland—and the fateful night I'd asked the speaker for help with my agonizing struggle. Here I was on the other side. *What would I say now to that "me" of long ago?* That was the question that inspired my talk.

By the time I stepped up to the podium to answer that question, I was alive with my message. I knew it wasn't standard fare and that some women may object or misunderstand. But I also knew that it could make them think, question, or perhaps, bring affirmation of their own feelings. So I spoke with passion about nourishing our own spiritual lives—aside from our husband's or the activities of the church. The room grew pin-drop quiet. Uncomfortably quiet or "hitting a chord" quiet? I couldn't tell, but didn't stray from my notes. "We need to seek our own spiritual path. To be our own high towers to catch the signals for what God has to teach us individually." I suggested ways to do this: books, keeping a journal, taking time alone for ourselves. I closed with Kahlil Gibran's words on marriage. "Love one another, but make not a bond of love…Fill each other's cup but drink not from one cup. Give one another of your bread but eat not from the same loaf…and stand together, but not too near together; for the pillars of the temple stand apart, and the oak tree and the cypress grow not in each other's shadow."

When I looked out, I saw a sea of faces that appeared to have been instantaneously and collectively slapped. There was complete silence. I took my seat on the stage while the District Superintendent's wife stepped up into my place. "Well, *that* was different wasn't it?" she said with an air of uncertainty. She'd probably been sitting there the whole time wondering how she was going to respond to "that." To her credit, she opted to be tactful.

I went home without the wide, feel-good cloak of approval

flapping about me. No one had approached me afterward to share her thoughts or to thank me. Seemingly, my twenty-five-year-old response to my own aching questions had touched no one. But in a few days, when my disappointment had passed, I realized the audience it *had* touched: me. With tears in my eyes, I recognized as never before that I was making spiritual progress on my own. What I'd shared in that room was real and true for me even if it wasn't true for anyone else. And for once, that was enough.

The following spring, Arnold and I received an anonymous invitation in the mail. We were invited to dessert and coffee at a lovely restaurant on the mezzanine of the new mall. Once there, we were part of an elite gathering: Dale and Linda, The Lairds, and Wendell and Ginger Bowes—Brad's older brother and his wife. We were looking for who else might arrive, when Brad and Maridel showed up, welcoming us with irrepressible twin smiles. Within minutes, they announced their engagement, and Brad put the ring on Maridel's finger to the music of our applause.

We had ninety days to create a wedding. Brad and Maridel planned to marry the day after graduation while all their friends were still in town. So the pliable stuff of possibilities had to be quickly turned into dedicated plans. Unlike my "mother of the bride" imaginings, I had very little time to dream with my only daughter over the vast satin sea of options. But she had already grasped the enormity of the task at hand and made plans to reduce her classes to a minimum as well as move home for her final semester.

What we were sure of and had been for a very long time was the wedding dress. One day when she was still in high school, she had raced over to me in the grocery store with a magazine flapping in her hands—a bridal magazine. "Mom, look!" she'd instructed. "This is the wedding dress I want!" I loved it too, but thought there would be a series of favorites by the time she was ready to marry. Maridel, however, had cut the picture out, filed it away, and had never considered another.

Even though I had long imagined making that dress, I quickly saw that I wouldn't be able to. Not only was our time frame short, and the demanding last term of school upon me, but I had also committed to a summer job for which I had not yet prepared—teaching a government-funded course in language arts. Sadly, I would have to hire a seamstress to turn the dress in the magazine into the gown of my daughter's dreams. Maridel and I still made a venture out of finding the right fabric, the perfect lace and the three patterns that would combine to reproduce the floor-length fitted lace dress with long sleeves and a full-length satin cape and train.

But ultimately, I couldn't agree to my own decision.

One weekend, while Maridel was away on a speech tournament, I felt the flash flood of mother love break loose in me. A seamstress might do a better job, but I was the one who still remembered the day she'd fallen in love with that dress. When she returned on Sunday evening, the basted form of the gown was hanging in her doorway.

The complicated project would require the kind of ingenuity that had once compelled me, at a much younger age, to upholster a chair. But with every step and every stitch, I knew it was mine to do.

Three months later, the whirlwind was over and all that was left behind was an unfurled banner of paper towel on our daughter's bed: "Thank you for twenty-one beautiful years." Her wedding gown hung behind me on the back of her door. She was gone—in a far different way than the year she'd left home for college. I paused in as I touched her gown on my way out of her room, grateful for her new life with an endearing young man. The beginning of an era for her, the end of one for me.

Life resumed and was precious. My students had become a

part of both my personal and professional worlds now. They showed up at my office door on scholastic business, but our conversations often went beyond the matters at hand. As they shared with me about their lives, I found myself talking about what I was learning, and offering the titles of books I was reading. Some days I could visibly see their young faces soften with relief and insight. I was still teaching the college Sunday school class, but this interaction was more meaningful. The realizations that had begun to grow in me were finding an outlet and nothing made me happier. My world was still small by most people's standards; as it had been from birth, its center was still the church. The only exceptions were my visits to surrounding grade schools to observe my student teachers. Yet within that world, I had changed immeasurably—and *that*, Robert Frost had written, made all the difference. Two roads had diverged in my life and I was indeed taking the one less traveled.

As the building fund for the new sanctuary mounted, Arnold's blood pressure did the same. He was on medication, but heeded none of the advice that went with the prescriptions. The only change was that Mondays, the traditional minister's day off, were now spent with his horses. In the past, only migraines had kept him from working seven days a week. I was grateful for that change, but didn't see how even Amy and Arrow were going to see him through another mammoth building project.

As we came to the close of our fifth year in Nampa, Arnold was deteriorating not just privately, but publically. His physical pain and inner turmoil had begun to show up in the pulpit. He was harsh and judgmental—his tone frequently angry. I felt more estranged from him than ever, helpless to break through the wall of his agony or share with him my own spiritual gains. Within our own walls, silence and withdrawal were becoming the norm, and I struggled to hold onto the thread of my own personal peace.

The pastoral vote was coming up again. With the exception

of that one experience in Muncie years before, Arnold had always received nearly unanimous votes. But this time I felt dread as the time approached. And I didn't know the worst. Behind the scenes, a single couple had initiated a campaign to vote Arnold out, and several members who had never attended under our ministry showed up to vote. They congregated up in the balcony to conceal their numbers, but one of the elderly ushers commented he'd never seen so many people he didn't know.

Despite the efforts of the disgruntled minority who launched the crusade, we were not voted out. However, it was the worst vote in our ministry. This was a staggering blow to a man already in trouble. His spirit crushed, anger turned to depression. Many of our members were outraged by what had happened, able to see beyond Arnold's liabilities to the herculean feat he was pulling off on behalf of the church. And many who had come to know him outside the church walls loved him dearly. He had entered their world of horses and camping, reveled in the Saddle Club parades, and shared their passion for riding. He had become "one of them" as no pastor ever had.

We could have stayed, but such a choice risked further dissension in the church—or even a split. Instead, Arnold made the difficult decision to resign. It was a decision made all the more agonizing by the desertion of the building project. Forsaking a vision was not in his nature. For several weeks we didn't know where we were going, but eventually Arnold received a call from a District Superintendent in California. He had been recommended to a much smaller, but prestigious church in Sacramento.

Through the years of our ministry, we had known other pastors who, after a bad vote or other circumstances, had been moved to a another area. Now it occurred to me, as it hadn't when I was less aware, that these men needed some kind of support. But there was never any counsel provided in the harrowing wake of collective rejection.

At fifty-one years old, he reluctantly accepted his new assignment. For him, it was utter defeat. For me, it was the loss of my beloved work and of proximity to any of our children.

When the parties and dinners of that last month ended, I was relieved. The long ritual of saying goodbye to so many people had been underscored by an old, familiar feeling. *What is this all about? If the mission of the church is to be compassionate and caring, why are pastors let go without a word from their superiors?* It was a question with deep roots. One of the five General Superintendents of the church had preached the message and held the recall vote. Neither he nor the District Superintendent offered any words of counsel or encouragement to Arnold—in fact, they said nothing. The General had the power to intervene and reach out to a man who had given his entire adult life to build and better this denomination—but he let him go without even a word of appreciation.

The contradiction of this to the scripture weighed heavily on me. One passage from Galatians kept coming to mind. "Brethren, if a man be overtaken in a fault, those of you who are spiritual should restore such a one in the spirit of meekness, considering yourself lest you also be tempted." Unquestionably, Arnold had needed counsel—had needed restoration—but none was offered. *What was I part of here*? I asked myself more intently than ever. I'd questioned for so long; but now the questions came with piercing pain, and in my heart of hearts, I had no idea how we were going to face another pastorate.

Unlike every other sojourn to a new locale, the journey to the capitol city of California would be a painful one.

Neither of us wanted to go.

HOUSE SIXTEEN

Monrovia Lane, Sacramento, CA

We had entered Nampa in glory and left in defeat.

Humbly, we entered Sacramento.

We hadn't seen the church nor had Arnold met with the board. As far as we knew, no one was even aware of our arrival on this weekday afternoon. The church was en route to the parsonage and visible from the freeway, so Arnold wanted to stop. We'd heard that the new sanctuary was beautiful, and I hoped it would ease our aching hearts even a little.

Ironically, our first steps into that space were like moving back in time. We entered a world of blue, set against dark wood. A sloping floor with a mezzanine was held within a soothing curved design. This sanctuary was Muncie's twin—that magnificent beauty we had left behind to go to Nampa. Feeling alienated from home, we were surrounded by the familiar. It had been designed by the same architect and bore his signature blue.

Next we made our way into the old sanctuary that sat directly behind this one. It had been renovated into a fellowship hall, offices and classrooms. There were more classrooms and a kitchen in the basement. To our surprise, a woman was down there working. "Well, you must be the new pastor and wife," she said with enthusiasm. "I'm Lois Anderson," and with that, promptly invited us to dinner that evening. We accepted the offer and headed out to find our own home.

The Sacramento parsonage was several miles from the church and was situated in a tree-lined, upscale suburban haven. People might be frantic or anxious behind these doors, but on the outside, all was well. Our house, too, was serenely beautiful. This U-shaped, one-story brick home was wrapped around a covered, rectangular patio that looked out on a manicured lawn and mature perennials. A last, small orange clung to its tree, as if assigned to stay behind and give us a proper California greeting. All the landscape, we'd been told, was maintained by the church.

I instantly loved the unusual floor plan. On one side of the house was a guest wing with a private bath and entrance to the patio. On the other, the master bedroom and two additional bedrooms joined by a bath. Between these wings was the living space: an open, spacious room that combined kitchen, dining area and family room, all of which looked out on the patio and the backyard. On the front of the house, the living room's large window looked out on the sedate views of the street. Nothing clashed, needed to be replaced or repaired. Despite my deep melancholy, I could feel my heart taking refuge here.

The first Sunday in a new church had always been infused with the fluttering wings of promise. But on this first Sunday, we walked a shadowed path, hoping promise would find us again. The vaulted beauty of the sanctuary had the capacity for 500 people, but today 150 were scattered throughout the pews. The sea of faces that Arnold was accustomed to was gone, and in its place was a congregation smaller than the one he'd left behind in Cleveland sixteen years ago. He had one secretary and no associate pastors. Except for the parsonage, it felt like starting over.

Arnold made it through Sunday—with a smaller congregation still at the evening service. But on Monday morning, he lay on the sofa in the family room and cried like a heartbroken child.

I ached for him. He didn't articulate his feelings, but I understood them nevertheless. I was feeling them too: hurt, anger, betrayal … disbelief. At a time when we needed to console and encourage each other, to share our mutual pain and disillusionment, we didn't know how. Our only expression of such emotional intimacy had been the threat of our children's demise: the night when Maridel was gravely ill in the hospital and the months that Dale was in Viet Nam. But when it came to nurturing each other, we both drew a blank. Even my life and death encounter on the back roads to Fort Wayne hadn't called up this most instinctive of human responses. And it was clear that we weren't going to start now.

Neither of us had been exposed to models of the open, honest exchange of feelings growing up—but then, who was? And in all our associations across the years, I couldn't think of anyone who demonstrated that—certainly no couples we knew. So what arose from the void instead, at least in me, was the inner voice of indoctrination: "It's no use complaining. What did we really have to be so sad about anyway? Wasn't our son alive and well? Wasn't our daughter happily married? Wasn't … wasn't …"

And so I kept my distance from Arnold's pain and when he got up from the couch, I wandered into the backyard to pick that last orange off the tree. I'd found a cake recipe that called for a cup of orange juice. But no matter how delicious the cake might be, I was afraid that it, too, would be eaten in silence.

In the weeks to come, Arnold proved his resilience once again: coming to terms with his responsibilities and working just as hard as he ever had. One of the first things he put his mind to was finding the right associate minister. This was a relatively affluent church, but the size of the congregation only allowed for one associate until Arnold could build it up to support others. So that one person needed to be diversely talented: able to head and build the music program as well as create a youth program from the ground up. In the meantime, it fell to me to take over the small choir and generate whatever enthusiasm I could until my replacement arrived. I also accepted a new challenge at my husband's request: supervising the children's Sunday school department. Other than running Vacation Bible Schools in Muncie, I had never had much to do with children's ministries. Nor had I wanted to—then or now.

Our joint struggle to adjust to this new post wasn't just that it was a fall from both grace and visibility; nor was it merely the adjustment to California after our love affair with Idaho. There was something more vexing than either of these. This congregation was fundamentally different than any we had pastored. We were accustomed to people for whom the church was central to their lives—a centrality that mirrored their commitment to God Himself. Only a minority of the members of this congregation shared this devotion.

The church constituency was made up largely of professionals with status, money, and a wealth of opportunities outside the church. Many of them had long histories together, including the marriage of each other's children. They loved the church and supported it financially—as evidenced by facilities that would usually require a much larger congregation. Yet they were independent from the life of this enterprise in a way that was foreign to us—and hard to accept. Sunday evening service wasn't a given; it was simply another option. Wednesday evening prayer meeting seemed to exist solely for a small, loyal core. Weekends away were frequent for many, which prevented them from committing to any regular roles or functions within the life of the church. And to our dismay, the members as a whole seemed oddly content with a new sanctuary that wasn't even half-full. For these good people it seemed to be enough to worship, see each other, and go home.

Yet they had called a pastor for whom growth was sacrosanct. He had built a reputation on it—and despite his weariness, didn't know how to do anything else. In the world of ecclesiastical matchmaking, this one didn't seem to be a fit for Arnold.

I felt it too. Even after discovering that I wasn't aligned with all the doctrines of the church, I still had always felt at home with the people. But here I was a guest at a large family gathering. As difficult as this was for me, it was doubly so for Arnold. What he had to give wasn't what they were looking for, which only deepened his despair. We needed something to give us a sense of mooring until Arnold could inspire this church to envision their potential.

My husband's flagging spirit and sense of rejection also caught up with our already troubled relationship. On the way to a weekend retreat for the young couples of our church, his mood suddenly shifted after we'd stopped for gas. I could feel the car's cabin pressure rising and myself tensing when he made a remark that I have long-since forgotten—but at the time stabbed just as if he'd drawn a knife and made my heart his target. I cried throughout the two-hour trip. He made no comment on my tears and I made no statement on my own behalf. Once we arrived, I left my dark glasses on in an attempt to conceal my puffy face—though they may have evoked even more silent questions.

The mood at the retreat was jovial, filled with games, teasing, and fun. I was an imposter who had shown up to imitate the pastor's wife. I saw my former self in their lively faces and their cheerful interactions, but inside I felt dead. The two days crawled by as if on all fours, each new activity an agony. *How did I start out like them and end up like this?*

When alone, the questions began barking at my heels—dogs that frightened me and threatened to tear to sheds what was left of my faith. It wasn't my belief in God that was at risk; but rather, this representation of Him. After a lifetime in this religious system, I had so little evidence of its veracity and so much evidence of its failure. If our doctrine, our understanding of God was right, how could I be living with an angry, miserable man who'd given up everything else to preach it? My angst didn't end with the weekend.

By February, though spring was showing up earlier than we could fathom—flaunting its cherry and almond blossoms like bridesmaids strewn all over town—it was still winter within our walls.

Adding to our uneasiness was the fact that Arnold and the board had been unsuccessful in procuring an associate minister. Either the candidate was just what he was looking for but didn't accept the position--or the man was eager and willing, but didn't suit Arnold, the board, or both. In the meantime we were continuing to carry the entire load of the ministry on our shoulders as we had when we were young. But of course, by now we didn't have the never-to-be-underestimated advantage of youth—or the zeal of the people we'd served in those years. However, in the midst of the board's frustrated efforts, they made another decision. This one served up what I imagined a "hot toddy" would be on a chilly day. I didn't even know what a toddy was, but it sounded so cozy to me—as if its warmth could seep right into one's bones, no matter how cold.

It had evidently come to the board's attention that there was a new trend in parsonage management. Why not just give the pastor's family a housing allowance and allow them to buy their *own* home? The board voted their nod and we were overjoyed. With nothing except the denomination's meager pension set aside for retirement, and no investments or securities, the idea of owning a house threw us a financial lifeline. For once, we wouldn't be moving out of a parsonage for the sake of the building fund, but for our own sakes. As much as I loved the current parsonage, the idea of joining the ranks of people with a home to call their own was indeed warming to the bone.

I hoped the acquisition of our own home would engender another kind of warmth. Maybe it would bring Arnold and me together in a new way—infuse us with the kind of shared joy that all first-time buyers must feel. I wanted to believe that in this foreign land in which we had been set down, another kind of redemption might await us. Then even before we could start our house-hunting in earnest, other news arrived. And with this, I could feel my own entry into spring and hope. We were going to be grandparents. Maridel was pregnant and due in October.

Somehow this news bestowed our search with a glow it hadn't possessed on its own. A family home it would be—a place our first grandchild would visit and remember as "grandma and grandpa's house." The ache inside me began to ease as the losses receded enough to make room for new and unexpected gains.

The prospective neighborhoods for our home would not be near the church, ensconced as it was in downtown Sacramento. Arnold had his heart set on property that would restore his beloved horses to him, and this agenda took us into outlying areas: the once-removed suburbs of Carmichael and Fair Oaks where horse property, while limited, did exist. We saw nothing that was acceptable in our price range until we came across a house on Winding Way. The home offered a wide circular drive separating the house from property developed specifically for keeping horses—complete with a small barn and wooded pasture. We smiled as we pulled into the driveway. The grounds were casual, but appealing; and while the house was obviously older, it had the look of a character with fascinating stories to tell.

Inside, it looked older still, was less fascinating and carried a peculiar odor. Even so, it wasn't without its charm: a small brick patio at the entry door (though less solid than one might hope); a raised flower bed under the staircase for an indoor garden (though its current emptiness was a visual casualty); an enormous family room that looked out on the woods (if you could look *past* the expanse of dingy, loosely woven drapes); and a separate living room with a parlor-like feel where I could nurse a quiet cup of coffee (even if the road noise could best be heard from there).

Perhaps this oldster's stories were ones we didn't really want to hear. Or smell. We turned it down.

A few days later, however, Arnold came to me and said he had reassessed the situation and thought we should make an offer. "I'm not sure where else we'll find horse property at that price—especially within driving distance of the church."

I knew he was right, even though the sudden sheen of ownership dulled at the thought of making this house our choice. Still, I reasoned, it would be our own—a place where we could paint and paper with abandon and *without* the approval of the board. Besides, Arnold needed Amy and Arrow's company. In their absence, he had returned, like a junkie, to his old habit of working on Monday. Unless a migraine took him down.

We drove out to Carmichael to look at the property again. The area was lovely, I realized. Overhanging trees and a profusion of flowering bushes created a wild, suburban jungle of color and life. Against this backdrop, I surveyed the house with new eyes, allowing my creative wheels to move, however reluctantly. Neither of us was overjoyed when our offer was accepted, but by the time we signed the papers, I was ready to turn this old character into an ally if not a friend.

In the interval between houses, Maridel flew her pregnant self to Sacramento for a visit. It was perfect timing for her to see both of our houses. I was excited to show her our acquisition, simply because, for the first time it was *ours*, but was disappointed by her response. "I'm glad you like it, Mom," she said when we left—no doubt recalling the more appealing parsonages from which we'd come. Citing the odd floor plan and low-hanging ceilings as her sources of dismay, she patted my shoulder and said, "But I know you. I'm sure it will be beautiful when your grandchild comes to see it." I agreed. She was looking at what was there, and I was looking at the projected image of a lovely country abode of casual sophistication.

When Maridel and Brad had settled in Seattle two years before, they had found a church home where their lively, youthful spirits had been a great boon to the pastor—and by this time, they were unofficially serving as associate ministers. Brad was leading the choir and together they were running the entire youth program. I noticed that my daughter's eyes lit up when she talked about two things: her unborn child and her "adopted children"—the teenagers she had so obviously fallen in love with. As Arnold and I listened to her recount all the innovative things that she and Brad were doing, I could almost hear Arnold's mind whirring. He said nothing to Maridel, but once she was gone, he told me that if the board didn't find someone soon, he was going to broach the subject of hiring Brad and Maridel to fill the position.

I didn't dare to hope.

But I went right ahead and did it anyway. In fact, I prayed while I packed.

HOUSE SEVENTEEN

Winding Way, Carmichael, California

The move into our first home was more arduous than joyful. *What have we done*? I asked myself with every load carried into a house on a par with the worst of parsonages. The situation struck me like arranged marriages that fare better than the chosen ones. But when the Fulchers pulled into our driveway a few weeks later bearing the live cargo of Amy and Arrow, I remembered what we had done and why. My resentment receded as I watched Arnold's high-stepping beauties strut from their stalls and pour their spirits into Arnold's diminished one—a transfusion of hope.

As we settled in the house, we waited out the slow-moving gears of locating an assistant minister. The latest one hadn't worked out, but another excellent prospect had come to the boards' attention in the meantime. Uncharacteristically, Arnold held back on his own recommendation, knowing that unless the candidate list was drained or the board got just plain weary of the process, it would be premature to suggest *family* as the perfect solution. I knew, too, that it would have to be the right thing—for the church as well as for Brad and Maridel—and yet I couldn't help imagining them pulling into that drive, and bursting with passion into our flagging lives. I couldn't help wanting the one thing that might salvage what we couldn't seem to salvage on our own.

Surprisingly, other than unpack and disperse our belongings, I wasn't even doing much with the house. I had plans, but each day I thought I might implement them tomorrow. For weeks, I'd convinced myself that setting up the indoor garden under the staircase would set me moving. But I hadn't bought plants. Even in the face of company arriving, I was unmotivated. And such company too! I'd stayed in contact with my friend Jeanne since leaving Cleveland, and she and her husband were coming to visit for a couple of days. I'd never met Ray and hadn't seen Jean in over seven years. Secretly, I wished they had come to see us when we were riding the wave of success instead of walking the disheartening shoreline of regret.

As I gave them the tour of the house, I made excuses for its appearance—"just moved in … lots of ideas … those curtains will have to go, of course …" The truth is, I was embarrassed. The following evening was prayer meeting night; and even then, for all my progress, it didn't occur to me to stay home with my guests. So the ancient wheel turned again: prayer meeting, choir practice and the long route home. The summer light was just beginning to fade when we pulled into the driveway. To my astonishment, our oatmeal curtains were hanging over the back fence, but were no longer lifeless and bland. Instead they were dripping a rich honeyed gold.

Jeanne and Ray came out to meet us, grinning. "We thought maybe you were praying for new drapes at church tonight," she said. "They'll be dry enough to hang by the time the sun goes down."

While we waited for the re-hanging of the drapes, Ray moved on to other things. "Let me show you something, Addie," he said after I'd poured us some iced tea. He picked up a small brass vase and asked, "Have any more brass pieces?" I got one from the parlor and sent Jean off to fetch another one upstairs. With deft flair, he arranged the pieces together on our round maple coffee table, adding a vine of artificial greenery. It looked stunning. "It's called 'grouping,' " he told me, and sent Jeanne off again to find anything else that caught her eye. Again, he created the same effect on my buffet with items that had just been stranded from each other, unnoticed. Things were going so well they asked permission to rearrange the furniture—quickly creating a cozy grouping of chairs that pulled you into its circle. By then, the curtains were dry enough to be hung, and once back up on the windows, gave the whole room a warm glow. "Let's enjoy!" Ray said, and with that, we took up residence in the room of new groupings and new life.

"That was the most productive prayer meeting I can ever recall," I quipped.

"That's what we like," said Jean, "Quick, dramatic results!"

When they climbed the stairs for bed, I stood alone—mesmerized by the transformation. Arnold had been outside tending to the horses most of the time and hadn't said much when he came in. It didn't matter. I couldn't wait to get up in the morning and see this beautiful gift in the light of day.

After Jeanne and Ray left the next day, I went out and bought plants. And when I walked in with them, I was coming home rather than into a house that held my things.

A few weeks later, after the next best candidate had turned down the associate minister's position, Arnold presented the board with the name of a young lay pastor he thought might be just right for the job. "Even though Brad Bowes is a layman, he's doing the work of an associate at our church in Renton and having great success—not only as choir director, but as an innovative youth minister. He has a college degree, deep roots in the church and is a young man of great character." Everyone was nodding and smiling, relieved they didn't have to start a new list.

"There's just one more thing I need to tell you about Brad

before we proceed. He also has a wonderful wife who is his partner in the youth ministry there in Renton—and she's my daughter."

I wasn't in the room, of course, but I was home imagining this moment, curious what the reception would be. When Arnold came home, he reported a mixture of responses. A few members had coalesced around the danger of relatives on the same church staff. A story with a sorry ending had followed as evidence. But the majority of the members, perhaps wearier than the others, took up the banner of "why should it matter?" "If the person is right for the job," one of them noted, "why should he be disqualified on the basis of being related to the pastor?" Eventually, a vote was taken on whether or not to invite Brad Bowes for an interview. Majority ruled. After giving me the report, Arnold headed for the phone and dialed up my hopes one digit at a time.

The difference of opinion on the board, as valid as it was, made me nervous. *What if they rejected Brad as a candidate? What if the majority ruled, but the displeased minority created an unfriendly climate? What if the church wanted them, but they didn't come—plunging Arnold further down the rabbit hole of his darkness*? I wanted to run—to resign from the role I had taken on thirty-one years ago with such naïve delight. Maybe what I really wanted was to be one of those people who sometimes showed and sometimes didn't—no explanation necessary. No wonder I resented and judged their "lack of faithfulness." I wanted that option for myself.

We'd been in Sacramento almost nine months when Brad flew in from Seattle for his interview with the board. We'd made a bit of progress by then if numbers reflect such a thing, but my greater concern continued to be Arnold himself. He was able to pull it together at church, but at home, he remained disconsolate and difficult. I knew it was too much to put on Brad—on any associate—to be the intermediary of his private pain; but I also knew that if anyone could, it would be our own children and our first grandchild. These were desperate thoughts; but in fact, I was desperate. How long could I bear going through the motions learned from decades past while living with a man who seemed to me to be sliding away from life? The horses, the house, the enthusiasm of the few—I counted on these things to shore him up *until* … there was that word again. "Until" was the word that, in my brain, had attached itself to five other words: *our children can get here.* Now that Brad was in our presence, it was even harder to imagine going on without them.

As I'd hoped, the board was impressed with the unassuming, talented young man who had a beautiful voice, played the trombone and came with a distinguished musical history. It pleased them that he came from a well-regarded family in our denomination and that his current pastor sent a glowing letter of recommendation. "I only wish that we had the means to hire him as minister of music and youth," struck a solid vote of confidence. Despite some continued rumblings over the familial issue involved, the members of the board extended Brad a call to join the staff as associate pastor.

Now we had another hurdle to cross: Brad's decision. He and Maridel had many factors to consider. He had an excellent job at Boeing Aircraft, which he'd managed to hold onto in the midst of a failing economy. Brad and Maridel also owned a house that was losing value every week. The pages of their local newspaper were glutted with owners eager to sell their homes, and "For Sale" signs cluttered most streets of Seattle and its outlying areas. It wasn't an ideal time, perhaps not even a viable time, to sell. These were matters we couldn't help them with. And so, we stepped back—or as far back as Arnold was capable of stepping—and let them take the reins of this decision into their own hands.

Again, I waited—hoping, like all those in the various waiting rooms of life, to be delivered to the sound of good news. In the meantime, I started working on what I hoped would be another source of redemption for Arnold and me. Someone in the church had told me that there were generous hosting programs for trips to the Holy Land. By signing up three other couples, we could have the trip at no cost. I'd set about getting the information, thinking that a true vacation might be just what we needed. We had never gone anywhere except back to New York to stay with our folks or spend an arduous week camping with Arnold's brothers. Spending time in the place where Christ had walked and lived, and sharing it with people from our church, could be just the balm we needed. We'd been in Sacramento almost a year, and our lives still felt haunted by spilled dreams that continued to seep into the ground beneath us.

In these days, the old experience of depression began haunting me again but at another level. I couldn't remember ever feeling so exhausted, so devoid of interest in anything. I seemed to be living for things that might rescue me instead of actually living. I could still light up at church temporarily, the old programmed commands coming to my aid on cue. But some days, as I fell back into the grey suit of my day-to-day self, I wondered how long I could even do that. I was a performer for whom the show had long since lost its luster, but there wasn't another thing in the world to do but continue. Even my spiritual progress seemed stalled. All that I had learned seemed ineffectual now, unable to pierce the shroud of my fears.

Arnold called Seattle every week. It had been three now, and the board was getting restless. Brad seemed to be leaning toward coming, Arnold told me each time, but no commitment yet. When I talked to Maridel, hoping for some inside information, she told me she had left the decision up to Brad, and that he was wrestling earnestly with it. As for herself, she seemed ambivalent—and who could blame her? After growing up in the parsonage, she'd married a math major and still ended up as an unofficial pastor's wife. Did she really want to make it official—with her father at the helm? If I hadn't wanted so badly to be helped back through the doorway of normalcy, I might have counseled her to flee while she could.

The call came the next week—and with it, a decisiveness that comes from waiting on the shining beam of clarity. With inner certainty, Brad had told Maridel—and then us—that he was accepting the position.

Suddenly, I was alive again, drenched in a downpour of relief and hope. The drought may not be over, I knew. But today it was raining.

Things needed to move quickly now as the board—not to mention Arnold—wanted Brad to take his post by the first of September, and July was already half over. The timeline was complicated not only by the necessary sale of their home, but by Maridel's decision to stay in Seattle for the mid-October birth. Despite the challenge of this situation, arrangements seem to make themselves. Once Brad arrived, he would live with us; and soon after, I would go to Seattle to be with Maridel. More precarious was the "plan" for Brad to return to Maridel's side for the birth of their child. This sudden, shifting wind lifted and carried me, setting me down in a place where the horizon looked like dawn instead of perpetual dusk. I was overwhelmed with a feeling that had gone missing for too long: utter and complete gratitude.

Within a few weeks Brad and Maridel had a buyer for their home. The couple was paying cash, thus insuring a speedy and certain sale. Brad had been laid off by Boeing even before he'd given notice, confirming the rightness of his choice. By the time he arrived in Sacramento, Maridel was living with a friend and looking for a temporary apartment to house the two of us. This divine co-ordination of events bolstered all our spirits, showing us the necessity of the whole process: the candidates who turned the position down, Brad and Maridel's internship in Seattle, Arnold's courage with the board, and their discernment despite some conflict. Right down to the young man who had made the choice alone, waiting on his own knowing in the face of pressure.

For the first time in a very, very long time, I thought about my angels.

The upcoming escape to Seattle was a delicacy on which I allowed myself to gorge. I ate it almost every hour, each bite as delicious as the last. For one shining month, I would be free. As I prepared Brad's living quarters upstairs, welcomed him into the house and worked to get him settled and comfortable, my mind never let it slip that we were exchanging places. And when the two of us sat down together to pass the choir baton from my weary, waving arms to his young, invigorated ones, the symbolism of our exchange was complete.

As I stepped on the plane one gorgeous September afternoon, my horizon was strewn with things to look forward to: time away from all my responsibilities, a respite from Arnold's pain, leisure time with my daughter at this momentous juncture in her life, the birth of my first grandchild followed by bringing her child and mine home with me. The dull, inner ache that had been my constant companion for months had vanished.

Maridel had secured a furnished upstairs apartment that looked out on a sea of green trees and, just as importantly, was close to the mall. The colors of the furniture were cheerful, the rooms spacious, and surprisingly homey. Maridel had kept back a few things to decorate the apartment for our month's stay: candles on the coffee table, framed pictures, a clock and artificial greens on the built-in shelves, and a flower arrangement on the little dinette.

We lived on this little interim island together, removed from our lives as we had known them. After a leisurely breakfast and second cup of coffee each morning, the most pressing questions of the day were, "What shall we have for dinner and does it need to be defrosted?" Most days, we left the house and headed straightaway or circuitously in the direction of the mall. Sometimes we had a specific item we were on the prowl to find, but usually we just grazed the aisles of stores that caught our slow-moving fancy. Sometimes we lunched in a favorite restaurant—alone or joined by one of Maridel's friends. Because she was tiring more easily now, we were always back to the apartment by early afternoon where she took a nap or rested on the couch while we "baby talked." In the evenings we watched TV or read, retiring early. These were magical days for me—what I imagined people experienced at a resort. And this was a "Five Star" resort for me: with my daughter in a beautiful place at a glorious time of the year, watching the sea of green outside our window turn bronze and red and gold before our eyes.

The only disruptions to this haven were the phone calls from Arnold whose mood ranged from sullen and irritable to desperate. On one call, he compelled me to come home. "I need you, Addie," he pleaded uncharacteristically.

"For *what*?" I asked, unable to imagine.

"Just come home."

"I can't, Arnold. Maridel needs me. The baby's due in a couple of weeks. She shouldn't be alone now."

"I need you too," he said, unnerving me with his urgency.

"I can't," I repeated and he finally relented.

I hung up feeling dislodged from my own reality. That was not the Arnold I knew—and even less recognizable was my response to this strange man who was calling himself my husband. It wasn't my habit to refuse Arnold anything, and while his vulnerability was foreign and frightening, my certainty was total. I wasn't leaving my daughter's side.

As the baby's due date got closer, I overheard Maridel's end of her earnest phone conversations with Brad. After every doctor appointment, they conferred, trying to maximize his chances to be present at the birth. Brad could only be away from his new post for a week, so waiting too long or not long enough could cost them their dream. I admired the passion of this young couple, so desirous of welcoming their child into the world together—something that wasn't done or even considered in the years our children were born. I felt a pang of jealousy as I listened, remembering that *I* wasn't even present for my first delivery. In the custom of the day, I'd been rendered completely unconscious. It seemed barbaric now. I'd missed an irreplaceable moment of my own history: the moment I'd graduated from wife to mother. I couldn't imagine having my husband there and seeing the sunrise of our child's face reflected in his beaming smile. But now, there was another chance for my daughter and her own young husband. I was pulling for them and for timing that would vicariously give me back a portion of what I'd lost.

A week before the baby's due date, Brad's father, Alpin, came to a conference in Seattle. His mother, Betty, came along too, hoping that their timing might be blessed by the sight of their first grandchild. In the meantime, she was an honored guest at the baby shower and had the pleasure of reminiscing with Maridel about Brad's birth. But early on a Sunday morning when their plane waited at the gate, she gave us both a tearful hug goodbye. Both her married sons lived in faraway places and this chance would likely never come again.

On Maridel's next doctor visit—the one she hoped would be the last—he corroborated those hopes. "The baby could come any day," he said, "Sometimes I'm fooled, but it's getting very close." Like two seasoned gamblers, she and Brad bet their odds. As soon as the weekend was over and his Sunday duties fulfilled, he'd fly to Seattle hoping for fair skies and perfect timing.

The next Monday evening, after a romantic dinner in a French restaurant with Maridel, Brad joined us in our prenatal hideaway.

The following day, they set out on some errands together, including another visit to the doctor. "I want to see you on Monday if you haven't delivered by the weekend. But I'm pretty sure we'll be meeting at the hospital before then." The two of them returned to the nest elated. The birth was imminent!

After a quiet dinner together in the apartment that evening, we watched Marcus Welby, M.D., and went to bed early. Within a few hours, I heard Brad and Maridel stirring. Then a quiet knock on my door. All sleep was now suspended as Brad called the doctor and we pulled ourselves together in wee hour darkness for the trip to the hospital. Maridel's contractions were already twenty minutes apart.

She cried en route to the hospital, sure it was a false alarm. In reality, I spent very little time in the barren waiting room. For once, the ambiance didn't affect me. I was in my own bubble, grappling with the collapse of years and giddy with the expansion of my heart. Twice, the doctor poked his head in--once to tell me he was going to take a short nap and a second time to keep me in the loop. "I'm headed to the delivery room to get that grandchild for you!" he said as cheerfully as a waitress headed for the coffee pot.

At daybreak, we had a baby boy: Justin Christopher Bowes. Brad bounded into the waiting room to tell me, his face lit up not with an ordinary grin, but with the full radiance of one who has stood for just an instant, between worlds. He had witnessed his first child emerge from one, mysterious realm and enter his.

With the news and Brad's embrace, I soared—flying untouched above everything that might try to win me back from bliss. Nothing else mattered but this translucent little being that slept swathed behind the nursery window where Brad and I stood entranced. I understood now what Arnold had felt the night Dale was born. He had been party to the raw wonder of this miracle while I had slept off the thief of anesthetic. For all my months of waiting and imagining, nothing had come close to the elation that guided my body through space without effort or thought. I was a grandmother and already in love with a child I had yet to touch.

A week later, Brad loaded the car with everything that had made the apartment ours—along with excess clothes and shower gifts—and drove south to California. Maridel, Justin and I would follow by plane in a few days. I savored this last phase of my hiatus, alone with my daughter and our darling babe. Several of her friends stopped by to see Justin and wish her well, and as I saw the reality of her life here ending, the reality of my awaiting life took hold. I tried to cheer myself with the fact that this new family would be living with us until their little parsonage was made ready. But underneath, I felt the pulse of returning to Arnold's impenetrable moods, waxing now far more than they were waning. That's when I reached for another comforting thought as one would for a sedative: the baby. Arnold had always loved babies and now that baby would be his own grandson.

Our departure from Seattle was unexpectedly emotional. Maridel's closest friends were at the airport where hugs and tears prevailed, leaving her weepy and shaky. Justin blessed us with sleep on the plane; but upon arrival in Sacramento, as Maridel carried her firstborn up the ramp to the terminal, she stumbled and fell. Close behind her, I saw her go down, but couldn't help. A wave of panic washed over me as real as a pounding wave. In a testament to the power of maternal instinct, she went down on one knee, simultaneously raising her arms to balance Justin and keep him safe. I took the baby from her and helped her up, and although she was shaken, she took him back and continued her proud march toward her husband and her father.

But when she presented his first grandchild to him, Arnold was indifferent.

"Looks like a Bowes," he said dismissively as we walked down the corridor together.

I was aghast at his response, hurt for my daughter and embarrassed for myself. It's also when I knew—when I let myself know—that my husband was in troubled waters. Yet even in his compromised state, Arnold couldn't resist Justin's considerable charms. Within a matter of hours, he was engaged—kissing Justin's downy head and talking to him as he held him in his arms. Over the months, he'd had periods of enthusiasm and excitement, all of them flashing and then fizzling like a second-rate sparkler. But this felt different. Justin's round-the-clock presence seemed to have opened a barred door within Arnold, creating a sustained loving response, a quiet joy. It appeared that our brand new babe was pulling him back from the thin edge of a steep slide.

By the time Brad and Maridel's own house had been readied by thc appropriate committee, Arnold had locked hearts with Justin and seemed guided by his infant light. The "little parsonage" was just halfway down the alley from the church, and Arnold dropped in almost every day to play with him—even babysitting sometimes when Maridel had an appointment.

When we left for the Holy Land a few months later, I thought perhaps the worst had passed. In fact, it lay dead ahead. Arnold seemed fine setting out, but once our group of eight was joined by a larger group from a Baptist church, his behavior suddenly pivoted. During the trip he sat at the back of the bus most of the time, dissociated from the group. When he did interact, his behavior was curt, and often rude. My embarrassment created such tension in my body that I became violently ill—vomiting while on the bus and then retreating to my hotel room. When I asked Arnold to go find me a cup of tea, he left and didn't come back for hours. In his absence, I vacillated between worry and an odd relief. He was acting like a stranger, and in the presence of such a stranger, I only wanted to escape.

After he refused to be in the group picture, and then derided me because I had chosen to be in it, I started coming apart inside. My only comfort was that I knew *we* couldn't and *I* wouldn't go on this way. Something had to change—never mind that I had no idea what it was.

I returned home not just tired in the ordinary jet-lagged, overstimulated way, but in another: emotionally bankrupt. Yet even in this critical state, I didn't know how to initiate change or confront my husband about his behavior. Coming back to home base and to our kids and grandchild, the default setting of simply "hanging on" took over. But one change did come, and for me it was no small one.

At the follow-up appointment of my annual exam, the doctor told me with alarm that my cholesterol was dangerously high. After explaining the risks to me and prescribing some major changes in my diet, he said, "Tell me this, Mrs. Woodcook, 'What are you doing that you don't *want* to be doing?' "

There were a dozen equally true responses to that question, but one rose rapidly to the top. "I really don't want to be supervising the children's Sunday School department," I told him.

"Then I hope you will give it up soon."

I left his office feeling much better than when I entered. What I really wanted was for my whole life to change, but at least now I had a stepping stone. I had permission to let go of the one thing that was most burdensome to me. And it secretly pleased me that the mind-body connection I'd made regarding my shoulder had been verified—this doctor had made the same kind of link.

With medical advice as my back-up, I told Arnold I was resigning from the children's department. I had just said "no" for the second time in a little over thirty years. *Well,* I told myself. *At least that's changing.* Yet in the days ahead, and even after I'd made my transition out of those duties, the suffering deepened. Every day I was stretching beyond what I could physically and emotionally do. Every day Arnold's behavior was erratic. Most days he was angry. I took repeated solace in Maridel's frequent visits to the house with the baby, and in our family gatherings. I leaned again and again on the fact that both the choir and the youth program were already making gains thanks to Brad's dedicated talent and Maridel's help. But even then it was clear to me that I was pushing with more strength than I had, and every time there was a private crisis with Arnold that strength diminished further.

The following Sunday, as we were getting into the car for church, a desperation gripped me that was new and almost total. Walking into the church and carrying on as usual seemed like sheer impossibility. Jittery, jumping beans words screamed inside my head. "I'm not going! Make any excuse you have to because I don't care what anyone thinks anymore. I just can't do it!" The car door still stood open, offering a getaway, but I closed it and swallowed, unable to speak my thoughts aloud.

On the way to church, Arnold was uncommunicative behind his wall of barely suppressed anger. The words were jammed tight in my throat now, but the tears couldn't be held back. I sobbed, hoping for some release of the pain. Beside me was a handsome, highly successful man who could have gone on to become a district superintendent—or even a general. But instead he was on a downward slide, and I was going with him. We were never going to rise again.

Once at church, Arnold got out without a word and I followed. Inside, I came to life within a few minutes—teaching, singing in the choir, interacting with people as if it were just another Sunday. I'm sure they never knew. I had managed, after all, to become Sara Bernhardt, the actress. But reaching that peak of emotion and declaring the raw truth to myself, even for a moment, served a purpose. I couldn't go on. The stark duality of our Sunday pose vs. our daily lives had burned through the fraying wires that had kept me in place. My life was becoming a non-stop re-creation of my "holy hell" in the Holy Land. Or maybe that hell and this *were* truly holy, bringing me to the point of no return.

Perhaps my life was a puzzle that would never go together, but was worth my attention anyway. Pieces kept flashing in my mind-- angles that might fit together if I could gather them all in once place. And maybe if I had the courage to expose what we were doing, it could all be put together in a whole different design.

A few weeks later, I was visiting Maridel at home when I saw a scripture verse above her sink. She'd hand-written it on a piece of stationery and taped it there. "I don't want your offerings, and I don't want your sacrifices; I want you to know Me and to love Me." It was a translation of a familiar verse from the Old Testament. The version I'd heard all my life had called for obedience. This one called for relationship. Suddenly, those words became a strategic piece of the puzzle, the one you find just under the edge of the couch that magically unites the others. I took it as a directive, a nod that I was once again moving in the right direction.

For a time, I'd had that sense of relationship over obedience. I'd had a spiritual intimacy that grew and shifted and opened to new terrain. My studies on self-esteem had been the fragile bridge to all of that, but somehow I'd managed to lose it. *How can something so vital get misplaced?* I wondered. *How can it disappear when you need it most?* What mattered now was that it had reappeared.

I carried this source of strength with me until the day Arnold came to me, and in a rare moment of honesty, confessed how tormented he felt, how disconnected from God. Even this was said with anger, as if God himself were to blame for his angst.

"You've got to get counseling, Arnold," I said. "You've got to deal with whatever's going on or you're going to destroy everything you stand for. Unless you get help, I can't go on."

He walked out without acknowledging the line I'd drawn in the shifting sands of our history. But I knew he'd heard, and whether he believed me or not, I vowed to believe myself.

Nothing changed immediately, except inside me. Acknowledged or unacknowledged by Arnold, I knew things would not go on as they were. I couldn't let them. And with that knowing, I began to relax, to be okay in a way that had nothing to do with the outer circumstances. As the weeks passed, church seemed less burdensome and its progress less imperative; although in fact, it did continue to grow. The most important thing for me was that I was no longer living a dichotomy. I was no longer letting the duplicity of my own life go unaddressed even if it looked much the same to others. And I felt something different in Arnold too--almost imperceptible, but there.

We'd been in Sacramento almost three years when Arnold's sister, Mary Ellen, and her husband, Ron came to visit. One evening after dinner, and in need of his preferred pain reliever, Ron asked where the nearest drug store was located. Rather than trying to direct them, we all decided to go. Arnold and I waited in the car, with me sitting directly behind him. Assured there wouldn't be a conversation, I began to shift into my own thoughts when he sighed in the silence. These sighs had become frequent in the last years, but this one came from an unfamiliar depth.

"Oh, Addie," he said, "I just can't go on any longer."

My heart leapt to attention and was off and running. Before I could find a response, he filled the gap.

"But what would I do?" he asked. The question was wrenching, coming as it was from the most hard-working, successful man I'd ever known--a man who had always known what to do. But oddly enough, I had an answer.

"I think you would make an excellent real estate agent."

"You do?" he asked, obviously surprised that I'd given it thought.

"Yes, I do." Every cell inside me was pulsing with the riotous hope of relief, but my voice was as calm as if I were reassuring one of my students of his full potential.

I saw Ron and Mary Ellen approaching out of the corner of my eye. "Here they come," I said.

They took their places in the car, Ron pleased that they'd found just what he was looking for. I was happy for him, but far happier for myself. My pain, too, had been enormously, miraculously, relieved.

When our guests left the next day, we seized the chance to talk. For the first time in a decade, there was aliveness in our conversation. He could go to real estate classes on Saturdays and a couple of evenings a week, we surmised, and probably get his license within a year—maybe less. We'd always agreed we wanted to move back to Nampa when we retired, so our destination was set. The pulse of our energy was so strong that we decided to act on it now. We would sell our house and rent a place to live in the interim.

It was so exhilarating to think about leaving the ministry that I was tempted to let the counseling slide. But remembering my promise to myself, I told Arnold again that I couldn't continue, even under these circumstances, unless he got help.

"I just got someone's name," he told me. "He's part of a group over in Pleasant Hill—they're all former ministers that have formed a counseling center."

It was almost too much good news for one week.

HOUSE EIGHTEEN

Topaz Way, Sacramento, CA

Giving up the sprawling comfort of our Winding Way ranch was a small sacrifice compared to the comforting vision of life outside the ministry. In the eyes of others, it no doubt looked as if we were losing ground: moving into a small, rented duplex in a neighborhood of units so similar, they were distinguishable mostly by means of their landscaping. Inside was the most modest home we'd lived in since Bellmore days. Stepping into a small square living room, you could look straight through to the kitchen/ dining area and out into the back yard. Mid-way through this space, a doorway to the right put you face-to-face with the hall bathroom. And on both ends of the hall, just a few paces from where you stood, were bedrooms.

I felt no pain about our reduced living quarters, and in fact, embraced them with relish. They represented something precious to me: a plan—and the heart of that plan was freedom. Not just freedom from the ministry with its never-ending duties, but from the years-long schism between my inherited religion and my inner longings. Like the proverbial school teacher coming to the end of a year of travail, I found my strength in knowing my days were numbered. I could go on because I knew it was almost over.

Arnold didn't even seem to mind the sacrifice of his horses.

They were taken back to Idaho and boarded once again at Marv's ranch. Nothing, it seemed, was as valuable to us as the relief of sipping from the elixir of promised freedom.

This little place, as humble as it was, offered some of the grace that had accompanied every parsonage across the years. Outside the sliding glass door on the back of the house was a sweet and private patio. There I nurtured the hanging vines and pots of flowers I'd brought from Winding Way, and took pleasure in watering the small patch of grass and its surrounding foliage. *This was our transition home*, I told myself, *and here in this little garden is the flowering of life to come.*

Once settled in our new home, Arnold and I began walking to a nearby coffee shop together most mornings. And while there were no stirring conversations over that coffee, the habit itself seemed to signal another way of life: a woman and her husband walking briskly toward a shared destination, companions in their expectation that tomorrow, they would do the same. Not since our first pastorate, where we'd played our rousing games of noon ping-pong on the dining table in Bellmore, had we shared in regular recreation outside of church.

Arnold had been in counseling for a few months by the time we made the move to Topaz Way. He'd eased into the experience by joining a therapy group facilitated by three counselors—all former ministers. I'd sensed a shift in him from the beginning, making it obvious how ready he was for support and for a place to speak freely among his peers. My mind went back to the night we'd pulled into our drive on Winding Way—after a particularly difficult Sunday—to find an unfamiliar car in our driveway. Before we could get out of our car, two figures emerged, unrecognizable at first in the darkness. It was a ministerial couple from a neighboring town. They'd driven fifty miles after their evening service to come talk with us. "We had a bad vote this morning," he said, his voice shaking. "We didn't know where else to turn."

We took them in, fed them, and soothed them as best we could from our own precarious perch. It had occurred to me that night that pastors in trouble, in pain, had nowhere to turn but to each other. And they rarely did that because the stigma of being a person in need was entirely unfamiliar—bred out of them by ministerial training and submission to a role. Now Arnold had found a haven among his colleagues and seemed to be responding to it well. I was pleased when he invited me to attend one of the group sessions with him. Besides giving me a chance to meet the psychologists he spoke of with such respect, I had the chance to experience for myself the warmth and support that was making my own life easier.

That summer Sacramento was on Dale and Linda's vacation itinerary. On the first evening of their visit, our family of seven crowded around the table for dinner, filling our miniature dining room to capacity. When we reconvened to the living room, Dale and Linda sat on the piano bench, forming a circle. A few weeks before, Brad and Maridel had called us over to their house after church one night to give us a present. Inside was a plastic baby in a plastic cradle. "You're going to be grandparents again!" the note inside read. I knew that Brad and Maridel were eager to announce to the rest of the family that another baby was on the way.

"We have something to tell you guys," Maridel said when we were all settled.

"So do we," Dale replied.

"Well our news is that we're expecting another baby!"

"Well," Dale retorted, "our news is that we're having our *first* baby!"

The room erupted in spontaneous celebration with Justin clapping his hands while we made the rounds hugging each other. When the exclamations ceased and due dates were compared, we were even more in shock: our second and third grandchildren were expected less than a week apart.

"Yeah, we finally figured out how it works," quipped Dale. "I left my socks on."

Now we erupted in laughter, and the four rooms of our little duplex suddenly seemed expansive. I'd been preparing myself for the fact that I'd be leaving not one, but two grandchildren with the move to Idaho. But now, at least, I'd be moving into the life and heart of another one.

A couple of months after joining the therapy group, Arnold had begun individual counseling with one of the therapists, a man named Mel. He didn't talk about his sessions, but it was enough that he was not only willing, but happy to go. I had feared he would go a few times, find fault with the therapist and use it as a reason to stop. And though our relationship didn't change that much as a result of his sessions, I was beginning to see signs of it elsewhere.

For the first time, Arnold seemed interested in meeting the needs of this *particular* church rather than forging ahead on auto-pilot. He stopped holding traditional revivals, and instead, brought in some unusual guests for weekend workshops. The first of these guests was a couple who represented a national organization called "Lay Witness Mission." Miraculously, this elderly couple got the people of the church intimately involved in small group sharing through the use of evocative questions. That simple tool affected people not only personally, but relationally, creating bridges and bonds between members who had little to do with each other. This, in turn, entirely transformed the tone of the Sunday evening services. At Arnold's bidding, people now came up to the microphone and very specifically shared the reality of God's love in their lives. The contrast to the Wednesday night testimonies of my childhood was stark—no rote words or signature suffering here. For the first time ever, what was going on *inside* the walls of the church had a direct relationship to our outside lives. And this resonated with my own hunger for honesty inside religion. As in the past, however, I wasn't among those who shared. How could I honestly reveal my life with the people we served?

Though no one in the church asked about the sale of our house and choice of rented abode, Arnold and I assumed people were drawing the obvious conclusion. Surely it was apparent, despite having our family on the staff, that we weren't growing roots in Sacramento. Yet it was equally clear that while he was here, their pastor wasn't letting up on his commitment to the church. In fact, thanks to the Lay Witness Mission, it was a pivitol time.

The church was growing, spirits were high and the atmosphere of the services had gone from formal and reserved to a casual liveliness.

Against all odds of reason, the year was proving to be a pivotal one for me as well. After Maridel attended a women's weekend seminar in town, she called me with the utterly unexpected: her certainty that I could become one of the seminar leaders for the growing enterprise of "Total Woman" –a book that turned into a movement. With my hibernating love of teaching jolted awake by this new possibility, she and I set out together for a "Total Woman" weekend. A short road trip and an overnight in a motel was fun in itself, but the thought of returning to teaching women was what drew me there. The speaker that weekend was not Marabel Morgan, the author of the book, but another young woman. On a break, I spoke with her about becoming a seminar leader and she gave me Marabel's contact information. The letter was forming in my head all the way home.

Even at that stage, I'm sure I knew I had some conflict with the message I so fervently hoped to deliver. And while this might have raised shiny, scarlet flags about my history as a messenger out of harmony with the message, I couldn't stop myself. My voice for spiritual growth had all but disappeared in this pastorate and I feared that if I didn't take this opportunity, I might never regain it.

Within a few weeks, Marabel called and hired me on the phone. I was elated to once again be something more than the minister's wife! "Total Woman" was growing so quickly that I started giving seminars within the month, loving the restoration of myself as a teacher as well as the buoyant energy of women eager to grow. I'd given three or four workshops in rapid succession before the glow began to wane. Once again, I saw with dismay, I was "skirting and substituting." How much could I make this material my own and still honor the author and her message? The focus of the book and workshop was completely on pleasing one's husband—something I'd tried diligently to do for over thirty-three years, but without the benefit of success. Even when I applied the specific suggestions of "Total Woman" teachings, it hadn't worked. After all these years, I was back to *that*—caught between wanting to teach and teaching someone else's truth. Now every time I taught a seminar, hypocrisy played its familiar tune at the edges of my mind. *But some of this is good,* I told myself. *And women seem to really love it.*

At the start of the following year, the year we hoped would be our last in the ministry, we acquired some new neighbors. Ordinarily, a young couple moving into the cul-de-sac around the corner from us wouldn't have been noticed. But this couple had a charming little boy named Justin. He was two by now, and though he had been instructed not to do so, he regularly escaped on his big wheels and rounded the bend to our door. One day when the bell rang, I opened it to empty space. "I knowed you was home," a little voice said, and I looked down to see the top of his shiny towhead.

In February of the following year two more grandsons turned our family into a tribe. First the phone call came from Idaho that

Tyler Jay Woodcook had been born, complete with the red hair that seemed to skip generations in our family. As much as I wanted to fly to Dale and Linda to celebrate their first child, I couldn't leave my due-any-minute daughter. And thirty-four hours later, I was glad I hadn't. At midnight, I crept into Brad and Maridel's duplex to stay with a slumbering Justin while Arnold made the trek to the hospital. Gavin Taylor Bowes made his debut just two hours later.

With the birth of her second child, Maridel plunged into the uncharted waters of soul-searching. She was not only puzzled, but alarmed, by the experience she had both times she gave birth. Over the course of her pregnancies, she'd become emotionally attached to her obstetricians—spending inordinate amounts of time obsessed with what they thought of her and whether they liked her. Following each birth, she grieved the loss of the relationship as one would the death of a friend. The first time she could forgive as romanticizing, but the second time left her disturbed. She confided her concern to me, asking about the counselors I'd met when I visited her father's group. I consulted Arnold and we agreed that while it didn't seem right for her to see Mel, another therapist named Ritch seemed just right for her.

In the meantime, I accompanied Arnold on one of his visits, entertaining myself with out-of-date magazines until he emerged from the hall. "Mrs. Woodcook," Dr. Jameson would like to talk to you." In shock, I scooped up my purse and followed her to his open door. I perched on the chair across from him, wondering why he had summoned me to this office. "Mrs. Woodcook, you're living with a very angry man," he said.

"Yes, I know," I heard myself say—while at the same time wondering if hearing someone *else* say it was what made it real. Mel's tone reminded me of the doctor's long ago in Muncie: a tone of warning. Then it had been about Arnold's physical health and my security. Now it was about his emotional health—and mine. Briefly, he shared his view of my husband as a man who was in danger both physically and emotionally. Mel had been a minister himself and knew the pressures. "All I can say is I'm glad he's retiring. It won't be a day too soon."

When I looked back on this moment months later, I was incredulous at my response. Or lack of one. Without comment, I thanked him and walked out.

Shortly thereafter, I was Maridel's chauffeur for her first appointment. Once again I climbed the stairs and sat in the waiting room on someone else's behalf. She had been anxious on the way there, sure that the therapist would make obvious sense of her problem in fifteen minutes and the rest of the time would be spent uncomfortably searching for things to talk about. Instead she came out relieved, and eager to go back.

Ever on the leading edge of things, Arnold made a trip to Nampa to go job-hunting. His real estate studies were coming to an end and he was eager to seek his prospects with a top real estate firm in Nampa. When I picked him up at the airport, he was flying high—a state I recognized as his natural habitat though I couldn't remember when I'd seen it last. Enthusiastically, he began to spill his good news. His first-pick firm was very interested in him and he expected to receive acceptance within a few days! He'd loved being back in Idaho again! And he'd bought a house! For the first time in my life, I didn't withhold my feelings.

"You did *what?*" I shouted. "I can't believe you would do that!"

"We can buy something else if you don't like it," he said as if he were speaking about a lamp.

But nothing could stop the torrent of tears. Even if we bought something else, the violation had been made: he'd bought a house without consulting me. And once the conversation resumed, it was clear that his choice had little to do with the house. It was just what came with this real estate rarity: a plot in town with barn and horse property. I wailed on. Our first purchased home had been chosen based on his need to have the horses close—now they were the primary consideration again. I hadn't even been part of the process! All I could feel was devastation and complete disregard, as if Amy and Arrow were more important to my husband than I was.

On the heels of this blow, my next "Total Woman" seminar faced me. This one was in Berkeley, and all the way there, I wished I was driving in the other direction. The initial joy of having a platform had all but disappeared. Straying from the script more and more, I was compromising the teaching, and even so, still compromising my own beliefs. In years to come, I would realize how life reflects what's going on inside us—but not on this day. Therefore, I was shocked when in the midst of the workshop, a woman stood up and challenged me. I'd made an off-handed, and in my mind, playful statement. "You girls know what I mean, right?"

"We're not girls, we're women!" she interjected and sat down.

I was embarrassed, but it didn't blur my recognition that my choice of words was demeaning. "You're right," I said back to the woman. "Thank you."

Afterward, she came up to speak to me, requesting that I read the book she thrust into my hands, "All We're Meant to Be," A *Biblical Approach to Women's' Liberation.* She was a friend of the authors, Letha Scanzoni and Nancy Hardesty.

"I think you'll find their work worth reading," she said.

I assured her I would read it.

"A liberated Christian woman is not content to settle without thought into the restricting pattern society expects of its members who happen to have been born female," the introduction began. "She is free to know herself, be herself, and develop herself in her own special way, creatively using to the full her intellect and talents." I eagerly read on, and as I did, "All We're Meant to Be," sealed my fate with "Total Woman." This book, so intelligently and incisively written, was diametrically opposed to what I was teaching—and I *completely* resonated with it.

Its outlook on partnership, in particular, was unlike anything I'd ever read or even heard. It spoke of eliminating the desire in relationship to dominate, exploit or manipulate. "Neither spouse will consider it a right to demand his or her own way, and such a concept will mean that each one will do as much as possible to help the other develop fully as God intends." This was the kind of relationship I wanted but hadn't dared to believe was possible! And I also saw that I'd been trying to get there through the wrong door. Following the traditional script handed down to me was never going to take me where I longed to go. The strange thing is, I didn't even have to resign from "Total Woman." I received no more requests to do the seminar.

As soon as I made this decision to face another direction, I was face-to-face with someone ready to take me on the next phase of my journey: my daughter. Maridel was sharing her therapy with me. Working with Ritch was beginning to widen her eyes to her past, particularly her beliefs about herself and God. Emotions were coming up for her that were foreign and uncomfortable, but even so I watched her thrive as self-honesty became her focus. Slowly, she was starting to understand that her strange attachment to her doctors had to do with a father, who while exceedingly proud of her, had never developed a relationship with her.

"Love is not the issue," Mitch told her. "I know your father. I believe he would die for you. But he only knows you as part of his world, part of his obsession with success. When other powerful men relate to you outside that context—as a worthy person in your own right—you feel that missing piece and don't want to let it go."

She was spoon-feeding me the very thing I'd craved for as long as I could remember: the nutrients of inner life shared between two people. I'd never had a dialogue like this except inwardly—and even *that* I now saw had been stunted by my own misgivings. The fact that Maridel was talking about my own husband, and reflecting so much of what I, too, had felt across the years, was the bonus. And still, interestingly enough, I didn't seek professional help for myself.

When Arnold and I went to Nampa together for a weekend, I got my own tour of the house he'd purchased. We saw it in the dusk of the evening, and while I knew it wasn't a true representation of the place—inside or out—I couldn't shake the impression it had left me with. Its low ceilings, small rooms and dark shadows felt much like my marriage itself: claustrophobic.

In the spring, Arnold resigned not just from another church, but from the ministry. Despite being his own worst enemy in this place, he'd done well here and people seemed genuinely sorry to see us go. As with every pastorate, he'd lifted this church to a new level and left it thriving in a way that it never had before. His body was broken and his early dreams of the ministry shattered. Yet over the course of the last year, as he'd struggled to deal with his pain, a new compassion had arisen in him. His sermons had grown softer and his sharing more personal. When he interacted with the parishioners, his manner was noticeably different—less like someone who was looking for the first opportunity to move on. It was clear that through his private and group therapy, the knot that had only loosened in Justin's presence, was coming slowly undone.

The real gift of this pastorate, I had begun to see, was not success as we had always measured it. We had arrived in humility and were leaving with respect, yes. But more importantly, something was emerging from our brokenness, our angst and pain. We had hit bottom here at a stage of life when many couples are in the prime of their ministry, and yet we had not been forsaken. For in this place, a new source of light had begun to shine on us.

As we packed up our duplex, I was torn between my unspeakable relief and the pain of leaving our little family just around the corner. Justin was now three years old and we'd recently celebrated Gavin's first birthday. I knew that while Arnold was still in pain, he was healing, and that he was also energized by the challenge of his new career. I wasn't as sure of myself. I'd surrendered my last platform with "Total Woman" and my only aspiration in Nampa was to reconnect with Dale, Linda, and Tyler. There were people I would be glad to see again, but I had no friends I could talk with the way Maridel and I did. Giving up those conversations felt like exchanging real food for rations. I didn't even have hopes of returning to my teaching position at the college. It had long since been filled.

This move from our last church ironically reminded me of leaving our first. As then, it was early spring and as then, I was eager for a release into a brighter world. The difference was that so many winters had passed in-between. I was no longer young. I knew myself far better, true—yet the vision of my own authentic life still eluded me.

HOUSE NINETEEN

Southside Boulevard, Nampa, Idaho

Retirement from the ministry had come earlier than I'd ever imagined, but not a day too soon. I was fifty-six years old when we drove away from the epicenter of our last little universe. This time, the trip was returning us to familiarity instead of plunging us into a foreign land where people awaited a miracle. Leaving Brad, Maridel and the boys was hard, but I instinctively hid out from the pain. Instead I reminded myself that I was heading toward my beloved mountains and Dale's family—and to the first home that wasn't connected to a church. I'd been born in a parsonage and lived my life in a series of them. Despite the flaws of our new home with its unattached barn, it had no attached church—literally or symbolically.

The red brick house on Southside Boulevard was not as bad as the memory of my first dimly-lit visit. The ceilings were not as low as I'd recalled nor the walls so close. Even so, it represented the greatest decorating challenge of my life. It had five rooms which were all less than generous in proportion, yet comically counter- balanced by a single room that resembled a warehouse. Five steps down from the kitchen, this giant stretched out across the whole back of the house. In addition to its lack of charm, there were other character flaws: no heat and no storage. The only way it redeemed itself was through the surprising relief of ten foot ceilings and two sliding glass doors that looked out onto the backyard. Since it had clearly been added onto this modest little house, I tried to imagine what its original purpose was. Evidently not for living as typically defined; but that was my challenge now—to turn its vast emptiness into something livable. We already had one barn on the premises.

On our first Sunday back in Nampa, we ventured out to church. The strangeness of it all banged loudly on the door of my liberation. For thirty-four years, church had meant one thing: the two of us and our accompanying ambitions, roles, and duties. Regardless of weather or emotion, these had propped us up into place because it *all* depended on us. Now no one would notice if we didn't show.

We chose a church of our own denomination of course—the other large church in town rather than the one we'd pastored. Its size would allow us to slip in and sit in the back row, hopefully unnoticed. In recent years, it had been a secret desire of mine to be one of those people who slip in late and duck out early, but I wasn't quite prepared to wish I wasn't there at all. The service was as drab as any from my childhood and those cell-bound feelings of the past began to drape themselves around me like a heavy, wool cape in summer. When Arnold signaled "let's leave" just before the close of the service, I knew he was feeling them too.

"I have a splitting headache!" he said. "I can't go back there."

"Fine with me," I countered. The truth is I would have *feigned* a headache to keep from returning. "Why don't we try the Cathedral of the Rockies in Boise? I've heard it's really wonderful."

Sure he would balk at attending a church outside our own, I hadn't mentioned this possibility to him. But like so many times before, my enigmatic husband surprised me.

"Let's try it," he said without hesitation. I was as floored as I was thankful. The Cathedral of the Rockies, a church I had only seen from the outside and heard about once, fascinated me—the name, the grandeur of the building, the draw of the forbidden. The thought of going there was so enticing that on that first churchless Sunday night of my life, I was happy at the thought of going back to church.

That week I turned my attention to the house. We'd agreed to paint and carpet the original house, but when it came to the *ware*house, I was stumped. Every time I passed by it, all I could do was stare—unable to envision converting it from "uh oh" to "ahhh."

Within a few days, however, a small pile of bricks in our backyard gave me an idea. I picked one up and turned it over in my hand, casting my eyes to the ground and my mind to the possibilities. As if in a dream, I noticed that the pile was merely the remainder of a whole cache of bricks buried in the dirt and grass. I suddenly had a vision of brick focal areas on the floor of our outsized room .

Fortunately, a vision is energizing. Across the next several weeks, I dug up and scrubbed hundreds of bricks by day. And at night, I doodled my designs; finally settling on a kidney-shaped area on one side of the room and a V-shaped one on the other. New carpeting would join it all together. The striking result in my mind's eye kept me at the tedious, nail-destroying work.

Our first Sunday at the Cathedral of the Rockies was more than a service—it was a revelation. Immediately I responded to the rows of stained-glass windows that called the senses to worship and created a quiet reverence in the sanctuary. The pastor, a man everyone just called "Fred," was practical, funny, and real. The personal honesty coming from the pulpit was, alone, worth the 20- mile trip to Boise. Fred's message didn't align with our doctrine or focus on any doctrine for that matter, but instead on things any human heart can relate to: like the need to be loved—including his own yearnings. With the thundering organ ushering us out after the pronouncement of the final "Amen," I knew we had found a church home. If I was reading him right, Arnold too had responded with satisfaction. I was right. Arnold loved the Cathedral as much as I did, and as the weeks unfolded, praised Fred's ministry more and more. Sunday became a joy: going to church without any responsibilities, out for lunch afterward, followed by a leisurely day. There were blessedly no Sunday evening services at the Cathedral.

Soon the whole week began to feel different to me. Arnold was occupied—obsessed really—with his new career in real estate. The form of work had changed, but he was still in overdrive. Thankfully, however, he seemed to be a natural at his new occupation—which in turn offered a far better return for his labors. He was fast becoming the most successful realtor in his large office.

My own successes were of a different kind. My cherished freedom now far exceeded my days in the upstairs apartment on Indiana Avenue. I had the liberty to go shopping, take long walks, meet former colleagues for lunch and spend days with Linda and Tyler. The rest of the time, I focused on my ugly duckling homestead, eager to see if I could, in fact, turn it into a swan.

My vision had now moved to the next stage. I'd laid the clean, dry bricks on the floor according to my patterns, and then hired a bricklayer to cement them together. On the kidney-shaped platform, luscious vines spilled out of the drawers of my hutch cupboard and antique sewing machine. Larger plants tumbled from baskets and pots, paired with the rocking chair that had once graced the cottage on Basket Island. For the V-shaped space, we bought a new, but old-fashioned-looking, black wood-burning stove. I hung tongs and various cooking utensils on the wall behind it. The remaining open space we filled with rust shag carpeting, and placed our casual furniture in a circular grouping between the two islands. More than any other room I'd ever decorated, this one pleased me most.

The good thing about old houses, I was beginning to discover, was that one could experiment fearlessly. It certainly wasn't going to look worse! Buoyed by the spirit of that realization, I single-handedly covered a bedroom wall with fabric and made a quilt to match. The results looked like a page out of a magazine.

But this odd little house wasn't the only thing undergoing renovation. As the weeks of attending the Cathedral progressed, Fred's vulnerability was giving me the courage to look at my own feelings. Maridel had opened that door through the sharing of her counseling, and now, like a guiding star, that theme had come back to me in the place I least expected to hear it: church. I was hearing from the pulpit the kinds of things I had secretly discovered for myself across the years. But this matter of examining feelings wasn't something I had come across in my reading. Fortunately, Maridel and I were continuing our Sacramento conversations and each one offered another inch of permission to be honest with myself emotionally.

Alone in the house one day, I felt irritable and angry without knowing why. In the past I would have simply judged my feelings with a quick *Isn't this the life you've wanted for years? What's the matter with you? You've got nothing to be angry about*! But on this day, primed by months of dialogue with my daughter and encouragement from my new pastor, I let the feelings come. Before I knew it, I was pounding the walls up and down the hall and screaming, "I'm angry! I'm angry!" over and over until the protest had drained from my body. If in fact, as I'd been taught, anger was a sin, then I was chief among sinners. But there was no time for reflection. As soon as my outburst ceased, I'd instantly burst into tears, slid to the floor and started sobbing. To my astonishment, when the tears subsided, I felt a greater sense of peace than I had felt in years. No not in years—ever.

Maridel had taken up journaling soon after she'd begun therapy and now I followed her lead. My writing was a mixture of feelings, insights and observations about myself. Fred had talked one Sunday about his own awareness of judging others and how it thwarted his relationship to God. Our years in the ministry, I saw now, were full of judgment: for people who didn't attend every service, came in late or left early, didn't actively participate, criticized our ministry, or were too needy. I'd read about being honest with oneself. I'd taught it too. But only now was I lifting the prohibition on myself.

I also wrote about my relationship with Arnold. While he seemed pleased with his new life in Nampa, things between us remained stagnant. As had always been true, he was working most of the time, but when we were together, we lived as if we inhabited homes on opposite sides of a chasm with a roof as the only link. We talked, but only of things that life necessitated; and although we now had the new luxury of uplifting church services, leisurely Sundays, and visiting our grandson together, none of this lifted the low-hanging cloud of estrangement for long. My fears, hurts, desires, and disappointments poured from pen to page. Surely we still loved each other, I reasoned, but even that love seemed like a ghost when I tried to find my way into its arms.

In reality, being left alone with my life wasn't so bad. In fact, I cherished the pace of it: the time to journal, walk, think, and excavate secrets I'd kept from myself. It would have been the perfect life if I'd been single. But I'd been married thirty-five years and felt I had little to show for that investment. Yes, we'd accomplished a lot and had a wonderful family. But what about us?

In mid-summer, I received a call that put that question on hold. I was offered my old job back at the college! My successor was moving and my classroom, as well as my office, were mine for the simple act of reclaiming. It wasn't the kind of offer that requires reflection. I was as ecstatic as I was the first time I'd been invited to teach, and flooded with even more gratitude. This time I knew exactly what I was agreeing to—and nothing could have been better.

As the summer moved toward fall, I completed my work on the house, and plunged into refurbishing my lesson plans and my wardrobe for my re-entry into the collegiate world. And when fall came, it was like sliding back into a favorite pair of shoes I thought I'd lost forever, mysteriously returned.

The next year, a "For Sale" sign appeared on the property next door. Arnold bought the small fixer-upper and its companion two-bedroom cabin. He took the project upon himself, and within months he'd sold it for a nice profit. It wasn't the only place he was turning into a handsome profit. By the time we'd been back in Nampa just over a year, a large picture of him appeared in the Nampa paper with the headline, "Million-Dollar Man." He was the first realtor in town to sell that much property in a year. I could only marvel.

We were both working full-time now, but unlike our years in the pastorate, our careers were our own. My fulfillment as a teacher and my relationships with my colleagues eased the emptiness I felt in my marriage. The questions to which there were no answers mercifully abated. Our history, our family and our comfortable life was the force-field that held us together. *Maybe it was enough*, I told myself. *Maybe it was all there was.*

We'd been back in Nampa almost two years when Arnold came home one day delirious with excitement. I thought he must have made his biggest sale ever; but instead, he wanted to show *me* a house.

"Come see it," he said. "You'll love it. It's perfect for both of us."

By now, I didn't have much faith in my husband's choice in houses. And I knew without asking that it was horse property. What kind of home with that requirement would possibly appeal to me? The ones I dreamed of—simply adored—were set in neighborhoods where the sight of a horse could only mean one thing: it was loose and someone was looking for it.

All this was galloping through my mind as a beaming Arnold drove five miles out of town, and then turned onto a country road. I realized that we were heading toward Lake Lowell, and instantly remembered a Sunday afternoon many years before when we'd driven this same route. On the way to see a parishioner, we'd passed a house that nearly made me weep with longing. It was directly across from the lake, set back on property with a long gravel drive that separated two sections of green, sprawling lawn. A huge oak dominated the yard, a guardian of tranquility. But what caught my eye as we'd passed was a chair in the window. *What would it be like*, I'd wondered, *to live there and not have to go to church tonight? What would it be like, instead, to just sit in that chair at dusk and look out across the lake?*

"I remember a house I saw out here one Sunday afternoon," I told Arnold as he made the next turn. "It faced the lake."

"We're headed that way."

"I'll show it to you," I said wistfully. "It was the color of coffee with cream."

But as it turned out, he showed it to *me* first.

"There it is!" he exclaimed just after we rounded the bend onto the lakefront. A "For Sale" sign swung back and forth in the breeze as we pulled into the long gravel drive that parted the vast seas of green.

HOUSE TWENTY

Lake Shore Drive, Nampa, Idaho

The house on Lake Shore Drive *was* the perfect house for both of us. At long last, and for the first time, we made the choice together and with inebriated enthusiasm. Yes, it had a pasture and a barn (tack shop and bunk house), but they were ancillary to the house itself, and barely visible from the road.

This was a home—such a home! It sat on three acres of property with white-railed fences running the perimeter, and a grove of large trees as its shelter. The far left end of the house was a two-story structure with a solid glass front—a gleaming tower that matched the magnitude of the oak tree in its reflection. The rest of the house was one story. Six tall windows lined up across the front, offering an elegant dignity to the casual design. I still remembered the one that had held the chair. No meager porch for this place! A wide, open deck ran from the driveway to the front double doors, which were offset from the middle of the house.

Inside, the six windows ran floor to ceiling across the twenty-five foot living room that overlooked both lake and the Boise Mountains. The open dining area was adjacent to this space; and from here, glass doors opened onto an expansive patio from which we could see the Owyhee Mountains.

The main home and its two-story portion, which had obviously been added on, were joined by a short hall. In a grand architectural gesture, someone had added this enormous room with its equally enormous window, to gain an unobstructed view of the lake. It greedily swallowed up almost all of our existing furniture, and we were delightfully obliged to purchase a five-piece sectional and two large hassocks. Even then, this rich brown beauty only filled half of the living room. On the other side, I placed three comfortable chairs around a large, round coffee table made from our old dining set. We bought a new traditional walnut set to take its rightful place in the dining area.

This wasn't a new house by any means and had its foibles: particularly the dated bathrooms and kitchen. But all was forgiven. The sheer spirit and blessedness of this place was reflected back to me through every window, evoking the thrill of emancipation.

After thirty-four years in the ministry with its city necessities and clamoring demands, here was my oasis. I lived in the country, across from a lake with two mountain ranges for my constant companions. It was quiet. And private. I spent hours sitting in my favorite chair, a rust recliner—just looking at the lake, watching the horses canter in the front pasture and listening to the flocks of geese overhead. Even when I was reading, I looked up frequently for the sheer pleasure of remembering where I was. The drive to school was seven miles, a transition between worlds that I loved equally. Back and forth I went, from the calming beauty of rippling water, mountain majesties, and fathomless green to the joy of engaging young, eager minds.

As a faculty member, I was urged to attend the three chapel services a week, but having gone to church out of duty for so many years, I excused myself on a regular basis. However, the week that I saw Fred Venable on the speaker's roster, no deliberation was necessary. The ever-honest, witty Fred connected well with the college crowd. Afterward, I joined the line of listeners waiting to thank him. He recognized me and in our exchange, I mentioned that Arnold and I had agreed to invite him and his wife, Joan, out for dinner. "We'd love that!" he said. "Give us a call."

It was odd to be on the other end of the pastor-parishioner continuum. "Taking the pastor and his wife out to eat," had always meant Arnold and me. I was pleased to be reciprocating. It was odd and it was lovely. A few weeks later, the dinner with Fred and Joan was lovely too, sharing our ministerial histories complete with trials and triumphs.

Fred called me a few days later and invited me to speak at the annual Lenten Lecture Series—noon-hour talks given once a week at the church during the Lenten season. As I delivered my talk about the possibility of rebirth at any age, a young woman's bright face kept catching my eye as I spoke. Afterward, she made her way to me and introduced herself as Patricia Kempthorne. "Could I take you to lunch some day?" she asked. "I'd really like to get to know you."

The lunch with Patricia, who turned out to be the Director of Children's Ministries at the church, led to another speaking engagement. Evidently over sandwiches and tea, she had been sufficiently impressed with me to recommend me as the speaker for the Cathedral's annual women's retreat.

Since my move to Nampa, my relationship with Linda had taken on new depth and by this time, I'd begun sharing with her my changing experience of God. Like my younger self, she seemed eager for a different perspective than the one of denominational rules and rote devotion. One weekend, thinking it would be fun to have a girls' getaway, she and I drove to Winnemucca, Nevada, to meet Maridel and her friend, Wendy. The four of us, never together before, formed an uncanny bond. The weekend was everything we'd hoped for and startlingly more. By the end of it, we had clearly formed a sacred circle—a place to question in safety the religious tenets with which we had all been raised. Like Arnold and me, Maridel and Brad had left our denomination and were attending a church with greater openness and freedom. That first weekend, Maridel and Wendy were fresh from a workshop where they learned about creating "affirmations" and "imagery books" that supported what one wanted in life. They'd toted along stacks of magazines and a four pairs of scissors. As we cut images from the pages, we shared them, talking intimately about what mattered to us. Before we parted that weekend, we set a date for another. Even with that stellar beginning, I couldn't foresee that I'd embarked on one of the most enriching ventures of my life.

Suddenly, I was receiving requests to speak—as if a stopped up spigot was suddenly running free! A college friend of Maridel's, Margi Galloway, invited me to hold a retreat for New Hope Community Church in Portland that her husband pastored. Next came a women's retreat for a church in Seattle, followed by a chain of invitations to speak locally in clubs and service organizations

When summer came, and with it, the cessation of teaching and retreats, our lakeside home took on another function: an idyllic summer vacation for our grandsons. We met Brad and Maridel in Winnemucca to pick up the boys and brought them back to the ranch for a month. Arnold had spent weeks eagerly bustling around outside, preparing the bunk house for his honored guests. Inside, he'd put three beds, a hamper, a place to hang their clothes and a little fridge. Tyler joined the boys for days at a time, leaving only to return again as soon as his mother would let him. "Three's too many for you, Mom," she would say. But within days, he was back, having pleaded to return. Arnold had also put a bell by the back door, which he rang mornings to wake them. They dressed, made their beds, tidied their quarters and lined up for inspection. Both "sergeant" and "soldiers" grinned their way through the pre-breakfast routine. He was making it a point to be a different kind of grandfather than father. He gave them childhood memories that neither he nor his own children had: horseback riding, tree house, snowmobiles in the winter and an official baseball diamond one summer.

Arnold had seemed to come alive in this place—not only with his grandsons, but riding his beloved horses on the lakefront road and on the service roads between surrounding fields. Sometimes I would watch him galloping off into the distance alone, and feel pleased that he was happy. But even the miracle of this house had done little to ease our strain. He still seemed self-absorbed, emotionally riding away from me too. It puzzled me. We had left the pounding pace and growing burden of the ministry, had acquired fulfilling jobs, and now had a home beyond either of our expectations. Yet nothing seemed to be healing the rift without a name.

Ours wasn't the only marriage in trouble. After fifteen years together, Dale and Linda divorced. The wound to our family unit was deeply painful, yet unlike other families, we didn't come apart. As our new family patterns unfolded, Linda remained our daughter—Tyler and her continuing to be as much a part of our lives as ever. When Dale remarried within a year and had a second son, we extended our hearts to his wife, Kathryn, and our new grandson, Jason. Our unusual arrangement wasn't always comfortable and to outsiders may have seemed strange, but for me, it was beautiful. It represented the breaking down of old paradigms and assumed agreements. Why couldn't we find our own way, expanding instead of contracting?

Only one thing was missing from my life now. I felt a longing for an experience I'd never had—except many years ago in a limited way with Jeanne. I wanted the kind of intimacy with other women that I'd developed with my daughters. Was it possible to have close women friends after decades of keeping my ministerial distance? On the next trip to Winnemucca, I brought up the subject in our motel therapy circle and surprised everyone, including myself, with my emotion. "I've never really had close friends!" I cried, startled by the truth.

"Is there someone on the faculty that seems interesting?" one of them asked.

"The young woman in the next office. But I'm sure she has lots of friends, and probably wouldn't be interested in someone her mother's age..." They stopped me and gave me an assignment to broach a friendship with Darlene.

Before I could get myself to move in that direction, Darlene came to my office door. "I know we've seen each other in the hall, but we've never talked." I invited her in and we chatted about life in the Communications Department where she worked, our classes, and our families. "Let's have lunch sometime, Addie," she said in parting.

The next week there was a brown paper bag in front of my office door. Inside, two cups and saucers holding tea bags and candy were nestled in beautiful fall leaves. To thank her, I took her to lunch. Amazingly, Darlene was reminiscent of Jeanne—raised in our denomination but by lenient parents who supported her to find her own experience of God. She had that refreshing sense of personal freedom to challenge what didn't feel right and come to her own conclusions. But this time, I had the freedom to be real too, and from that first lunch, we stopped thinking of each other as merely colleagues. We were friends.

The following spring I was asked to deliver the Mother's Day sermon at the Cathedral of the Rockies. I used the book, "The Giving Tree" by Shel Silverstein as the text. This simple story of a tree that thrived when it offered a young boy its shade, apples, and limbs to climb—but became useless when it sacrificed its trunk for him to build a boat—was the perfect metaphor for mothers who give too much. "When we give from what we can replenish, we continue to be life-giving year after year," I exhorted, "but when we give from our very life-source, we are cut off from our own vitality and ability to thrive." I closed by reading Paul's admonition from Ephesians: "Let your roots go down deep into the soil of God's marvelous love."

Arnold made no comment about my sermon afterward, which called up my mother's ghostly silence when I'd won the oratory contest. But neither past nor present kept me from feeling proud of myself. At last, I was beginning to realize that my value wasn't defined by others. Although I was honored to speak to all audiences, my in-depth weekends with women were most fulfilling. My topic, wherever I spoke, was self-esteem. But on retreats, I could share my own experiences of the years—my gradual but momentous climb out of doctrine and duty. Always, this sharing evoked deep emotion in women and brought their own inner conflicts to the surface.

When I was invited to hold a second women's retreat in Portland, I went deeper than ever before—recounting the time I took on the supervision of the Children's Department in Sacramento despite my total lack of desire.

"It weighed on me every Sunday," I told them. "And when my cholesterol count went off the charts, I was fortunate enough to have a doctor who asked me, 'What is it you're doing that you don't want to be doing?' That's the day I gave my resignation to my husband and pastor. My own health had become more important to me than pleasing him."

A woman stood to her feet. "I have the same problem with teaching kindergarten children in Sunday School. It ruins my Sunday." I was aware as she spoke that her minister's wife and other staff members were in the audience. If I'd opened a can of unwanted worms, it was too late now. "But my brother-in-law is the Sunday School Superintendent, and I don't want to let him down."

Before I could speak in support, one of the assistant minister's wives spoke up. "We're not doing *anyone* a favor by doing what we don't want to be doing. What we feel in our hearts is what we need to be doing."

"Yes," I continued, "And there's no doubt that there is someone who would love teaching kindergarteners, but the job's not available!"

My talks and retreats were no longer fueled by a meager supply of books. Now a whole library of spiritual material had opened up to me, including classic texts that had been there all along but I hadn't known existed. Maridel was feeding me a steady stream of titles: "Living in the Light" by Shakti Gawain, and "Circle of Stones" by Judith Duerk were two that allowed me to experience God's love not as a belief, but as reality. No amount of underlining or highlighting was sufficient to acknowledge the gratitude I felt as I read words that perfectly described my early depression and its true meaning:

"At these times we usually feel emotionally that we are hitting bottom, but as we actually hit the bottom, we fall into a trap door into a bright new world—the realm of spiritual truth. Only by moving fully into the darkness can we move through it and into the light."

Often, I simply sat and sobbed with utter, grateful joy.

In the midst of deepening my relationship to the feminine, a new woman came into my life. After the birth of four grandsons, Courtney Woodcook was born into our widening circle. A granddaughter felt like another flowering of my spirit, launching me into fantasies of tea parties on rainy afternoons. With my own daughter, I hadn't known who I was or how to share what mattered most to me. We'd found our way to that in time, but now, I had a fresh start, another opportunity to heal the lineage of which I was a part.

As my work with women grew, I could feel myself preparing to let go of my work at the college—as if a calling that had once been primary was giving way to another. I was more challenged in that arena than in this one—particularly to grow spiritually. Before I made that final decision however, my work presented me with one of the deepest healings of my life. I got a call one day from Keith, the head of the department, and as I blithely walked the corridor to his office, I didn't feel the approaching specter of a primal wound.

"Addie," Keith said when I was seated, "I have a favor to ask. We really need someone to do a school evaluation out at Springwood. I know this isn't in the scope of your regular duties, but I was wondering if you would do it this time."

I hated school evaluations. They were tedious and took enormous amounts of time—both to observe and write up. "I really don't want to do it, Keith," I heard myself say.

"You don't have to, Addie. We just needed someone and I knew you'd do a good job. Don't worry about it."

That was easy, I told myself as I walked away. But I didn't feel good. Over the weekend, a stew began to simmer in the old cauldron: *I'm so fortunate to even have this job. And Keith's always been so supportive. The least I can do is honor his request.* The litany continued until, by Monday morning, I went to his office and told him I would do it. Within a few hours, I began to feel depressed. The next day it was worse. By Wednesday, I felt black inside. After forcing myself through my morning classes, I locked my office, put a note on the door and drove out into the country. Dense fog surrounded me as I crept along, climbing a small incline and then gently finding my way to the bottom of a hill where I had to go left or right. The weight in my chest was crushing, and in an attempt to lift it, I cried out, "Oh God, help me!"

Suddenly I remembered the "Sunday showdown" with my mother in the campground cottage over fifty years before. I'd dared to say "No," and had suffered the consequences. Quarantined for all those years, uncontrollable emotion arose like a screaming beast at last released. When the eruption subsided, the fog cocooned me as I sobbed inconsolably. All that time ago, I'd concluded that I should always co-operate with people in authority, subverting my will to theirs. Keith hadn't even been coercive or tried in the least to make me feel guilty. I had done it to myself.

I turned around and found my way home, but inwardly, I was already home. Such glorious insight and such welcome relief! But I still had the final step to take. I walked to Keith's office the next day to tell him I wouldn't be doing the evaluation, but I didn't get the chance. "Hey, Addie, he said waving me into his office with a smile, "Springwood cancelled that evaluation request! So you don't have to do it after all."

I was in awe. The Spirit had set that whole thing up for my sake—giving me the chance to heal one of my oldest wounds.

The next year, at age sixty-five, with a total of fifteen years as a college professor, I decided to retire. It wasn't a popular decision with students, colleagues, or the head of the department. Even my own feelings were a mixture of loss and eagerness. I would miss college life, but dreamed of a new calling: teaching women who were ready for spiritual change. I was ready, too, for freedom at yet another level—not only in terms of my time, but with regard to breaking my last official tie to the church.

In honor of my retirement Arnold planned a big "surprise" party. I had caught wind of it in one of his phone conversations, but didn't let on. But when I came home from shopping one day and found Brad and Maridel in the guest room, I knew the day had come. Later Dale arrived with his family. Linda, now remarried to husband Jerry, was also there. We all made a promenade along Lake Shore Drive to the neighborhood steak house. When we returned, the left half of the front yard was filled with cars and the other half filled with people. Our deck became the platform for the evening's events. Brad and Maridel sang; several people from my personal and professional life offered tributes, including my nine year-old-grandson, Gavin. Afterward, we feasted on homemade pies baked by friends. As I wandered through the throng of people, receiving hugs and congratulations, I felt the richness of my life: the connections and interconnections, the support and love that was mine. Here on the lawn of a house that was once just a passerby's wish, I was surrounded by not only the life I'd created, but the spirit of the one into which I was walking.

With more time in my home, itself a reflection of love, my spiritual life was evolving yet again, seeping ever more deeply into my everyday reality. Walking alone in a two-mile circle of adjoining country roads was my new early morning ritual. Far more than exercise, it was a time of communion for me as I gathered wild asparagus for dinner, watched the geese overhead, and marveled at the changing tableau of color and texture from day to day. I'd repeatedly tried to have the requisite "devotions" over the years, but reading the Bible and praying under guilty duress never lasted for long—and seldom brought me closer to God. But the moving devotion of walking did that naturally, becoming an act of daily communion. And unlike the required practices of old, I felt bereft when weather or the rare morning appointment prevented it.

When I'd left the college, I'd broken my last tie with the religion I'd inherited by birth and perpetuated through marriage. Now a more private ritual seemed in order. Years before, I'd had my grandfather's ordination picture and certificate professionally framed for the walls of our home. I'd been proud to display these mementos of a man who had not only been present at the birth of our denomination, but in whose home I had been birthed. "Goo Goo," as I would always remember him, had been a gentle presence in the first decade of my life, and I would always think of him fondly. But it was time to let these two visual ties go and let new symbols of my faith adorn the wall. As I took them down and packed them to send to my cousin, who was a historian of the church, my feelings were mixed. The resonating symbolism of letting go was tinged with a fleeting sense of irreverence, but by the time I made my jaunt to the post office, all I was feeling was freedom—and one step closer into authenticity.

Now, as if freed to go deeper into my healing, my process noticeably accelerated. Layers of hidden attitudes toward myself were exposed. As accepting as I thought I'd become toward myself, I now faced the undergrowth of self-criticism, feelings of inferiority and unworthiness. I steadily supplanted them with the perennials of acceptance. I saw again that my outer life, no matter how desirable, wasn't capable of removing the stain of old beliefs about myself.

In this context, the relationship with Arnold began to change too, though not in the way I'd always imagined. Outwardly, things were much the same; but inwardly I realized that I had always lived my life around his pain—whether physical or emotional—and that this focus had kept my own denied pain at bay. The emotional purging in the hallway on Southside Boulevard had opened the door, and for awhile, I'd written more freely about my feelings. But like a person who confuses progress with a cure, I was ignorant of how much pain I held in lock-down with my body as its keeper. I had developed arthritis and while diet had originally controlled my cholesterol, it was now a continuing battle. The old doctor's question once again came to mind. "What is it you don't want to be doing?" Then, it had been as simple as resigning from supervising the children's department at church. But now I was playing for bigger stakes. I needed to resign from the old relationship roles that been breathed into me like oxygen—and that I had kept alive. But *how*?

After years of incremental steps with long periods of drought in-between, my spiritual path was indistinguishable from my life.

I knew the answer to my question was just to keep going—to stay as honest with myself as possible and use every opportunity to walk through the next door to healing. For me, this door had cracked open and closed many times, but now could not be shut again—as I learned one day at lunch with two acquaintances.

The pair had just returned from a Ladies' retreat at their church. Since I was doing this kind of work myself, I asked about the speaker. They both glowed with admiration as they praised her warmth, her ability to get her point across with humor and her obvious connection to God. "I think it was the best retreat I've ever been to!" one of them said, and the other concurred.

I'd enjoyed the account of their experience, but on the way home, I suddenly felt depressed. Perplexed, I told myself, "Oh, just get off at the next exit and have some pie and coffee." I felt momentarily better—then instantly awful again. My old ploy of covering up feelings with sugar and fat didn't set well—and I knew wouldn't help. As I drove by the exit, passing up my opportunity for distraction, my depression deepened and I screamed out, "Oh God, *what* is wrong with me?" No sooner were the words out when the response erupted from my own lips.

"I'm jealous!"

This discovery, this release of my own honest feeling, set me free immediately. I was euphoric! I saw that I'd unconsciously compared myself to this amazing speaker and in my own mind had come up wanting—needing people to feel that way about me and afraid they didn't. But by naming the feeling, I had demonstrated that I had the power to change it! Admitting this supposedly sinful and therefore forbidden emotion had not brought shame, but joy!

This was the most exciting epiphany I'd had so far and I was eager to use it again—just as I once had felt about wearing a new, stylish dress. My feelings about my marriage, so long protected by the ruts of our unspoken agreements and my own reticence to disturb the waters, were emerging too. I saw that I often complained to others, but didn't ever speak up to Arnold. I was forever trying to work around things, withdrawing physically or verbally without conveying my hurt or anger to him. Now with my growing bank account of integrity, I saw that I couldn't continue to be an accomplice to our dysfunctional ways.

As had been predicted years before, Arnold's health problems were compounding. He was driving himself in real estate just as he had in the ministry: relentlessly. His migraines and neck pain still plagued him as did his rising blood pressure, and I made these physical problems my excuse for not confronting him—even when I saw that it was costing me as well.

I was shocked into an answer the day Arnold came home from a doctor appointment and told me he'd been scheduled for an immediate open heart surgery. Suddenly, I saw the possibility of a fate worse than my own death: becoming my husband's caretaker. As we made our way, with our family's help, through the trauma of the heart surgery, I stared at the very real possibility that his life was shrinking. And I also stared at the truth about myself: I wouldn't desert him. Whether driven by obligation or plagued by resentment, I would become his caretaker.

As I nursed him back to health and watched his remarkable recovery (even healing from heart surgery got his Type A treatment), I considered myself warned. Arnold was not going to stop his relentless pursuit of his work for the sake of his health. This surgery that should have been a red flag for him, was instead, one for me. The tension he created in his life often manifested in cutting remarks to me. Across our years together I'd always handled it the same way: swallowing back the hurt, crying in private, and then, like my mother, creating emotional distance.

But one day a few months after the surgery, Arnold lashed out at me with such anger that for the first time, I felt threatened. The life-changing ground upon which I stood shifted. If I was teaching others about emotional honesty, I had to exercise it for myself when it was most scary. My integrity was on the line even if no one else knew what I saw when I looked into the mirror. I floundered, reaching for something—anything—that would be keep me from rolling into the involuntary rut of the past.

"If you ever talk to me that way again," I told him, "I'm going to do something about it." It was hardly a convincing retort. But it was all I had, and was enough to elicit a serious response.

"You wouldn't divorce me, would you?" he asked.

"Yes," I said. "I would."

I'd said the words, but didn't know if they were true. Would I really follow through if he lashed out at me again? I didn't know. But at least I'd put the word out there between us—the word that neither of us had dared to place on the wobbly table of our relationship. Once again, I had changed how I felt by expressing my feelings. In the past, I'd walked away shaken and hurt. Today, I was outwardly shaking, but strong inside.

These were the experiences that began to challenge my indoctrination to be compliant. Others' expectations had always been more real to me than my own needs and feelings. In fact, for many years, they were all that existed. Even my musical talent had been surrendered to a religious system that I didn't feel part of in my deepest heart. I didn't know that I had the choice to use it another way. I didn't realize that it belonged to me. And without that awareness, there was no way to choose.

As a result of all this, things were tenser in our household than ever. We weren't fighting outwardly, but an unspoken and pending clash of wills pervaded the atmosphere when we were both home. As spring arrived, I had no plans to divorce or even separate, but I knew that something had to give—and soon.

Mother's Day weekend was coming up, and with it, special plans. Arnold had agreed to take me to Winnemucca, Nevada, where Maridel would pick me up the next day. From there, we would embark on an overnight celebration en route back to Sacramento. Arnold and I set out early, and uncharacteristically, he asked me to drive. He feigned sleep for over an hour, but in the midst of the desert, he bolted upright in his seat. "Look at those mountains!" I said. The sun was shining directly on the massive range, lighting up their snowy peaks—a postcard in the midst of a wasteland.

"I've found someone who is crazy about me," he blurted out in response.

My response was telling. It was the response of a woman who had been lost in an insoluble maze—and had just been handed a map with the exit clearly marked. I put my hand on his knee, and said, "Tell me about her."

Instead, he started to cry.

And didn't stop.

He sobbed, doubled over in his seat until we reached the town of McDermott an hour later. Usually we stopped for coffee there, but today only to use the restrooms. When I got back to the car, he was back in the passenger seat, crying uncontrollably. Even when it waned, it returned again—all the way to Winnemucca. Once there, we went into the Red Lion Inn and ordered soup, but he excused himself when it came. I stayed and ate, paid the bill and returned to the car to find him sobbing again.

At the motel, he carried my luggage into the room and then told me he had to leave. "You've done your crying, haven't you?" he asked. It was the first thing he'd said since he'd made his announcement.

"Yes," I replied. *Throughout our whole marriage* I thought. He hugged me and then headed for the door, obviously in a hurry to leave.

"Are you going to cry?" he asked.

"I will if I need to."

That evening, I walked the main thoroughfare of Winnemucca

from one end to the other, only stopping to try on some hats. All I felt was relief.

My difficulties with sleep, originating in childhood and complicated by Dale's tour of duty in Viet Nam, were persistent in my life. But that night, alone in a humble room at Motel 6, I slept the "deep and dreamless" sleep of the Christmas carol I'd sung a thousand times.

Maridel arrived the next morning and we headed off to a hotel in Reno, hoping to arrive in time for our brunch reservations. She had arisen early that morning to come get me, and after about fifty miles, asked me to drive. I'd planned to wait until after brunch to tell her my life-changing news, but decisions are of the mind and emotions don't play by its rules. I hadn't driven far before I burst into tears. "Mom! What's wrong?" she asked, sitting up straight in her seat just as Arnold had done the day before. I pulled over, and between sobs, told her what had happened. We sat by the side of the road until my story and its belated feelings had been emptied out. Her reaction was not typical either. Having walked through years of struggle and grief with me—sometimes encouraging me to leave—she was relieved as well. "When I'm alone with either you or Dad, I have a parent. But when you're together, I can't enjoy either of you," she'd told me once.

We arrived late to a beautiful old hotel where Maridel had made brunch and room reservations. Our table had been given away, but they accommodated us apologetically with a small table in a bay window, away from the main dining room. It was perfect. In this quiet corner, we continued our celebration—not only of motherhood, but of release into a brighter future. How could it have been orchestrated better? In the wake of a forty-seven year marriage coming undone, I was out of town and with the one person who required no explanation for my elation.

When I arrived home from Sacramento a week later, there was no discussion about the next step. None needed. We both knew that divorce was the choice each of us had already made. Arnold said he would get all the forms and do the necessary paperwork, for which I was grateful. But the day he brought them home and sat at our dining room table filling them out, I couldn't stay. I went out into the yard, sat on the bench on the far side of the tack shop and cried as if I'd just received the worst news imaginable. For some part of me, it absolutely was. But for another part—the woman who had found herself against all odds—it was the *best* news imaginable too.

I steeled myself to call my sister, Rhea, with the news, fearing she may embrace her religious convictions instead of me. She was still a loyal member of the religion we'd grown up in, and divorce was not on the roster of acceptable responses to marital catastrophe. But to my relief, she seemed far more concerned about practical matters.

"Where will you live?" she asked almost immediately. "Will you get an apartment?"

"No, I'm going to buy a house."

"With *what*, Addie?" Her tone unmistakably flirted with sarcasm.

"I don't know," I admitted. I'd never been involved in the finances of our marriage, and only had the vaguest notion what I might walk away with.

But unlike my sister, not knowing didn't bother me. For many years, I had pictured living alone someday. And it wasn't in an apartment. It was in an older, classic house of my own. Ignorant of my fiscal stature though I was, I had no fear that scarcity would be my lot. It might have been naïve, but it served me well. That singular thought left no room for any other to take root.

After years and years of so little movement in our relationship, the process now went into high gear. Simultaneously, we put the house on the market and Arnold bought a brick bungalow in town. He took very little from the house—our old round table, a couple of chairs, his clothes. We'd agreed that I would stay on at the lake, inhabiting our once-upon-a-time dream home until it sold. It was equal parts odd and liberating to be the sole resident of the last home—the most beautiful home—we had shared together. Most of the time it was peaceful for me, although there were moments when the sorrow of it all would sneak up on me like a purse snatcher and run away with my serenity. Then I would cry deep, rending sobs for the dashing couple that sat on my dresser in their black and white joy. For them, I grieved. I was free, but their dream had perished, and with it, a part of myself.

Arnold continued taking care of the grounds with their formidable needs for mowing, irrigating and animal maintenance. We were in contact by phone most days as well. He was taking dance lessons and when at the house, would try in his awkward way to show me the steps he was learning. I had never seen him glow with enthusiasm over anything at which he was so inept. It was sheer joy for him I saw—no matter that he wasn't good at it.

When the neighbor next to us came to my door delivering tomatoes one day, I also learned how deep Arnold's allegiance went—married or not. I invited the man in as I would anyone bearing a gift, and continued my work at the stove while he stood nearby.

"You're lonely, aren't you?" he asked.

"No, I'm not really," I said casually.

"Yes, you are," he said, moving toward me and grabbing me. He held me so tightly I couldn't move, forcing a hard kiss on me. When I fought back and didn't stop, he took his bowl of tomatoes and left.

I called Arnold and he was at the man's door in less than an hour. "You're never to enter that yard, again!" he told him. "And if you do, I'll call the police."

Until that moment, I'd never imagined myself to be in danger. Nor did I realize that I still had a man who would come to my rescue when I found myself in the role of an unwitting, but nonetheless, distressed damsel.

Once the grieving shock of our decision had passed, my life took on its own lilting cadence—a rhythm that had no doubt been there all along. I'd had hints of it for sure: my years in the upstairs apartment; not being the only pastor's wife in the Nampa church; and the release from the ministry itself. But none had been as complete as this. This was release even from marriage—from the tie that I knew would always bind us after forty-seven years together, but loosely now and without the day-to-day cost.

My time, my choices, my schedule, my "yeses" and "no-thanks" were entirely my own. I gardened, walked, and read without knowing what I might do next. I entertained, but only as a medium to friendship. I wrote too—for myself and for talks that I hoped yet to give. My audiences were gone now, yet I felt like I had more to say than ever and pledged to get it down on paper. But as the months unfolded, I saw that my audiences hadn't so much disappeared as they had changed. There were audiences of one—like my friend, Dianna. She was a clerk in the Media Center at the college and we'd formed a bond over film catalogs and audio-visual equipment. In gratitude for her patience with my technologically-challenged ways, I'd asked her to lunch. There I learned, though I never would have guessed it, that she felt stuck in her current job. But as a single mother of two adolescent daughters and a paycheck that didn't always stretch to the next payday, she was not enamored of her future.

"So what would you like to do?" I asked.

She knew. She wanted to be in charge of the career center at the college: helping students choose a career, guiding them with their curriculum and eventually placing them in the right job. She was brimming with ideas and innovations.

"But I'd have to go back to school to do it, and if I give up my current job, I'll lose the benefit of having the girls' college education subsidized.

"What about you?" I pressed. "As an employee, wouldn't the college cover *your* classes as well?"

It was a question that changed her life.

By the time I'd retired and Dianna was making the jaunt out to the ranch for long evenings of dinner and even longer conversations, she was finishing her degree. Through this relationship, I discovered another way to share the spiritual growth that was both behind me and in front of me. Gradually, the relationship with Dianna became more and more mutual, but in the process, I had become a mentor.

I turned seventy just two years after Arnold and I divorced. I wanted to create a celebration for myself that would be unlike any party I had ever had—outside of church, outside of marriage, outside of age itself. I sent out invitations to my daughters and twelve of my closest friends. On the front was the photo of me escaping through the corn stalks with my grandfather hand-on-hip behind me. "Guess Who's Turning Seventy?" it asked.

When the day arrived, I was electric with happiness. As the house filled with friends whose greatest gift was merely their presence, I saw for myself how much my life had changed. For some of my guests, I'd been a pastor's wife; for others, a teacher; for some a colleague; for one, a mentor; for two, a mother. But as I sat in the circle, all those roles diminished and fell away. In the glow of connection to people who loved me dearly, each for their own reasons, I was just myself.

I'd invited my guests to bring a memory of our relationship to share and most of them chose a gift that reflected that memory. But one gift would be a lifelong treasure—a poem about my visitation of angels. Maridel had composed it for the occasion and Gavin had written it in calligraphy on color-washed parchment.

Angels knew
to come to you in silence
piercing the confinement
of crib and dark around you …
If angels knew
to bring to you
a glimpse of Something More
that never faded …

Then what does it matter
if walls and doubts
people and years, fears and forms
exerted all their power against you?
As long as they could not hold you
as long as they could not keep you
from becoming …
An angel
who brings to those
cribbed and alone
The Light of Something More.

Far more than a birthday party, this gathering was an affirmation of every step I'd ever taken to be whole and a living affirmation of my new life, my ever-growing path.

The following spring, the house on Lakeshore Drive sold, and my once-skeptical sister loaned me $15,000 for a down payment on a dream: a home of my very own.

HOUSE TWENTY ONE

State Street, Boise, Idaho

Maybe a home of my own is what I'd been dreaming about forever. Inside the parsonages, inside the houses I bought by default and the one I co-signed for with an open heart—maybe a home of my own was always the deeper wish. Like a woman, crazy in love, who finds every excuse to say her beloved's name, I loved saying the words, "home of my own." Now I had to find it.

I met my realtor wearing an eager smile, but by the time we'd looked at two houses, it had dramatically faded. The first house was little more than a cluster of small rooms with a sloping back porch that overlooked a patch of weedy yard—and, just to keep things consistent, a kitchen that discouraged all forms of cooking. The second house wasn't much better. For two years, I'd been envisioning my own home and neither of these resembled the small, but elegant beauty I'd had in mind.

"I guess $15,000 down doesn't buy much," I said as we headed for the third house. "Hold on, Addie. This third house will knock your socks off!" *Were houses one and two a set-up? I would have been completely willing to have my socks knocked off on house one!*

I was feeling a bit played, as we turned onto State Street. But when the car stopped in front of a white house with two columns and a small portico that sheltered an antique door, a smile once again took possession of my face. "It was built in the thirties," he said. "I think it's just your style."

Inside I was greeted by original chandeliers, a brick fireplace with a wood mantel, and two stressed-glass windows gracing either side. Wide white molding added character to the living and dining rooms. The bright, updated kitchen had a darling breakfast nook just big enough for a round table and two chairs. The main bedroom had a deep closet seldom seen in houses of this age. The other bedroom was on the front of the home, and looked out on the street. It would make an ideal study.

"The owner will let you have it for $15,000 down and taking over her payment of $349.00 a month." The smile had now become a grin that would fade only when sleep released it. I bought this beauty, who was not much younger than me, for $65,000.

On moving day, Dale and his family arrived at the ranch with a van. We caravanned the twenty miles to Boise, with me driving along behind the rolling container of all my worldly goods. In the midst of our unloading, Arnold suddenly appeared. I invited him in and he sat in the just-furnished living room, looking forlorn while we bustled around him. On the next trip out, I walked over to him.

"You did this all by yourself," he said. His statement was simple, his tone disbelieving.

"Yes, I did."

There had never been a moment like this between us. Always, he had been the one in charge or at the very least, the one making my endeavor possible. Freedom took on new meaning.

But I wasn't free yet. A few days later, I went to the store and came back humming, only to realize that I'd locked the door handle, but had failed to pack along a key. I called a friend with more guts and experience than I. She assessed the situation and then took her shoe and broke the small window above the doorknob. Well, that's something I wouldn't have thought of! I immediately had the glass replaced only to lock myself out again a few days later. This time, I vowed to handle it myself. Wielding a ladder from the garage, I propped it up against the outer wall nearest the kitchen window. I was certain I'd locked it, but had to start somewhere. I could see the key on the counter. Evidently the part of me that thought I'd brought my key had also been mistaken about the window. It was open, and stretching my arm through it, I was barely able to reach my little metal miracle.

Climbing down, I felt triumphant—grateful that my own ingenuity had solved the problem. But as I unlocked the door a question appeared. *What is this about anyway? Why am I locking myself out of my own home?* I knew what it was. Leaving a key behind once? Okay. Leaving it behind twice, after paying to repair a window? Suspicious. Not putting the house key on my ring to begin with? A message. My mother's voice suddenly arose in my head. "Who do you think you are to own your own house? It's unseemly, Adelaide. I didn't raise you to live this kind of life!"

I climbed the steps from the back door, dumped my bags on the counter and headed for the foot of my bed. Down on my hands and knees, I screamed at my mother, "Stop it! Stop trying to control my life! I have every right to have a home of my own!" I was sobbing now, and shaking uncontrollably. "I deserve this, Mother! Leave me alone! I have every right … I have every right …" I repeated until all the anger had drained from my body and I lay empty and spent on the floor.

When I was calm, I reached for the bed and crawled onto it, making it mine. With time, I would make this whole room, this whole house, this whole life, my own. My mother, I realized, had no power to take anything away from me. It was I who was sabotaging my days, and locking myself out of joy. It was I who had become the shaming mother. It was myself that I was screaming at.

A few weeks later, my friend, Judy, came by to see the house. Judy had once been my husband's secretary, but now was a decorator extraordinaire. I awaited her guidance, knowing that with a few salient ideas, this house could exceed my own expectations for a home of my own. Judy whooped with delight when she stepped inside, hugged me and started to roam. After touring the rooms she offered her wisdom. "Do two things, Addie. First, paint that crown molding a glossy white. Then get new carpeting. I'll help you choose the color – maybe green, maybe teal. I'll get you a good deal."

I could see it all. With the old, non-descript carpet gone and a new one coloring the floor, with eight inches of glossy-white molding, all my antiques and dark furniture would have the perfect backdrop. I saw no reason not to take on the painting myself—after all, there would be no new carpet until that was done. The painting was therapeutic. Foot by foot, I smoothed on the glossy paint stroke by stroke to the accompaniment of classical music. And every time I moved the ladder, I stepped back briefly to survey the transformation of the room's new crowning glory.

On one of my descents, my ring caught on a nail in the ladder, bending it's roundness into an oval. I was flooded with a stab of instantaneous pain and started to cry, but shortly, I realized that my finger was no longer hurting. Still, the crying deepened. Something else had been triggered. Just before I'd moved, I'd bought myself this Australian blue topaz ring, now misshapen on my dining room table, as a symbol of my new life and freedom. Again, I headed for the foot of my bed and began railing at my mother for manipulating me into letting go of that little ring—that beloved gift from the Starkeys. The pain was the pain of an inconsolable ten-year-old and once it had abated, I could see, as I had with the key, my participation. Who wears a beautiful new ring while painting? Then something even more stunning came through: there was wisdom in these seemingly errant acts. Each of them had allowed me to release one more layer of stored anger, hurt and sadness.

A few weeks later, it occurred to me that I hadn't seen my deed since I'd moved in. I searched the house over, but couldn't find it and decided to let it go for the time being. A month went by before the import of a deed washed over me again. I looked once more—in all the same places. Again, I decided not to worry, telling myself it had to be somewhere in the house.

In the meantime, the painting had been completed and Judy and I had chosen the most elegant, easy shade of teal carpet. Once its beauty was flung from baseboard to baseboard, the crown molding popped and the fireplace seemed to take on a new dignity, like an old gentleman standing tall in his best suit. My antiques looked beautiful against the vibrant color, and I stood in the middle of it all realizing that I couldn't imagine wanting to live anywhere else.

It was after this heart-settling moment that I found the deed. I was, of course, looking for something else. Riffling through a pile of stationery housed in the antique secretary, there it sat underneath the marriage certificate of my paternal grandfather and grandmother, Goo-Goo and Mary. I had to laugh. It had been buried in and under the oldest artifacts of my history. Now it had been freed from the past! I took full possession of my house that day, and whether or not it was true, I imagined Mary—the grandmother who had refused to wear the role of the minister's wife—smiling down on me.

Although I had frequented Boise over the years, it was new to me in the way a town is until it becomes home. I began to find my way around, replacing my former shopping haunts with new ones and discovering the treasures of the city in the process. But I also spent a lot of time alone in my home. Part of the seclusion came from the fact that my friends from the college, Dianna and Darlene, were no longer as accessible. We still got together, but not in the spontaneous way that proximity had made possible. The other reason for my solitude was that I felt drawn to write. I spent hours at the desk in my den writing about what I'd learned over the years: chapters on feelings, fear, self-esteem and faith. The spiritual knowledge of the last eighteen years coalesced with experience as I wrote, the words flowing onto page after page of legal pads. I was doing this for myself, yet hoped it might be of use to others as well. Over the months, the pages grew into a high yellow stack that resembled a manuscript. I titled it "The Spiritual Journey of a Minister's Wife," had it typed up and sent it off to a publisher. It came back just as I'd sent it, except for the black stamp of rejection: "Unsolicited Manuscript." Although unread, and without any reason to believe it ever would be, I cherished the experience. Disappointment trailed far behind the value of solidifying the principles that now guided my life. They were much more deeply rooted in me than the day I sat down at my desk with an empty tablet in front of me.

Now that the writing had run its course, my energy and interests turned outward again. I began to major in friendship. I hadn't set out to do so; but suddenly, solitude gave way to the kind of socialization I'd missed in my sheltered years as a child, a teen, and minister's wife. I began both attracting and deepening relationships with women who were very different from me—and from each other.

I'd met Shirley at the Cathedral when I taught a series of classes there called "Living from Within." She was almost ten years younger than I and initiated our friendship as straightforwardly as she initiated everything else in her life. After the first class, she charged up to the front full of enthusiasm and eager to engage. The second week she brought a friend and suggested we all meet for lunch. At lunch, she proposed that I hold a self-esteem seminar at her house. And soon after that, Shirley showed up at my back door with ice cream sundaes on a regular basis.

While our histories and personalities had little in common, we bonded over a common endeavor: healing from the wounds of a domineering parent. She had left home at an early age to join the Navy, and was still invested in a long, distinguished career as an innovative physical therapist. Shirley helped children others had given up on. She was quick, sometimes boisterous, and unlike me, had little interest in fashion or style. Yet I'd never known anyone so warm, so embracing. She challenged me with her courage, her willingness to initiate and confront. And most of all, her willingness to look at herself. Just as in her outer life, Shirley charged into her own depths with seemingly fearless vigor.

My relationship with my mother was a long-running show on the marquee of my life now. Whether locking myself out or catching my ring on a ladder, all emotional roads led back to that relationship. It was puzzling. I would have said the year before that I'd come to terms with her. Yet even now, my new relationship with Shirley seemed to have its taproot in histories of a domineering parent. Just to be talking about it so frequently and deeply, dredging up stories and feelings I hadn't thought of in years, signaled that I wasn't through yet.

And then the theme arrived via another friendship. Life had changed drastically for my young friend Patricia since I'd met her at the Cathedral some years ago. Her husband had become the mayor of Boise and she was deeply involved in the public life of the city. Thrust into a spotlight that she didn't always relish, my home became a refuge for her—a place where she could retreat for a long lunch and the luxury of divulging her true feelings. I'd known that Patricia's mother had died when she was an infant, but until now, we'd never talked about the pain that lived on underneath the enticing cover story of her life. As she shared her pain, I felt inadequate to be enough in the face of her loss. How could I nurture her, support her as her mother might have? But gradually, I realized that Patricia wasn't asking me to be her mother or make up for what she'd missed. She was simply relishing what I had to give: a shelter from the storms and complexity of her public life and inner world. The delicious lunch and eager, listening ear were things the mother of a girl of any age might offer. But I could also offer what most mothers can't: support for freeing herself from the burden of loss. Unlike her, I'd had a mother. Unlike her, I'd been over-mothered. But now I was seeing that emotionally, I'd been unmothered too. We were more alike than different.

Since the day I'd set boxes on the floor of this house, my mother seemed more present than she'd been since I left *her* house on Washington Avenue. Some days, I couldn't turn off my running tally of grievances toward her. Then, after weeks of feeling captive to it, I decided to confront her Gestalt style—a method I'd heard about from Maridel. Positioned in my emerald green chair on one side of the fireplace, I placed her in the green-and-gold-striped one on the other, noticing that I'd chosen the high-backed seat of authority. Prepared to unleash fury as I had before, I was surprised when my words, emotional as they were, weren't angry ones. I was asking questions this time, sincerely seeking answers to the riddles of my childhood. "Why did you beat me, mother? And why did you beat my frail little sister? Why did you make us wear cotton stockings on vacation and deny us those beach pajamas from Cousin Lois? Why wouldn't you let me join the Girl Scouts? Why couldn't I have had the chance to be on the Ed Sullivan show? Why were you always holding back the expression of my talents? Why were you always so stern and unfeeling?" The questions flowed out of me, spilling as if from a secret urn. When I was quiet at last, something inside me said, "Go sit in the other chair."

At first all I felt was my own emptiness as I awaited her defenses. But none came. When I began to speak as my mother, responding to my queries, I was astonished. "I loved you. I just wanted you to be a good woman and I thought that was the way to do it. I only wanted to keep you safe, to protect you from a world that frightened me. I never meant to hurt you."

Her response dismantled me. I cried first like a little girl and then like a woman almost the age my mother was the day she died. I cried for the regrets, the losses, and the relationship that would never be. And then I cried in gratitude for the first real sense of the woman who was my mother—a product of her fears and of the environment that produced them.

It was the day I began to make real peace with Elizabeth Caldwell Blauvelt. And I hoped, the day her soul found a measure of peace with me.

On the other side of the generational landscape, I was seizing opportunities to make my youngest grandchildren, Jason and Courtney, a part of the new life I was creating for myself. The older boys had been so central to our years on the ranch, but now were teenagers who had absorbing lives of their own. I still cherished my time with them—Tyler dropping by for dinner or coffee, and Justin and Gavin visiting each year—but with Jason and Courtney, the pleasures of young grandchildren were sweetly extended. I particularly loved their overnight visits: outings to the grocery store for special food, creating picnics in front of the fire, and trips to the corner ice cream shop. The two of them not only left their loving mark on me each time they visited, but left one on the house as well. To my delight, they painted a mural in my basement—a remarkably beautiful countryside complete with mountains, streams and a bright red barn. Without knowing it, they made my home all the more mine and all the more treasured.

One day Arnold showed up direct from the doctor's office delivering bad news. He'd been given an ultimatum: go on dialysis or plan to die within six months. One of his kidneys wasn't functioning at all. Dialysis not only meant restrictions of many kinds, but the endgame to a long journey of compromised and declining health. He looked like a weary warrior, facing certain defeat. The feelings inside me were many, but in that moment, just one found its way to words: "Arnold, when we divorced, I told you that if you ever needed me, I'd be there. And I will." His other relationship had just ended after breaking off and reviving many times in the last several months. Now he was heading down a dark tunnel alone. I could have walked away, relieved that I had no further obligation. True, but not real. Real was our history, our family, and the bond that spanned almost half a century.

He took me up on my offer for help, and to make matters easier for both of us, he bought a condo in Boise ten minutes from me. Inexplicably, we were involved again—not without conflicting emotions on my part, but not without certainty either. Fortunately, he was as independent as ever some days; and on the days he was compromised, I took over: driving, shopping, and cooking. After my run of independence, it was a difficult, but necessary place to be.

The truce we'd worked out in our separated state didn't hold when put to the test of ongoing contact. Old patterns surfaced like thin paint over wallpaper and with them, I vacillated between compassion and annoyance, between willingness and resentment. I had an escape hatch now, of course: an address with my name on it. But often I retreated to feeling hurt by his hostility and guilty over my reactions. He was ill. He was dying. He was in pain. Why couldn't I just be supportive and not take offense? Why wasn't I more loving and forgiving after all my spiritual growth? And to make matters worse, he still loved me and wanted me to sell my home and move in with him. But that I could not do.

In my days of making new Boise bonds with women of varying ages and mindsets, I'd met a young woman at a Christmas party. Ginny was in her early thirties, and unlike almost everyone else I knew, didn't take life so seriously. For the last couple of years, we'd spent many Sunday evenings together gabbing, feasting and laughing. A favorite topic was our shared love of decorating. I'd also shared my spiritual process with her from time to time, and watched her become more curious about her own inner workings. The depth of our dialogue was steadily increasing when she fell in love and got married. As a matter of life's course, our Sunday evenings together became infrequent.

A few months after Arnold's announcement, Ginny too showed up at my back door with bad news. She had advanced breast cancer. Her life was now measured in months, not years. Most of her remaining time was, of course, given to her husband, but we talked most weeks by phone and she came to the house a few times. When the phone call came that Ginny was in the hospital and in her last days of life, I felt a strong impulse to go see her. I was apprehensive, as I hadn't seen her for some weeks, and though her voice was always calm and cheerful when we talked, I knew seeing her now would be neither cheery nor calming. On a Saturday evening, I knew it was time. I made my way to the hospital and sat with her while her weary husband slept nearby. Our conversation drifted back and forth with the tides of her consciousness. Mostly I sat in the quiet and held vigil, hoping my presence was a comfort.

"Addie, we never went to The Grape Escape," she said at one point.

"We always talked about it, but we never made plans," I responded.

"Maybe we …" I knew she'd started to imagine it might still be possible, but had stopped herself.

I took the moment as my chance to ask the question that had been playing in my mind for the last half-hour.

"Ginny," I said, "would you like to just slip away?"

"Yes," she answered. I sat with her until she fell asleep again, then stood by her bed and whispered my goodbyes. She died the next morning.

I'd never sat with a dying person. I'd never even lost a friend. Now, through my youngest friend, I'd crossed a threshold into a corridor where another loss, a more complex one, waited. I wanted to be ready for Arnold's passing, but didn't know how to prepare myself.

My life was more regimented now. All my plans were made with Arnold and his needs in mind—and those tentatively. The inner assurance that I was doing the right thing was like a trusty, woven cloak that has weathered many seasons and outlasted a closet full of other garments. But the friction and conflict of our interactions was so painful, so disheartening that I longed to cast it off even at the cost of my own shivering guilt. The pull of deep, emotional ambivalence was wearing. I still had a life of my own of course—friends, events, family, my spiritual books—but I was tethered again like the two-year-old tied to the porch with the world passing her by on Route 45. The next year, just two years after his first surgery, Arnold had another five bypass heart surgery and became increasingly dependent on dialysis. Once again, his recovery was astonishing for someone of his age and condition, but even so, his future—and mine—had become a narrowing path.

Most men in this state wouldn't consider traveling, but family had now become as sacred and compelling to Arnold as the church had once been. Making his plans to receive dialysis as part of our journey, we flew together to California for a long weekend at Dillon Beach in celebration of our first grandson's college graduation. In the presence of our children and grandchildren, the light of his old spirit flooded back into him—as if he'd been given a transfusion of blood from the gods rather than mere mortals.

The following year our first grandson brought the family together again. Arnold wouldn't consider missing Justin's marriage to Nikki, a vivacious young woman from Coos Bay, Oregon, despite the risk and everyone else's concern. With our family nurse, Linda, on board, we flew to Oregon for the wedding. Despite his limitations and in the face of all predictions to the contrary, Arnold danced with shine and pluck at the reception.

But it would be his last time.

Just short of a year later, he called me at five o'clock in the morning. "Addie, I'm in trouble," he said. As had often been true, he'd had too much fluid over the weekend and needed an emergency dialysis. Characteristically, he choreographed everything from the moment I arrived: which shirt and pants to pull from the closet, which shoes from under the bed. But uncharacteristically, he wanted me to get the walker from its exile in the garage. I'd never seen him use it except immediately after heart surgery. I watched him as he rushed crazily down the hall, not wanting help, but when he started to navigate the walker down the two steps into the garage, I intervened.

As we pulled out of the drive, late summer's beauty caught his eye even in the midst of his crisis. "Isn't this a beautiful morning?" he asked. In these latter years, he'd begun noticing the things he had always whizzed past in pursuit of success. He'd even planted roses in his front yard and down the walk that extended from his patio. It was a part of Arnold I thought I'd never see: stopping to smell the roses. We spent most of the short jaunt in quiet with Arnold silently surveying the spill of color around him. But just before we got to the hospital, he said, "Oh, Addie, I wish I'd died in my sleep last night." I reached over and took his hand.

Once we arrived at our destination, he took command again: telling me where to park and where to get the wheelchair. "Did you put the brake on?" he asked as we trundled away from the car. When we arrived at the nurse's station, he seemed more like the person on duty than she did. From memory, he seamlessly named—and spelled when necessary—every prescription on the daunting list. He was at ease now, comfortable in these familiar surroundings and their history of rescue.

We sat in the waiting room with little to do except watch a TV one could hardly ignore. I suddenly realized that I was not only hungry, but that we could be waiting awhile.

"I think I'll run upstairs and get some breakfast," I told him. "Want anything?"

He nodded. "Toast." Feeling better after some coffee and breakfast, I headed back downstairs with the requested toast in one hand and a bonus bowl of strawberries in the other.

When he wasn't in the waiting room, I was relieved. They'd already gotten him in for treatment.

"The nurse wants to see you," the receptionist said, and as if she'd summoned her up, the door opened and she appeared. I walked toward her with the toast and berries, but as soon as I got within reach, she took them out of my hands.

"Mr. Woodcook's had a heart attack," she said. She led me into the back where a doctor and nurses were trying to revive him.

"Please don't do that!" I called from the doorway. The doctor turned toward me. "He has a living will on file across the street and doesn't want to be resuscitated."

With a nod to the others to continue, he came over to me. "I'm his wife. On the way here this morning, he told me he wished he'd died in the night."

"We'll be less aggressive," he said, and returned to his post.

The nurse took me into a little room down the hall and within moments, a chaplain came and sat with me. I knew from this, and from my own soul, that Arnold had died. Soon the doctor came in and pulled up a straight chair, sitting close and eye-to-eye. I can still feel his knees against mine. "Mr. Woodcook's dead," he said. "If there's anyone you want to call to be with you, there's a phone at the nurses' station."

I thanked him and the Chaplin, stood and walked down the hall to call Linda. While I waited, an odd, almost humorous thought came to me. I wished that I could call the doctor who first warned me about Arnold dying an early death if he didn't change—just to tell him, "Well, Doc, he never let up and he *still* made old bones." I think Arnold would have liked that. Because in the end, it wasn't *in* his bones to do anything else but go after life like a hungry hunter in pursuit of the prize.

Linda arrived faster than I thought and had Tyler with her. "I want some time with him," she said, as we prepared to go into the room together. I knew she wanted to make him look presentable—the act of a nurse, the care of a daughter. When she came out, I went in alone. I just stood there beside him, unable to feel anything except that numbing wall of shock that in the face of death, moves in like blinding fog. In the way that such moments dangle in space, without grounding or anchor, I wondered where the strawberries were. And that musing led to another: after fifty-five years of being together in one form or another, his last spoken word to me was "Toast." I took a deep breath, put my hand over his battered heart, and kissed him goodbye.

I was relieved and grateful for both of us. He'd been ready to die. And I was ready to live my life untethered at last.

After Dale arrived, the four of us stood together in the hallway waiting for further instructions. A nurse approached us apologetically. "I'm sorry," she said, "but I have to ask. Would you give permission to donate his organs?" We didn't laugh then, but would later. "I don't think there's anything left you'd want," Dale told her. "He used it all up."

Courtesy of the Ada County Sheriff's Department and my Lieutenant son, their long-time employee, Arnold had a twelve-motorcycle escort from the church he pastored in Nampa to his resting place in Boise—a distance of twenty miles. Police cars held back traffic at lights and on freeway ramps as the hearse and its entourage of cars sped down the road uninterrupted. No doubt onlookers were wondering what important person had died and made a note to check the evening news. "Wouldn't Bapa have loved this?!" we kept exclaiming to each other. It seemed fitting to me. He'd left Nampa years before steeped in hurt and humiliation. This time he was leaving with the honor and dignity that his efforts of a lifetime deserved. It was the only part of the meticulously planned funeral that he *hadn't* planned and we all hoped he had the aerial view.

It was not the pomp of these circumstances that left the biggest impression on me, however. It was, instead, the way love found its way into the beating heart of this day. Irving, Arnold's right- hand man in two churches and his best match in all those years, officiated at the service. Irving, the little live-wire that had once startled the constituency of the Beacon church on a regular basis was with us, part of our family and part of our loss. The funeral itself was held in the sanctuary that Arnold had single-handedly made space for in the neighborhood through his own iconoclastic brand of charm and confrontation. As the people we had once pastored formed a long line to greet me, as they had so many times in years past, I was stunned by the enveloping grace of their love. Most said, "We love you." Many embraced me. All were genuinely warm.

The most tangible thing from that day, what we would hold in our hands for years to come, was Arnold's own words. He had communicated his wishes for his funeral to all of us, but none had seen the words he'd written for the back of the funeral program. He called it his "final message to family, friends and all who hear."

In part it read, "I believe that it is good to be part of a fellowship that meets your needs. However, throughout my lifetime, I came to feel that it is Christ within me that is the important thing and not the church. I was raised in the days of guilt-producing sermons and became part of that institution. But at fifty years of age, I began to see from reading the New Testament, how little guilt and how much grace is in the Scriptures. None of us needs religion. We need the Christ as our Companion, our Lover, our Spiritual Counselor. Ours is a New Testament faith—one of joy, of happiness, of the realization of the best of life."

This was his legacy, the place to which he'd come not through success as he'd envisioned it, but through seeing those visions die—and then reaching out for the help his soul so desperately needed. Neither his change nor mine had resulted in a relationship that matured into deep love and understanding. But each of us, in our own way, had found a greater peace than we'd known existed when we'd started out together fifty-five years before.

And now Arnold deeply affected my life in another way. He'd left me his new Buick and his duplex—both of which were free and clear—along with his savings. It wasn't a fortune, but it was an enormous boon to my life. It took some months and the help of my family before the process of emptying, transferring and selling had cleared. But at the end of it, Arnold had done as he'd wished: given me something that a loving husband would—security and independence.

I had thought that when he was gone, the conflict that I carried so long would be gone too. I'd imagined myself as a free agent again and this time, completely. That was the theme of my life. I saw it more clearly than ever now: always looking for release from the clothesline around my waist, always looking for a way to run free. But it didn't prove to be that easy. Unable to sleep at night, I would run long monologues directed at my divorced and now deceased husband. Over and over, I poured out my hurt and anger, telling him all the things I never had—then berating myself for not doing it when he was alive and then for wasting my time doing it now.

During the day, I felt good, resuming my friendships, my walks, and my voracious appetite for reading and spiritual growth. But many nights, just as the shadows fell across the mountains, so they fell across my psyche, pulling me into a compulsive wrestling: how I should have been different, how *he* should have been different, how the church had failed us and how we failed each other. We had never talked about our deepest conflict and pain, had never had closure. Now I had to find a way to create it for myself.

In some ways, the old blackness was back. I had a name for it now and knew the cause, but didn't know how to dispel it. For days, sometimes weeks at a time, it would lift intermittently, and each time I hoped I was free of it. But inevitably, it returned.

By the next spring, I was ready to fulfill my long-denied wanderlust. For years, my sister and I had been talking about making a sojourn back to Maine with the intent of revisiting Basket Island. We decided that this was the perfect year to do it. In September, I flew to Kansas City, and accompanied by Rhea's friend, Betty, we set out on a road trip to Maine. Arriving on an island requires more forethought than the average vacation. Reservations have to be made with the tides. Betty had done the research and the next morning, we timed our arrival to correspond with our window of tidal opportunity. The old excitement jangled in my blood as we approached the one opening in a thicket of bushes where our past, like a fairy tale mirror, could be accessed. We slowed as we approached, all of us looking for the spot and wondering if we would recognize it. All at once, there it was! Changed by the loss of the makeshift wharf, but still our unmistakable entrance to heaven. Through the car window, our first glimpse rewarded us with our fondest wish. Across the sands sat an island with seven little cottages—unchanged by the ravages of wind, sea and sixty-two years.

Scrambling from the car, a closer look brought disappointment. It's cold in Maine by September and the cottages were boarded up. Summer residents had already fled.

"Wait," Betty said. "The far one doesn't look like it's closed up! Someone must still be there."

Together, the three of us made the journey across the sand on foot, an undertaking more difficult for Rhea than for me. I wanted to run with arms wide open, to stand again in the middle of this tiny world that had once been mine. Instead, I walked with my sister, holding onto her, but with my eyes transfixed upon our cottage. With our shoes full of sand, our little procession it made to the well in the center of the island. There we were again, surrounded by cottages, sky and sea. Only the sands had shifted. The crush of nostalgia came with every breath.

From there, we wandered slowly, as if in a dream, to our own cottage. The place was boarded up with the same storm windows that had been ours, and the same blackberry bushes bordered the house. We were helping ourselves to the few berries still clinging to the branches when we heard shouting. A young man was walking across the island toward us, delivering his message as he approached.

"This is private property!" he called. "You're trespassing." He'd no doubt delivered the speech before, but I doubt to three women his grandmother's age.

"We know it is," I said. "We don't mean to trespass, but…"

"I'm sorry, but I have to ask you to leave."

"Of course. But before we go, may I show you some pictures?"

I pulled black-and-white photos from my bag and offered them without a word: one of my sister and me in front of our cottage; my father in the dory; my mother on the porch. When realization struck, his adamancy turned to hilarity; and Andrew, the historian of Basket Island, started jumping up and down with joy.

"Come, come!" he said, motioning toward the house from which he'd sprinted. "Come have tea!" Inside, with the tea kettle whistling in the kitchen, Andrew pored over the photos, questioning us about dates and details. "I can't believe this!" he exclaimed repeatedly." He darted toward the kitchen as if the tea was a screeching child in need of tending, but continued to talk with us across the distance. "We have almost nothing from this era!" he shouted. "This is amazing!" He returned, grinning and wide-eyed, the pot trembling with his excitement. I offered to relieve him of the task of pouring hot tea—for all our sakes—but he declined, eager I'm sure to be a good host to his benefactors. Settled back in his seat, he looked once more through the pictures, asking more questions. Then he looked at me and asked soberly, "I know this is asking a lot, but could I borrow these?" His face pleaded along with his words. "I promise to return them. I just *have* to show them to my folks!" Who could say "no" to such a recklessly jubilant historian?

Before we made our exit from island and past, Andrew took pictures of Rhea and me in front of our cottage. "Please come back," he said in parting. "Everyone will want to meet you. Come back next summer."

Oh, how I hoped we could.

I returned home to unsettling news. Someone had tried to break into the house while I was gone—a reflection, I feared, of a neighborhood in decline. The city had also widened the street in recent months, bringing the noise of the traffic much closer to my sanctuary. Dale was concerned about my safety and urged me to think about moving. Even with the troubling changes, I might have been content to stay on. But the idea of moving to a place that required less care did appeal to me. With the funds Arnold had left to me and the sale of my home, my choices would be greatly expanded. I thought a condo would be perfect—smaller, safer and without yard duty. Beyond that, I didn't have a guiding vision like the one that had led me to State Street. But of this I was certain: I'd know my next home when I saw it.

HOUSE TWENTY TWO

Heron Cove, Boise, Idaho

Who could resist a view of water from the front door? I didn't know that a condo with its intimation of closure and confinement could look like this! Upon entry, my realtor steered me toward the kitchen on the left but I declined, walking through the living-dining area and straight back to the wall of windows. A small, sheltered patio was right outside the sliding door, and a few feet beyond that lay a small lake formed by the tributary of the Boise River. Between the lake and the river was a greenbelt.

"Are those herons?" I asked, spying large grey birds swimming and diving in the lake.

"Yes. It turns out that 'Heron Cove' isn't just a pretty name. They live on the property along with wood ducks and quite a variety of birds, I'm told." People were out on the footpath, talking as they walked along together. I envisioned myself out there early mornings alone or in the afternoon with a friend.

"Want to look at the place, Addie?"

Since I was already living here in my mind, I might as well take the tour.

I walked back toward the kitchen that sat off the entry hall. It was small and square, but blessedly open on both ends. Over the sink, a large opening allowed me to feast my eyes on the whole panorama of the living area and wooded world beyond. There was that water again! When I turned around, a garden window let in the light, and just outside it, I could see the delicate dogwood tree that would greet my guests before I did. As my realtor pointed out the features of the kitchen and I pretended to listen, my real attention was on the things I'd missed when I'd made a beeline for the lake: a fireplace and what appeared to be a hand-painted chandelier. *Perhaps Italian*?

"Does the chandelier go with the house I asked?"

"It isn't listed as an exception so it must be."

The master bedroom was bigger than the one in my house and a waterfall sang its trickling refrain right outside the window! I mentally placed my bed in the room and imagined being lulled to sleep by that luscious sound. Outside the window itself, of course, was the ever-present lake. I felt like it was following me wherever I went, offering its flowing beauty to me with every glance. On the other end of the room, a corridor of mirrored closet doors formed a passageway between bedroom and bath. Two pocket doors made the bathroom available from both the hall and my bedroom.

The end of the tour was the only disappointment. The "second bedroom" was actually an open area that sat between the hall and the entry to the garage. Fine for an office, but not private enough for a guest room. It might do for weekend visits, but I had hoped to have a place where my sister could come and stay for a few weeks. I was disappointed, but undaunted.

This was the place.

Even before I moved in, I started bringing my vision to life. The living-dining area looked even larger in its new coat of seafoam green and was the perfect backdrop for my new living room couch and its collection of large, comfortable pillows. The subtle design of salmon and green blended deliciously with the walls and the view. A chair-and-a-half made of the same fabric, along with my antiques and dining table, completed the room. And in the bedroom, more good news: there was space for a round table in front of the window. On it, I placed my antique tablecloth and dressed it with books and a small lamp.

As for the back "room," I gave up on turning it into a bedroom and opted instead for a cozy den with two comfortable chairs, a TV, and my desk.

Only after moving in did I notice the almost total lack of storage in the house. No second-bedroom closet of course, but no linen or storage cabinet either! Just a small coat closet in the entry. I was deeply upset with myself. *Why hadn't I paid more attention to something so vital? Where was I going to put everything I'd had stored in my house?* Fortunately, Maridel had come to help me get settled, and came to my rescue with some creative solutions—like using the antique dresser, which graced my living room, as storage for my linens. It also prompted me to get rid of things I really didn't need, and Shirley assured me she would install shelves in the narrow garage. I was tempted to believe I'd made a mistake, but the lake wouldn't let me. I had my lake back—how could *storage space* compete with that?

And so my days on Heron Cove took shape. The quiet was a luxury after the growing noise of traffic on State Street. When Patricia knocked on my door early mornings, our conversation was "a moveable feast" as we traipsed the trail together and marveled at the life around us. A bench along the way was perched near a waterfall and if her schedule permitted, we stopped to talk or just let the water speak to us. But almost every day, I walked the path alone, enjoying the simplicity of the smiles and greetings offered by my fellow travelers. Most mornings, too, I sat on my little patio and drank my morning coffee, entranced by the wildlife and the water. Mother ducks with their waddling broods came right up to the patio, and one day, I saw a deer go right by my patio. I'd found far more than I'd been looking for. I'd found a haven.

The one thing these peaceful living quarters and their serene surroundings could not give me was *inner* peace. With Arnold's death, I thought things would be different. I thought my inner waters would calm because he was gone and our relationship was over. But while the rest of my life was active and fulfilling, the inner war waged on. Things that Arnold had done or said erupted into my psyche like geysers, bringing with them a flood of negative emotion. In the grip of such memories, I fantasized about what I *should* have said and *should* have done. This self-punishment was followed by another: berating myself for not doing it when I had the chance. Without realizing it, I was making myself into a victim in my own head, creating my own prison. All the focus was on how he'd treated me and how I'd sacrificed myself for him and his success. I knew it wasn't true that I'd gotten nothing in return, but that's what I told myself. Round and round it went—blaming him and then blaming myself. I desperately wanted to move forward but felt helpless to let it go. Sometimes the intervals between sieges were longer than others and each time, I prayed it was the last. I was miserable. I couldn't let go of the old feelings and didn't know what else to do.

For Maridel's fiftieth birthday, I decided to splurge and take the two of us on a cruise. The real appeal was that it was a spiritual cruise, "The Inner Voyage," that sailed from Ft. Lauderdale and went through the Florida Keys, stopping at several ports. Many well-known spiritual authors and speakers filled the roster of the colorful brochure. Inside, I hoped I might find a solution to my suffering—some experience that would free me from the torment of my mind.

Amidst the bountiful dinners, the warm conversations, the uplifting speakers and thought-provoking classes, an answer did come—but not in the way I'd envisioned. I'd carefully chosen each of my classes with an eye to what might speak to the knotted dilemma within me, and so naturally, chose the one on forgiveness. The teacher's outlook of forgiving for the sake of your *own* healing quickened my heart with the hope that she could help me if I could just get a few minutes alone with her. The group waiting to speak with her after class was daunting, and so I asked God to give me an opportunity during the cruise if it was meant to be. That night, I saw her talking with a young man out in the hall and told Maridel that I was going to try to speak with her. I stood nearby, the way one does when waiting to petition the ear of another.

After waiting for a considerable length of time, I gradually became more and more embarrassed by my own lingering presence. I felt like she was ignoring me, laughing and talking with the young man, occasionally glancing to see if I was still there. When she asked him to open his attaché and show her pictures of his family, I slipped into a nearby doorway to make my getaway. Maridel had been nearby waiting for me and together, we returned to our cabin. I was angry! "She let me stand there all that time without so much as an acknowledgment!" I said. "I felt so foolish—like a shamed child."

Maridel listened to my anger and blame, but instead of colluding with me, suggested that I had just staged a re-creation of an old drama: not feeling worthy of the attention of someone more important. She recalled the times that her counseling colleague and friend, Paul, had met us for coffee when I visited Sacramento—and how each time, I remarked that I didn't know why with his busy schedule, he would take time to be with me. Instantly, I saw how tonight's experience, as reflected in this recent scenario, went back to my marriage and echoed down the corridors of my childhood: my needs never seen as important, in fact, rarely acknowledged. I began to sob. *Was there a bottom to this pit?* Part of my deep pain was the fact of my collusion—that all these years, part of me had believed that my unworthiness was real.

I returned home from this seaworthy adventure with something more than another round of release. For one thing, I had allowed another person to witness my pain. Always before, these deep releases had been alone. There was something healing about the exposure and the comfort of another person's acceptance. The other thing I took home was a little, bright pink, spiral-bound book with an attached pink cassette. "Emotional Fitness for Emotivated Living" by Elisa Lodge. In contrast to all of the professional materials of the cruise, this one was simple, almost homemade-looking. Elisa, the young woman who had written this book and given the workshop, had offered me a tool for healing that I'd never considered: my own body. In her workshop, she'd guided us to express our feelings merely through movement. She would call out an emotion, "Fear," and give us time to let the body form to the inner feeling. When we felt we'd gotten it just right, she encouraged us to sustain it. And through the body pose, the feeling ran its own course: intensifying, peaking and then releasing. When the body relaxed, the shift was palpable both emotionally and physically.

Once back home, I was eager to actually read the book. It started with a bold statement by Dr. Bernie Siegel. "Repression of our emotions is the Number One health hazard." I believed it. Adding to his statement, Elisa herself wrote, "Repressing emotions and blocking the physical actions that accompany them has created not only emotional pain, but physical pain." I looked down at my arthritic hands. It was a condition associated in mind-body theory with anger. Elisa provided a welcome promise: "As you learn to exercise your emotional range, you will become much more sensitive to feeling each emotion as it surfaces in your body."

I began regularly using the book's accompanying cassette—not just as an abstract exercise—but as an applied tool when memories brought up old feelings. Instead of assuming I was stuck with them, I took the pose of the feeling itself. One day, in the course of my routine, I remembered an incident when I was extremely embarrassed by something Arnold had said to me in front of other people. I hadn't thought of it for years, but suddenly, there it was! I let the feeling take form in my body: head down, turned in, and bent over. I held this, focusing on nothing else, and feeling the hurt of his remark in my body. When I released the pose, it was as if the story had been released from my mind, no longer able to hold me in its grip. I was grateful to have a tool that I could use whenever I needed it to keep setting myself free.

I had lived at Heron Cove a year when I received a call one evening. Propped up comfortably in bed, reading, I reached for the phone, but answered the call of destiny. "Addie," my sister's weary voice said, "I can't live alone any longer." Rhea was single and still living in Kansas City where my friend, Jeanne, and I had taken her some forty years ago. In recent years, I had invited her to live with me, but she had wanted to maintain a measure of independence—living in her own quarters in the house of her friend, Betty.

"I'll get another place," I told her. "One where we can each have our own bedroom and bathroom." She assured me that she would help me financially and encouraged me to find something I loved. "It needs to be for you too, Addie."

I heard between the lines. My sister's health, which had never been good, was irreparably poor following a major heart attack and open heart surgery.

"I'll take care of you, Rea. Just give me a couple of months to get moved."

My feelings were like a stew made of ingredients that didn't blend well together. I wanted to be what my sister needed and I was grateful to have the means, the health and the heart to do so. But I knew what it meant: once again, I would be a necessity in someone else's life. Like Arnold, Rhea would be dependent on me for almost everything except money. It wasn't so much the giving up of my cove by the lake, as it was the relinquishing of my independence. Yet I was clear that this was mine to do and that it was a worthy sacrifice. I had the chance to give my sister the best home she'd ever had.

HOUSE TWENTY THREE

Old Saybrook Drive, Boise, Idaho

Imagine my realtor's surprise. Every time he'd driven by Herring Cove for the last year, he'd envisioned me happily ensconced in my condo by the river. Yet one year later, off we went again in search of the perfect home not for one, but two. After a quick look at available places in Herring Cove—none of which suited, we drove down the road and around two corners where the ideal home awaited.

This condo didn't have the "old house" charm of State Street or the watery, hypnotizing lure of Heron Cove, but it did have exactly what we needed: three bedrooms and two baths all on one floor. It was the only unit in the complex that met all of those specifications, and beyond its functionality, it had both appeal and potential. The front door opened to a small entry area that led down a short, angled, hardwood passage and into the lift of vaulted ceilings and a large living and dining area. The kitchen was part of this space too, separated only a short bar. The gas fireplace pleased me as did the sliding glass doors that led out onto a grassy area with a wood fence creating privacy.

Best of all, Rhea would have her own compact quarters. A small square hallway off the living room opened to a bath and bedroom. From her sliding glass doors, she would look out on a sweet enclosed patio. I loved this little luxury of opening up her room to nature and giving her a private spot to sit outside.

Down the wide hall, the master bedroom beckoned from wide double doors, and opened onto an oversized space with adjoining dressing area, bath and walk-in closet. A third set of glass doors led out onto the grassy area, which I now saw extended all the way to the back of the house. In almost every room, the outdoors was only a step away, liberating me to green and sky at every turn.

At the end of the hall was the third bedroom, the smallest, but perfect for a TV room or den.

My mind had already taken a visionary snapshot of a large patio, flower garden and trees where the yard of grass was now, uninspired and uninspiring.

"I think this will work!" I told the realtor. "There's private space for each of us while still feeling open and expansive."

I only had six weeks to move and get ready for Rhea before her arrival in July. My friend, Jeannie, an interior decorator, helped me arrange the furniture. I marveled how my antique pieces always seemed to find their places in every house, as if each one had just been waiting for their arrival. It could be argued that they looked most at home on State Street, but they were as stately and gracious as ever in this more contemporary setting. The secretary, that had once needed to be cut down to size to fit in our new parsonage, had room to spare here. In fact, I would be able to garnish its top with greens or pottery. The marble-top dresser greeted my guests with its glowing lamp and a few cherished pictures while serving as a sofa table for the couch which faced the fireplace. And next to my big, comfortable half-chair, the marble-top washstand held the green hurricane lamp that had been delivered to my doorstep by a grieving widower so many years ago.

As I settled into this place, preparing to share it with my sister, I found many things to appreciate—a large laundry room off the kitchen, an enormous pantry, a lazy-susan built into the cabinets, and a living space with a couple of angled walls—giving the space a unique, artsy feel. All of this was contained in an end unit which meant I only had a neighbor on one side. But nothing pleased me more than the window above the kitchen sink, where a view of the Boise Mountains was mine with every glance.

Soon after Rhea's decision, we learned that some family friends from Nampa were driving back to Kansas City for a summer visit just about a month before her arrival. They agreed to drive her car back on the return trip, as well as pull a trailer with her bedroom furniture in it. Her car carried the rest of her possessions: her clothes, lamps, linens, and TV. Receiving her belongings before her arrival allowed me to get her white French provincial bedroom set in place and all her belongings put away. The transition into her new world of sister and strangers would, at least outwardly, be smooth.

On the day of Rhea's arrival, I stood with Linda and Shirley, watching as the passengers flowed out into the terminal. When the corridor was empty, our little welcoming committee—flowers and balloons at the ready—was growing impatient. I peered down the empty jet way for some sign of my little sister. Just then a young attendant wheeled a smiling Rhea into view! This was her triumphal entry into Boise and back into family life. Growing up in a home with parents who couldn't connect emotionally, we were all we'd ever had and now we were together again. We laughed, cheered, and hugged, creating a bit of celebratory attention as waiting passengers and passersby peered curiously at the commotion. Once the flash of cameras had ceased and the luggage collected, we escorted Rhea to her new home. A big sign, "Welcome Home, Rhea!" hung across the garage door. Tacking it up there had reminded me of the day our Dale had come home from Viet Nam. Such different feelings now. He had escaped death and my sister had come here to die.

Physically compromised all her life, Rhea crossed my threshold not just as my sister, but as a patient. She had survived a precarious open heart surgery the year before that left her heart permanently damaged. She was on drugs to thin her blood because of high blood pressure. Her eyesight had been poor for years, but she was now blind in one eye. To me she was a classic example of what unaddressed oppression and abuse can do to a quiet, gentle soul. Once she'd had dreams of being a nurse, but was too emotionally and physically broken to even attempt it—and the saddest part is that she would have made an excellent one.

Looking at her now, I heard my mother say, "Rhea's going to be an old maid and stay home with her mother." My friend, Jeanne, and I had rescued her from that particular fate, but nothing could rescue her from the crippling effects of all the pain she had taken with her when she made her getaway. Nothing, that is, except herself—her own growth and change. But that option, too, had escaped her.

As I settled into my new life with my sister, I felt the familiar pull of old patterns, of commitment to someone whose survival depended on me. But knowing that our time together would most likely be short, I vowed to make it good for both of us. A comfortable routine emerged for me: walking every day for both exercise and solitude; grocery shopping a couple of times a week; taking Rhea to her medical appointments; and fixing our meals. Though she had always been a far better cook than I, she seemed to savor my meals. Most evenings we ate our dinner on TV trays in the den at the back of the house, synchronizing them with *Jeopardy* and *Wheel of Fortune*. I rarely knew an answer, but my sister, now in her late seventies, often did better than some of the contestants. Then another nocturnal habit emerged: reading. I got books from both library and bookstore and read to her before bed. Our favorite was the Mitford series by Jan Karon. Ironically enough for me, it was about a minister and his wife and all of their funny, endearing parishioners. Rhea loved this ritual and I hoped that some fragment of her childhood was being restored to her in this simple act of bedtime stories.

As the months of the first year progressed, another side of Rhea emerged. I knew from her life in Kansas City and the continued communication by phone and mail, that she was much loved. She drew people to her and had a host of friends. But few, if any, knew her pain. With me, however, she felt safe enough to vent her fury and unload her anger about her lost life, her lack of education, and her feelings of worthlessness. The years of agony and pain came spewing out as she told and retold me stories of her childhood and her years of captivity as an adult in my parents' home. Unlike me, she was angry not just at my mother, but at my father too. She resented his escaping into his own world and not standing up for us. These bitter tales were hard for me to hear, reminding me as they did of my own painful past. Almost daily, I was dragged back into the force- field of my childhood—something I had worked so long and hard to free myself from. Believing so firmly by now that everything has a reason, I wondered why this darkness had once again found me within my own walls.

After long spells of listening and sympathizing, I talked to her about my journey, recounting the ways I'd been able to free myself from my own unhappiness. I suggested she seek her own healing in whatever way she could, and told her how talking aloud to our mother had brought me such relief. "She was dealing with her own past, Rhea. Underneath all her control, she was wounded too." While she conceded that Mom didn't know any better, she was too buried in anger and remorse to find her way out. She only wanted to die her way out of the misery. After awhile,

I abandoned my attempts to help her change and did my best to focus on the one thing I knew would not be lost: loving her.

This love was not only critical for her to have and for me to offer, but crucial for another reason. My sister was still an attending member of the church we grew up in, and when she moved to Boise, I'd imagined that part of my commitment would be taking her to church each Sunday. Though she had her car, she very quickly realized that she wasn't up to driving in a strange city. I'd wondered how she would feel about me not attending with her once I'd helped her get acclimated. She knew, of course, that I didn't go to church anymore and had on occasion expressed concern for my spiritual well-being. But after attending a few of the churches, none of which she liked, she allowed herself to bypass her religious obligation based on her health. I was outwardly supportive and inwardly rejoicing. However, not going to church was the least of the matter. Rhea still embraced the hard-line fundamentals of the church, and while she didn't flaunt her disapproval of my life and beliefs, which I shared from time to time, she did bring the rigidity of those values back into my home. It wasn't, of course, her belief in God that I struggled with, but with the unchanged and unchanging version of God as a rule-keeper and an almighty authority who judged us. Love didn't enter much into the equation—as it never had in our childhood. If I couldn't live love now, with my body-broken and heart-broken sister, she would leave this world without ever feeling it from her family and perhaps, without seeing another view of God.

In spite of the heavy shadow that moved about the house, hovering close by, my sister and I did turn some of our shared past pain into hilarity by laughing about our crazy childhood.

"Remember the time we begged Mom to let us trick or treat and she finally relented by letting us exchange coats and go to the neighbor's?" I asked.

"What must they have thought?" she said, barely able to get

the words out.

"When I told that to Maridel, she couldn't stop laughing—went into the bank and had to leave," I added.

"The neighbors must have thought Mom was a nutcase!"

"Wasn't she?"

We howled with healing laughter. Other nights we reminisced about the people in the church and when we really got going, did spot-on imitations of their repetitive testimonies.

"I just want to do some little thing for Jesus," Rhea whined, then held up a sliver of invisible pie on a plate, recounting dear old Mrs. Ladue's paltry contribution to my mother's recovery.

I was grateful for those times, for while they didn't outweigh the surfeit of negativity about the past, they did bring relief to my heart and a feeling that being together was helping to heal my sister's heart a bit after all.

When the anniversary of Rhea's arrival in Boise came, we were both surprised. In her mind, she had come here to die, and while it wasn't something I wished to hasten, she regularly reminded me that she did. Her health was failing bit by bit and at one point became critical enough for her to need oxygen, a walker, and a few weeks of Hospice care. But to her dismay, her strength came back and Hospice informed us she no longer qualified for their services. "Guess you'll need to take me shoe-shopping, Addie," she said, laughing. She'd given all but one pair away when her demise seemed certain.

Rhea's recovery brought mixed feelings for me. I didn't want my sister to die, but I did want her to have what she so dearly longed for. And I was finding it increasingly depressing to live with someone who wanted to die when I wanted so much to fully live. Early in the second year, I became painfully aware that her negativity, sadness, and anger were taking a toll on me. Her litanies were pitiful, but also familiar. The depression of my early days, the days of my own complete unconsciousness, threatened to become my companion again. And I was physically compromised too. My blood pressure had elevated again to an alarming level. I'd always had problems with sleep, but now found myself thinking of it as the enemy. The added weight of responsibility for my sister's every need pressed down on me and I no longer had the contact with my friends that had buoyed me through such times with Arnold. They kept in touch but it was hard for me to leave the house for more than the necessary errands and appointments. Neither was it the same when they came over as I didn't have the freedom to talk about my conflicts; and the truth was, I didn't want them to see that I was struggling. Linda was my only consistent source of support. She lived just a few miles away now and often popped in after work to cheer things up with her smile and upbeat spirit. And she also managed Rhea's complicated web of medications, keeping them organized for her and helping with the many adjustments month to month.

I'd always known that I wanted to return to Basket Island with Maridel and made plans to go in the summer of 2000. I'd kept in touch with Andy, the island historian, and his family, ensuring that this time we wouldn't need to wave our photographic credentials lest we be booted off the island. And of course, this time we'd be arriving "in season" while the island was occupied. "We're letting everyone know you're coming," said Andy's mother, Cyndi.

As we drove along the coast, my excitement was different this time. Before, I'd wondered if the houses would still be there or if seventy years of ocean weather would have had its way with them. But this time, I was feeling an emotion for which the dictionary has no word. To be returning to this place with my grown daughter and sharing this idyllic window of my childhood with her felt like a tale from a children's storybook. But I wasn't reading it from a book. I wasn't being transported to a world that didn't exist except in my imagination. I was being escorted by my child back into a world that had once belonged to me, and by some miracle, still did.

We walked first to the cottage that had been our family's home. I introduced myself to the man in the yard, Bill Seavers. My reputation preceded me and he took us around the front of the house to meet his wife, Carrie. "We heard you were coming!" she said. "Tell us what the island was like when you were here." As we chatted, I felt comfortable asking to see the cottage.

"Oh, yes. It was given to us as a wedding gift from my father, and since we're soon to celebrate our fiftieth, we've made quite a few changes to accommodate our family."

The little house was now two stories. They had put a stairway in the entry that invited a climb to two bedrooms above and the back porch had been enclosed to create a bathroom. The kitchen had been updated of course—probably more than once—yet I could still sense the house as it had been. And when I looked out the picture window at the unchanged view of sky and rock and water, I could still feel myself there in that room, waiting for breakfast to end so that I could be loosed out into the magic of my island kingdom.

"Here's our address," Carrie said, nudging me out of my reverie. "Please keep in touch."

When we stepped outside, the screeching of the eagles overhead brought such a wave of nostalgia that for an instant, it was as if I had never left and my father would soon be gliding up in his dory with a fresh catch of flounder.

Out in the center of the island, we found Cyndi, eager to show us around and introduce us to the islanders—each of them giving us a bit of their own history with the place. One woman came down from a ladder to meet us when Cyndi made the long-range introduction.

"I used to see two little boys from this house running around the island," I told her. "I wasn't allowed to play with them, but I remember watching them."

"One of them was my grandfather!" she said, laughing heartily.

It seemed impossible—preposterous even—that time had played such a trick on me.

"Come have tea," Cyndi beckoned, after the woman headed back to her ladder. My mind flashed back on the day that Andy, in a state of ecstasy, had made tea for three old ladies. We passed a pleasant hour with Cyndi sharing the history of their house and telling us about the people on the island as if they were old neighbors we had just recently lost touch with.

"Can't you stay for dinner?" she asked. I so loved the gesture, but knew that after several hours on the island, it was time to head back to our hotel.

"Well, then plan to come back and spend the night next time!" she announced as if issuing a friendly edict. "Some of the folks will be so disappointed they missed you."

"I would love that!" I said, wondering if in fact, I could pull off another visit to Basket Island and once more sleep to the sound of crashing waves and wake to the miracle of being surrounded by nothing but sea and sky.

"Be sure to check out the empty house before you go," she called. "It's for sale."

Maridel and I leaned into the windows of the largest of the houses, using our hands as blinders from the sun. It was far more open than the others and much larger as well. I remembered the family who lived there, the Knights._

"Wouldn't it be great to own a house here again and have a family summer gathering here?" I asked Maridel.

"And what a place to write!"

My mind ran with the images of my grandchildren and perhaps one day, great grandchildren running toward the dunes with their sand buckets or picking blackberries and bringing them back to the house. The image was unbearably sweet and I felt myself longing for its poetry, its deep abiding fulfillment. Just the way a storybook should end. But I also knew it was not to be. The island had been mine once, before I could even appreciate what a privilege it was, but now, my best hope was to return one more time and spend the night. Once off the island and back in our lovely old hotel, a strangeness came over me—an unsettling feeling that it had all been a dream.

After leaving Maine, we set out on the road to make a tour of the houses where I'd lived throughout my childhood. We started with the house of my birth. One is never sure what to expect when making a pilgrimage to places inhabited eight-four years before. Of course, I had been back to Spring Valley a handful of times, but didn't look up my natal address. But there it was, still standing on Route 45, looking pretty much like the sepia-tone pictures I have of it—including that damnable porch where I was first tied to something that cramped my style. To my surprise, a young man answered the door when I knocked. I introduced myself and said, "You might be interested in knowing that I was born in one of your upstairs bedrooms eighty-four years ago." It was obviously not an announcement he was prepared for, but didn't hesitate. "Well, come in, come in!" he said. I declined his invitation, but talked amiably with him at the door, happy to hear about the history of the house.

"He told me it was built in 1915," I told Maridel when I got back to the car. "That would have been five years before I was born." I wished I'd brought that picture of myself standing in the driveway to show him, but it was enough to hold it in my mind's eye and reflect on how far I'd come since my days on the once literal—now symbolic—clothesline.

A short distance away, of course, was my grandma's house—the place I so diligently attempted to run back to after we'd moved to the campgrounds outside Beacon. It was still in the family and still the home of my Uncle Frank who lived in the upstairs living quarters. Downstairs was the home of a family business. No smell of baking cookies or grandfather clock in the hall, but my cousin Janet's husband had beautifully refurbished the house and it looked more elegant than ever.

Uncle Frank, now in his late nineties, was looking fairly good too—beaming as always and engaging me and Maridel in bright conversation on the big porch. I hadn't seen him for twenty years and as we snapped pictures, I tried to imagine what it would be like to live not just in the same house, but in its upstairs apartment for your entire and very long adult life. I would have died long ago, but it seemed to suit my uncle just fine.

The next day we set out for Beacon. Skipping the cottage on the Beacon campgrounds, which I knew was no longer in existence, we showed up on Washington Avenue—the home where I lived three times in my life. With Maridel at her outpost, I knocked on the door, glancing at the yard where my wedding reception had been the big event of the neighborhood. An older lady came to the door and when I introduced myself and told her I'd once had my wedding reception in her yard and lived there three times, she excitedly called to her family to come. Abandoning their Sunday lunch, her husband, son and his wife all appeared at the door, eager to see what was worthy of interrupting a meal.

"This lady lived here when she was two years old! And again when she was…" she turned to me for the details.

"When I was twelve and again after a year of college while I was waiting to get married."

"She had her wedding reception in our yard!" she exclaimed, sounding as jubilant as if it had just occurred.

"Come in! Come in!" they chimed as if I were a family member believed to be dead. I waved Maridel in from the car and together we entered the house where angels had left their spirits imprinted on my consciousness in the space of mere seconds.

Their story came spilling out as we walked the rooms. The son and his wife owned the house now, but the father was in charge of showing me all the changes they had made. Some changes predated them, however; they were surprised to learn that there had once been a door from the kitchen to the entry way. The house had been extensively remodeled over the years and the six of us moved together, comparing the way it had been with its new incarnation.

"Oh, I see that old pipe is still coming down from this corner," I said.

The son laughed. "That's our next project!"

Their welcoming warmth, their interest in every detail of how the house had changed emboldened me. I wanted to visit my nursery again. To see the window where the angels had flown as one being up and away from my crib.

"If I could," I said to the mother, "I'd love to go into the room at the head of the stairs. It was my nursery when I was a baby and I had a visitation of angels there one night."

The lively conversation hushed as they all murmured their support, stepping aside to make way for my ascent. The mother escorted me, and Maridel trailed behind. I stepped alone into the room, cluttered with the business of life, but all that fell away when my eyes fixed on the window. It was not square as I'd recalled, but oblong, yet obviously the original. I took a breath and envisioned the crib where it had sat along the wall. It wasn't a cathedral or a window of stained glass, but I had the same feeling that I'd had in those places. For me, it was the most sacred of spots. Maridel then joined me in the room for just a moment as I pointed to the window and the position of my bed. That moment had always been full-blown for me, as real year in and year out as it had been that first night. Now, it was sealed in my heart.

The family urged us to stay and have lunch with them, but

settled for a few pictures in the yard with their camera and mine. I needed to be alone with Maridel. I needed to let the moment sink into my being.

When I was ready, we drove toward town and up the side street to my favorite address: 9 Davis Street—the home with all the best memories because of the Starkeys. I hardly recognized the house. All the ironwork, the wisteria, shutters were gone. It looked like a plain white cube of wood and windows. The man who answered the door, however, was willing to let us inside and showed us with enthusiasm all the changes he had made in his almost fifty years of living there. We didn't go upstairs, but standing in those rooms was surreal for me. I was envisioning the ghostly version of how it all had been: my Dad's radio in the corner, his desk amidst the massive furniture, the Christmas tree in the bay window, the front parlor where I had been quarantined, and the corner where I'd learned to play the piano.

"My mother told me the facts of life while I was looking out that window at the garden," I said to the man. "She told me that "God plants a little seed and I thought it meant that babies grew on cornstalks." The man laughed, but Maridel asked for a good suggestion for lunch. She evidently thought all the nostalgia was impairing my conversational judgment.

In the middle of town, the former bank—a stalwart brick building—had been converted to a barbeque restaurant with a covered patio. "The Piggy Bank" it was called, and over plates of pulled pork sandwiches and slaw, we laughed about the name.

"Sounds like the kind of 'clever' that shows up only in movies," Maridel said.

"But then, this whole day could be a movie," I remarked.

"I'll say," she replied. "Everything from angels to sex ed."

After lunch we visited the library of my youth—now the Beacon Historical Society—and shopped in boutiques housed in what was once the railroad station. Beacon, it seemed, was being refurbished as a quaint little getaway town for people fleeing the city for a weekend. There was even word that the old hat factory where I worked was being turned into a world-class art museum.

In one of the boutiques, I found an amazing collection of dolls made by "Small Wonder." They were newborns of such life-like attributes that if they hadn't been lying on a shelf, I could have been fooled. I immediately thought of Rhea who loved babies more than anyone I knew. Though not a typical gift for an elderly sister, I knew instantly that this was the perfect gift. Once home, I carried the doll in my arms, took it into her room and placed it in her arms. Her eyes filled with tears and she cooed over it as if it were her own.

Re-entry from the trip was hard, reminding me as it had of my lack of freedom in my daily life. I could feel my conflict increasing and decided to see a counselor. After I poured out my situation and my angst, she told me she really couldn't help me—that I seemed to be handling it very, very well. Hurting enough to seek help, was that all I got for my investment? Or had I, once again, in a display of old habits, come across as strong and together instead of breaking down and allowing my feelings to show? A comment Maridel had made to me on the trip made me wonder:

"Mom, every time people ask you how you're doing with Rhea, you just always tell them how easy it is—and how some nights you just make oatmeal for dinner. Why don't you just tell them you're struggling? They care about you. They want to know the truth."

For the most part, I did suffer alone. Often, feeling under duress, I would sit in the car after walking and sob my heart out. I cried in the night too, hoping my heavy, double doors prevented my sister from hearing me. I felt so bad for her, but I felt bad for myself too. I would be eighty soon and felt trapped once again.

There was so much I wanted to do, but I was tethered on the old clothesline. My nemesis. At times, after my walk, I banged the steering wheel of the car at the far end of the parking lot. *Foiled again*, I thought to myself, but knew it wasn't the whole truth. I knew it was right for my sister to be with me. I knew it was right to take this opportunity to pour into her the love and acceptance that she'd never had. Yet the conflict ate at my bones. What was I supposed to be learning?

My trip back to Maine had been hard for Rhea. In her long-honed way of communicating, she didn't complain outright but made it clear that despite her friend, Betty, spending a week with her, things were not to her liking. I vowed not to leave her for that length of time again, which only felt more binding.

When the holiday season arrived and with it my eightieth birthday, I was harboring a secret that I was dying to share. When I'd turned seventy-nine, I'd decided to write a pictorial memoir for my family. During the year I had turned the dining room table into my desk, using it both to sort pictures and write on yellow legal tablets as was my custom. Of course, when anyone from the family came over, I had a method for whisking it off the table and out of sight. The truth is that regardless of whether or not all my family appreciated this labor of love, I was grateful for it. It had saved me from the tedium of my life, giving me a place to go that was all my own and lifting me out of my confines. I'd been not only inspired to do this by Shirley's mother, but was able to hire the same couple who produced her memoir. As each chapter was typed up from my longhand, it was sent to Colorado to be edited and the corresponding pictures scanned.

Before the big family celebration and my debut as an author, I was feted by my friends. Two of them, Judy Stallcop, who had helped me decorate my house on State Street, and Jeannie Kineley, who had helped me decorate this one, hosted the event. It was held at Judy's home, a gorgeous old house all decked out for Christmas. The table with its clusters of poinsettias looked like something straight out of *Martha Stewart Living*. Each guest had been asked to bring an ornament that symbolized our relationship or reflected a memory we'd shared. My eyes filled with tears many times as women of all ages and from all stages of my life took her ornament from the tree and shared its meaning.

"Remember when we wore these to church?" Beverly Laird said, holding up a pair of ornamental gloves."

I laughed.

"Yes, Addie and I do go that far back and in every phase of our friendship, she has supported me to be who I am."

When it was Shirley's turn, she held up a saw ornament.

"This saw symbolizes just one way that Addie and I spend time together because I'm her handywoman as well as her friend. But, truly, the time spent with her while I work is far more important than the pay!"

After each person shared, the ornament was given to Judy, who placed it on an artificial evergreen swag. "That way, we will all be with Addie every birthday from here on out—hanging from her mantle and reminding her of how much we love her."

I was overcome with the love from the crowded room of women of all ages—some, like Beverly, I'd known for much of my life. Others, like Becky, I'd recently met. "I can't believe how all those women mingled as if they'd always known each other," I told Maridel when we got in the car. "I'd actually felt a bit nervous about all of them meeting, but I didn't even have to introduce anyone. They were all talking like old friends by the time we got there."

"Well, they all had you in common, Mom. They knew just what to talk about from the moment they met. Besides, you drew each and every one of them into your life so no matter how different they all are, they reflect some part of you."

As the night of my big family party drew closer, I was reeling with excitement. I couldn't think of anything more special than presenting them with my beautiful bound version of my life's story complete with a hundred pictures. I'd completed it in October and it had been sent to the publisher. When I'd received the handsome, leather-bound copies of "Between the Portals" in the mail early in December, I didn't know how I was going to wait seven days to deliver them.

The party was to be held at Linda and Jerry's spacious home with all of the Boise family in attendance: Tyler, Dale and his wife, Kathryn, and their two children, Jason and Courtney. But those who didn't live there flew or drove in to celebrate my eightieth birthday: Maridel, Justin and his wife, Nikki, and Gavin. I felt so blessed to have my whole integrated family there. Despite divorces and Brad's absence in our midst, we blended as one family—laughing, joking, and eating a delicious catered dinner. Few, I knew, had that privilege when families had come apart. I felt the beauty of it, especially when the candles were shining on the cake and everyone was looking at me with love and singing full force.

One person who lived in town was missing: Rhea. She didn't feel well enough these days to go out into a group of people and yet, her presence was felt as I handed out beautifully wrapped copies of my book. Rhea had paid for half of the sizeable printing cost as a birthday present to me. I'd dreamed all year of my family's reactions to opening my book and was rewarded with their gasps of delight and astonishment. We sat together for a long time, paging through the photos and talking about the memories they evoked. I even felt Arnold's presence as his grandchildren pointed out some of his characteristic poses and imitated him.

They presented me with a gift too—a throw and accompanying pillows in all of my favorite colors: rusts, greens, and golds. Blended into the weave were a grand piano and a violin—the instruments that had given me and my father so much pleasure.

Once the anticipation of my birthday celebrations and the holidays had passed, reality set in again. It wasn't that reality was bad so much as it reminded me that my daily life did not reflect my inner spirit at eighty years old. My zest for living! My love of travel! My desire for expansion rather than comfort with contraction!

"You've got to do more for yourself, Mom. Rhea spends so much of her time alone anyway. Why do you feel like you have to be there so much?" Maridel had asked during her visit. She'd noticed how emotionally tethered I was to my sister even when we went out shopping for a few hours. I had no answer, but her question stayed with me after she had gone home. The truth was, I felt guilty when I was away for "too long" and always felt the need to check in on her while I was out. Rhea certainly wasn't complaining. In fact, sometimes she encouraged me to go out more, but I didn't feel comfortable doing it.

The next time Maridel came to town, we planned to go out for the day—out for lunch and to the mall to shop. Mid-afternoon, we got a cup of coffee and stopped in See's for a couple of candies. Deciding to go up to a comfortable lounge area to enjoy our treat, we hopped on the escalator. My brain was suddenly tasked with balancing a quick hop in the moving stairway with the added factors of hot coffee in one hand and a piece of candy in the other. Unable to calculate the equation quickly enough, I fell backward, the coffee flying as my head hit the metal steps and the stairs kept rolling. "Mom!" Maridel screamed, which brought the attention and fast action of the crowd. Someone hit the button to stop the escalator and others rushed toward me, telling me not to move. One woman stepped through the crowd and got down by me, talking to me gently and holding my head up as it was hanging off the step. She said very little but her presence calmed me. Every muscle in my body wanted to jump up and shout, "I'm okay!" but I knew I had to heed the consensual warnings. By the time the medics had gently lifted me, asked me several questions before seating me in a chair, and many more once seated, it became clear that I really was okay. They wanted to call an ambulance, but I persuaded them not to. "My other daughter is a nurse," I told them repeatedly, "she'll look out for me." So they settled for educating me about signs of concussion and dispersed.

Maridel and I walked through the store, found a bench out in the mall, drank our cold coffee (mine was miraculously half full), and ate our candy. She had pried mine from my hand as I'd lay waiting for the medics. We meekly laughed at ourselves, but taking time to sit was no longer about the treat and drink. We needed to process what had just happened. We both knew it could have been—by all rights should have been—catastrophic.

With the encouragement of both my daughters *and* my fall, which I saw as a metaphysical statement of losing balance in my life, I did make plans a few months later for a long weekend in Portland to see Justin and Nikki. I had to give myself this much reprieve from the sameness of my days and the often stifling atmosphere of the house. I noticed that when I got away—especially on a plane—and let the landscapes, rhythms, and faces of new places in, I felt like me again. The contrast always startled me, making me aware of how much of myself slipped into the background in the duty-driven routines of my life. What I really wanted was to be myself at home—right there in the midst of living with my sister. Right there in the midst of her physical and emotional suffering. Instead, I felt pulled back into the oldest desire I knew: the longing to escape.

Life puttered on. Unremarkable, and for me, isolated. My friends were outposts in this world that I'd created. The few who made friends with Rhea—Linda and Shirley primarily--were the only ones I saw on a regular basis, and each time they arrived at the door bearing fresh food or just fresh energy, I was awash in gratitude.

Late in 2001, news arrived that didn't change my daily life, but did bring new brightness to it, the way a new lamp can make a whole room feel different. Nikki and Justin were expecting! My little Maridel would be a grandmother and I a great grandmother. I was over the moon, and since Rhea had always loved babies, it gave us something uplifting to talk about.

When Maridel called one day with a sudden impression that the baby was a boy, I reminded her of a dream I'd had the year before. I was standing outside in front of an old house when suddenly I saw Justin walking down the road toward me, holding the hand of a little boy. It had felt prophetic and perhaps was a nudge on the part of my psyche to hold out for new life—not just that of my first great grandchild's, but my own.

When that baby came into the world in July of 2002, he was not only a boy as predicted, but he was born on Rhea's birthday. It pleased her so! As I listened to Maridel's jubilant voice describing to me the cell-reverberating experience of her grandson's birth, my eyes filled with tears. They were tears of happiness… and tears of sadness. *Why wasn't I there? How could I have missed this?* And even more astonishing to me was the fact that it hadn't occurred to me to be there. I'd gone to the shower four months before, but hadn't considered going to the birth? There it was again.

Deciding to live more fully again, I made a trip to see Jaden Quincy Bowes before he was a month old. Gavin flew into Portland for the occasion too. Looking at my first great grandchild was like breathing rarified air. I couldn't see him simply as a baby. He was gorgeous but he was, to me, something so much more than that. It was as if he'd landed here in this house and fallen into my willing arms, carrying a message my brain couldn't decode but my heart understood perfectly. He belonged to me, was a part of me and yet not mine at all. He was a piece of my yet-unlived legacy. And I knew I had to return soon.

When Thanksgiving came, I was back with two of my Idaho grandchildren in tow—Tyler and Courtney. Gavin had moved to Portland by then and joined us with his girlfriend and her son. Including Maridel, who showed up from California, and the three residents of the house, we filled the leafed-out maple table that had once been mine. The satisfaction was bone deep. My life was coming full circle in a new way and I vowed not to miss it.

Even as I pledged to expand my world, I knew I must begin to love that world itself, creating newness within it. To walking, I added working out at a nearby gym and found I loved the feeling of growing stronger at an age when most women accept growing weaker. I was feeling more physically fit than I ever had which contributed to a greater sense of well-being in my circumstances. I also began spending more time with my circle of friends whose company energized me with talk of books, movies, and their own changing lives.

As I took on the responsibility of keeping my own life vital, it was reflected back to me through others. My cousin, Paul, contacted me and asked if he could come out from New York for a week's visit. I fondly remembered playing with him in his backyard when he was a little boy and I was a teenager. He was now a father, a grandfather and a family historian. Rhea and I were intrigued to meet this man we hadn't seen since our teens. The three of us connected easily, slipping into lively reminiscence. He had packed his suitcase not only with memorabilia—like Goo Goo's last report to the District Assembly, written from his death bed—but also stories we'd never heard. He brought something else with him too: a very different view of our mother.

"I'll never forget how good your mother was to us," he said with love in his voice. "She always had time to talk to us and made us feel special. All of us just loved to go see her."

Rhea didn't hide the laughter I was trying to suppress. "That's not the woman who raised us," she said, and launched into her own stories of Elizabeth Caldwell, mother-at-large.

Paul was as shocked by our experience of her as we were of his. As if reading two outrageously different books by the same title, Rhea and I couldn't imagine the soft, caring woman whose memory he honored any more than he could relate to our version. Later in the week, Paul's brother, John, joined us from California. The first night at dinner he expressed the same sentiment for our mother. "I don't know where all of us would be if it wasn't for Aunt Lizzy," he said. "She made such a difference in all of our lives." I suddenly recalled that Paul's sister, Doris, had once written an article about her experiences as a missionary in India, noting the spiritual influences of her Aunt Lizzy as part of her journey.

I felt so strange—a bit like the adult children who discover after their father's death that he had another family. Evidently my mother had a whole different side to her—one that was lavished on nieces and nephews, but that barely flickered for us. It gave me deep pause. Whatever your experience is of someone, it doesn't mean you truly know them. The part is not the whole.

A few months later, as I walked out of the gym, I tripped on a rise in the sidewalk near the door. I tried to catch myself by running to get my balance, but only gained speed on the long downward walkway. At the street, I fell and hit my head. As with my last fall, I refused the ambulance but wasn't able to avoid the emergency room at St. Al's. An employee of the gym offered to take me to the hospital when I insisted that no ambulance be called. The CT scan revealed that when I'd hit my head, the jar on the left side had spurted blood to the right hemisphere of my brain. I was transferred to the trauma unit and kept overnight for observation and several more scans.

When the doctor showed up in my room that afternoon, he greeted me and pulled up a chair. My heart appropriately started to step up its dance. The last time a doctor had come into the room and pulled up a chair, Arnold had died.

"How old was your mother when she died?" he asked.

"Seventy-three." This couldn't be good.

"And your father?"

"Eighty-one."

"Well, all I have to say is you have some kind of genes. You're fine. You can go home."

My face was swollen and black and blue. The sight of me scared my sister, but as unnerving as it was to look in a mirror, something else scared me more. I'd fallen again—doing something even more ordinary than getting on an elevator with candy and coffee in my hands. I knew it was symbolic. People my age fall all the time but they're weak, unsteady, and unbalanced. I'd been coming out of a 24 Hour Fitness Center. Why was I falling?

In the fall of 2003, during my routine colonoscopy, a malignant tumor was discovered. The surgery, I was told, should be a relatively easy one as it was not attached to the wall of my colon. I felt grateful, disturbed, and unsettled all at the same time. Yes, I had a family history of colon cancer. I was nine when it had taken my gentle Goo Goo from this world. But I had trusted I would avoid it with a healthy lifestyle and the emotional process of "cleaning out the old crap" in my psyche. The unsettled feeling came from knowing that I wouldn't be able to care for Rhea for a period of weeks and would have to rely on friends and family to do it.

The surgery was successful. No other treatment was required. Maridel came for ten days. Family supported. Friends rallied. And gradually, I regained my strength. I seemed to be doing a better job of flirting with death than my sister seemed to be. I could only assume that the independent, free-wheeling traveler and pilgrim in me was making it clear that while the life I was living was noble and good, it didn't work for her. It was, in fact, making her sick.

These were days when I wrestled deeply, as I had in years past, but on a whole new level. I wrestled with the enigmatic nature of being true to my complex self. How do I honor all my parts without guilt? How do I listen to the selves that were neglected if not abandoned? How do I inch my way out of old patterns and still live on the right side of my values—like taking care of my sick and slowly dying sister.

Rhea had gone through a series of declines by now, but always rallied to a point just below her previous state. The cumulative effect was that much of the time she required oxygen and depended on a four-pronged walker to get around. Some days she used neither. Other days both. Over time she'd suffered numerous mini-strokes, which left her feeling weak for days.

Every Christmas, she hoped it would be her last and as this Christmas came and went, I didn't see how she could last another year. On New Year's Day morning, I went into her room as I did every day, but found her unable to move or speak. Linda was by my side within minutes. Her presence, as always, was a source of strength and comfort—not just because she herself was comfortable in the situation but because she loved both Rhea and me. Even though we knew Rhea's wish not to receive any life-sustaining treatment, we confirmed her decision.

"Rhea, you've had a severe stroke. We're not going to feed you or give you any medication. Is this what you want?"

She nodded her approval.

Over the next week, Linda and Shirley took turns being with her at night so that I could sleep and be ready to care for her by day. Hospice came back to the room they'd vacated a couple of years before. Their involvement allowed me to run some errands during the day and have some time to myself.

I was in and out of her room continually through the days, heartbroken by her attempts to tell me something that I couldn't understand. I knew her efforts must mean she felt strongly about her message, but none of my attempts to interpret were right. She shook her head, just barely enough to be observable, and gave up until the next time. On Dale's birthday, the seventh of January, I passed by her door on the way down the hall, but felt impressed to turn around and go back. She was gasping for breath. I tried to adjust her head, but it didn't help and so I just leaned over her face as her body struggled, no doubt against her will, to breathe. I kissed her as she breathed her last. Until Linda arrived, there we were together, big and little sister regardless of our advanced years. After all the years apart, we had found our way back to each other in the end, and I knew, despite my inner conflict, that it had been the right thing for both of us. The best thing.

Throughout the next few days, as Maridel arrived and she, Linda, and I planned the funeral, my emotions were a strange concoction—substances that found their way into the same bottle, but didn't mix. I was happy for Rhea's release from this world that had been so painful for her, but the sadness of her life pressed in on me in the dark. The funeral, held at a church in a nearby mall, was presided over by Irving—who had known us both all his life. There was such comfort in that and in my family and friends all gathered in tribute to her life. Maridel stayed on for several days, helping me to get started on the financial, legal, and household tasks that faced me.

Once everyone had gone home and I'd begun to find the new strands of living that would now be mine, I made it though the difficult days by journaling all my feelings and thoughts. In the early morning, I would open my heart to the voice of Spirit, listening. And I would pour out my own gratitude for all that Rhea's time with me had brought: a renewed thankfulness for escaping the rigidity of my parent's religion; for healing the relationship with my mother when I did; for the opportunity to learn about myself and address my own shadow, my own losses. I was also grateful for the things Rhea's presence had helped me see and face: the residue of my own pain from the past, the strengthening of my hard-won beliefs about the nature of God and the shedding, perhaps at last, of my nemesis: the struggle between caring for someone I loved and needing to be free. I also began with surprising immediacy to reconnect fully with my friends and found that our long talks and the sharing of good food and laughter eased my transition.

Rhea had left me the money she'd saved for her retirement. In retrospect, I believe that she had always planned it that way. Her instructions were simple: "Spend it all and enjoy it, Addie." Ironically, this was the very thing she wouldn't do for herself. Once I had the energy to take it on, I made her bedroom into a den with my big lounge chairs and a wall of all my books. The television was moved in there to make a proper guest room at the end of the hall. I hired a painter to freshen the house with colors of sea foam green, terra cotta, and bronzy browns, and then put down a spirited cinnamon carpet that drew the palate of hues altogether. The new energy breathed into my home lifted my spirits and supported the feeling that, at the age of eighty-three, I was entering the best era of my life.

I was free again. I had no one to please but myself…when I came and went, what I ate and when, who I saw, and how I spent my time.

After recreating the house to reflect my refurbished life, a big trip was the next thing on the agenda. Like a homing pigeon let loose, I flew back to Maine with Gavin, the fourth generation to experience my paradise. This time we accepted Cyndi's invitation to stay overnight and went to sleep with the roaring lull of the ocean as our lullaby. The next afternoon, we were sitting on Cyndi and Tom's porch enjoying a glass of wine when Carrie and Bill Seavers, the owners of our childhood cottage, came around the corner with appetizers. As the sun flooded the land around the house and made a path of diamonds on the water, I felt I could explode with sheer happiness. When it was time for dinner, we traipsed from one end of the island to the other for a barbeque at the Seavers' cottage with Andrew, the island historian, as our cook. As the evening lengthened, we shared stories spanning eighty years—laughing together like old friends who'd met on this magical island for decades. In some inexplicable way, I had come full circle. I had come home.

The following year, I was scheduled for another colonoscopy. Because of my history, I had them more frequently than usual. And after some years of struggling with growing bouts of a weak and raspy voice that made it almost impossible to speak at times, the decision was made to do an endoscopy as well to look for any polyps in my throat. I had the procedure in the morning and by afternoon, was feeling weak and sick. Assuming it was just part of the recovery, I settled into bed. Linda had called after work and I'd told her I was okay, but the sound of my voice troubled her. Even though she was weary from the day at work and just wanted to get home after meeting her husband, Jerry, for dinner, she felt impressed to come by the house. By then I was feeling worse and she called Dale and Tyler to come. She asked me all her nurse questions, worried about the possibility of an internal bleed, but I said "no" to all of them. As we talked, I rallied and thought the worst had passed. Even so, she decided to spend the night with me and left my son and grandson to keep me company while she went home to get her things.

When she returned, Tyler was out in the driveway waiting for her. "Mom, something's terribly wrong with Grandma!" She came inside to find me almost comatose and got up on the bed with me, ready to perform CPR while Tyler called 911. This time the ambulance ride couldn't be avoided. In the emergency room, waiting, I threw up copious amounts of dark blood which eliminated the need for testing. It was a bleed. I'd lost five pints of blood and was given a transfusion of three. The gastroenterologist was called for an emergency surgery to repair the bleed. My children were consulted about my legal request to be resuscitated.

"You're fortunate to be alive," the doctor told me the next day. "I didn't know if you were going to make it or not."

I was as grateful as I was stunned. For someone who was so enthusiastic about life, I was doing more than my share of dramatic brushes with death.

The next year: another trip. I was feeling good enough to keep up with my world-traveler friend, Darlene, who had once been my colleague at the college. Despite the distance between Boise and Spokane, Washington, we had managed to keep the relationship vital through letters and phone calls. Now we would be able to physically connect again. Darlene, the master planner, booked us for a European cruise on the North Sea. When we arrived on the ship, our accommodations had been upgraded. Instead of the standard room, ours was large and open with a balcony! Across the seven days, we visited the nine surrounding capitols of Northern Europe—as far as Oslo and Copenhagen. I felt more like fifty than eighty, climbing steep stairways and easily managing walking long distances. I adored the beautiful gardens and home of Monet. I was inspired by the windmills everywhere—giving me such a heartening sense of progress with the environment. But the place that touched me most deeply and left its mark on me was the home of Anne Frank. I'd read her diaries of course—likely more than once. As transporting as they were, walking through the place where she lived and wrote was far beyond what the page could capture. I was sobered and felt such sorrow, not just for her, but for the millions of people who lived in such a consuming state of fear. Tears kept rolling down my face in reverence for this sacred place of courage and transcendence.

The Center for Spiritual Living had become an integral part of my life by now and I was still enjoying the *Science of Mind* magazine too. Originally, it had been a source of inspiration—then the catalyst for nudging me to take seriously the instruction to go to Cathy's church. Now it was the ongoing link between my private spiritual life and my visits to the Center. But it had yet to serve its full purpose. One day as I crossed my living room, the latest edition caught my eye and I stopped to peruse it. It opened to an ad for a cruise to Panama. The name, "Oceans of Gratitude," seemed to vibrate on the page. The speakers were spiritual teachers and authors, some of whose books I had read. The main speaker was Michael Beckwith, founder and spiritual director of the International Agape Movement. I recognized him from the movie, "The Secret." I knew I was supposed to go.

A few nights later when my book club gathered, I announced to the group that I was going on the cruise. Supportive as always, they bypassed the typical fear-oriented questions that most friends might ask an eighty-six-year-old woman who planned to go on a cruise alone. Perhaps some of them even had those questions, but among my friends now, it was always assumed that where there is guidance and something feels right, all is well—without knowing the particulars. At the end of the meeting, however, I had a sudden impression to invite my friend, Victoria, to go with me. Her raised eyebrows sent a message: "not likely," but she did add that she would check it out online and let me know in a couple of weeks

Within a few days she called. "Addie, the truth is I can't afford to go on the cruise, but after looking at the information online, I know I must go."

Victoria took care of everything—arrangements for the cruise, the hotel, flights, and ground transportation. Before we ever left town, I saw that it would have been a daunting process for me, especially without a computer. It was a realization that deepened on the day of departure and bloomed larger every day of the trip. I'd not only been guided to take this trip, but Spirit had provided the perfect human guide—and impeccable companionship.

One day we attended a session on "Prosperity Consciousness" by a young woman named Christiane Schull. I wanted to tell her how much I had enjoyed her talk, but had decided not to wait in the circle of people surrounding her. The next night as we entered the auditorium, Victoria led us closer to the front than we'd sat before and as I turned to take my seat, I saw Christiane just behind me.

"I wanted to tell you yesterday how much I enjoyed your session. I came to true spirituality later in life, and it's such a joy to keep learning and growing."

"What is your name?" she asked.

"And where do you live, Addie?"

"In Boise, Idaho"

She smiled, as if intrigued. "Tell me your story."

It was an odd request coming from a stranger and there was little time to fulfill it, but I gave her a quick synopsis.

"Addie, you must tell your story. Have you spoken or written about it?" There was an urgency in her voice that shocked me and caused a stir deep inside. The program began but I couldn't keep my attention on the speaker. *What had I said that had caused this stranger to urge me to tell my story?*

The next day, Victoria and I had plans to go to the city of Panama on a tour. Wasn't that part of why we had come? To see the destination city? But when I awoke, the pulse of my experience with Christiane was so strong that I wanted to be alone to think and write. Victoria understood completely—as self-aware friends do—and left at 7:30. I quickly showered, dressed, and grabbed my camera, happy to have a chance to take pictures on the almost deserted ship. I got on the elevator and automatically pushed Floor #5, where most of our lectures took place. When I got off, there stood Christiane with coffee in her hand as if waiting for me.

"Do you have a moment?" I asked. "I want to tell you something important that I left out last night."

"Let's sit down," she said, and went to get me a cup of coffee.

I'd forgotten to tell her about my visitation of angels. Of course that story opened wide a spirited and intimate conversation about spirituality and each of our unfolding paths. For over three hours, we talked, huddled together like two old friends on an almost empty ship. Perhaps a few people walked by but if they did, we were unaware of them. When we parted, she repeated her message with an even greater sense of urgency. Several times during the last year, I had felt this urge myself—to rewrite my biography as a spiritual memoir, the long journey from confinement to freedom. In fact, I'd made attempts to get started, but couldn't get more than a few lines.

I saw Christiane a couple of other times—an unlikely repetition on that huge ship of thousands of people. The first time, she joined Victoria and me at our lunch table and said to my friend, "This lady must tell her story." Since meeting her, I was vibrating inside with the feeling that she was right—that something was deeply unfulfilled in me and would be until I wrote my spiritual memoir. Each time I saw her, the feeling grew stronger, as if waking, restless, after a deep slumber.

Just before I saw her for the last time, I'd sat down in our cabin and looked through the packet of the presenters' material

Coming across Christiane's card, I saw that besides being a speaker and author, she was also a ghostwriter, which she hadn't mentioned to me. This added credibility. So when I encountered her again, I suggested that I send my biography to her. We agreed to talk on the phone once she'd had a chance to read it.

By the time I got home, it was dawning on me that when I'd presented my family with that bound copy of "Between the Portals," I had tried to make it enough, but now I knew it wasn't. My real story was about my transformation. It was clear that meeting Christiane was the reason for going on that trip. This was evident to me every time I talked to a close friend about my trip—all I wanted to tell them was about this compelling eruption in my life, and each time, tears accompanied my story.

A few days after sending a copy of the book off to Christiane, I headed to California to visit Maridel. In one of our conversations, I confessed to her that I did feel uncomfortable about one thing: Christiane's geographical and religious background was entirely different from mine. Regardless of how skilled she was as a ghostwriter, how could she truly understand my life? Maridel assured me that a good ghostwriter would get inside my world through interviewing me and becoming part of that life herself.

I'd given Christiane Maridel's phone number and was eager to hear from her. I was curious about the cost of the project and how long it would take—and whether she was even willing to take it on. When the phone call came, Maridel slipped out of the house to take a walk and give me some privacy.

I was eager to hear about her reaction to the book and discuss the process of ghostwriting, but instead we talked about the cruise and what had gone on in our lives since then. When I broached the topic of the book, she seemed hesitant. "I think it may be too difficult for you financially, Addie," she said. "I charge $25,000 for 150 finished pages and my printer charges $25,000 for 1,000 copies."

I wasn't sure why she had made that assumption, but it was true. While I could actually come up with the money, it would greatly deplete my reserves.

"I'll understand if you don't want to move forward with it."

We agreed that I would think about it and let her know what I decided.

"How did it go?" Maridel asked when she got back from her walk.

"Fine."

"You don't look like it went fine," she commented. This surprised me because I did feel at peace about it—but perhaps disappointed.

"Well actually, I think I got confirmation that Christiane isn't the right person to write my book. The bottom line is $50,000—25,000 for her work and another $25,000 for the printing."

"Whoa, wait a minute. I can help you greatly reduce the printing costs. When I self-published last year, it cost me a fraction of that."

"Well, right now I just need to sit with it. But I'm feeling that Christiane's purpose was mainly as the catalyst for getting this book written. And from our conversation, I think she feels that too."

Maridel settled into the couch. "Mom, tell me again why it is that you feel so strongly now about writing this book."

I surprised myself by spontaneously recounting half a dozen experiences that had shaped my spiritual life: the salient moments of being totally honest with myself and with God—like the time I'd had lunch with the two women and felt miserable afterward, only to discover that underneath, I felt jealous—and how admitting it to myself had completely freed me. Soon Maridel was recounting other milestones and agreeing with me that this seemed like the legacy I needed to leave behind.

A couple of days later, we were sitting on her porch having

tea. "While you were on the phone earlier," I said, "I wrote a note to Christiane and thanked her for being the catalyst for getting my book written—and that I knew another way would be provided for that to happen."

She looked into my eyes. "Mom, if you know that this book is the right thing for you, I'm the person to write it."

My hands flew to my face and tears gathered in my eyes. For a moment I stared at her unable to find my voice. There were tears in her eyes too.

"Oh Honey, I've thought about this and wished you could write it, but I didn't ask because I know how busy you are with your work."

"Well, that's the thing you don't know. I've had a lot of guidance to cut back on my astrological counseling and start writing full time—but I had no idea how that was going to happen. In fact, the request for astrology readings has come to a halt, and when I took that walk while you were on the phone, I surrendered the whole situation to Spirit for provision."

We rose from our chairs and embraced, tears running down both of our faces. At this moment on our spiritual paths, we were both strongly guided to take an enormous step—and we were each other's provision.

As the project of turning "Between the Portals" into the deeper saga of my spiritual evolution got underway, it was tempting to believe that the book itself was the reason I'd received the cryptic message to "Go to Cathy's church." After all, it wasn't that hard to connect the dots between that directive and the genesis of the book.

The church's "Science of Mind" magazine, which had served as a direct confirmation to follow my guidance, was also the source that led me to the "Oceans of Gratitude" cruise. On the cruise, I'd met Christiane and everything else had unfolded from there, including the provision of my own daughter as the ideal writer.

As a bonus, the book became the catalyst for a personal connection with George. He frequented the Sunday morning services at the Center but I had never personally spoken to him. One day I had an urge to send him the opening pages of the manuscript, thinking that he would be intrigued with the story of how I'd come to The Center. My gesture resulted in an invitation to meet for coffee, something we've done several times. It's been delightful to share our spiritual histories and the joy of living our faith. George, the once imaginary friend from my childhood has become real in this world.

But neither the book nor the friendship with George was the ultimate purpose behind the original message to attend Cathy's church. "No one expects a miracle standing at the kitchen sink," the book begins. And as miraculous as this book is for me, it's what came out of the process of *creating* it that constitutes a miracle…

The Mystery Revealed

The Center for Spiritual Living now seems to me like a new womb from which I could be born once more into the arms of the church, but this time into an atmosphere of freedom, love and joy. Into an atmosphere of such profound acceptance—of all people, of all faiths—that I could begin to see, by contrast, that there were still places in my soul that needed healing.

Sunday after Sunday, as I allowed the light of expansiveness to fill and flood me, that same light began to shine on my own buried patterns and unresolved issues. Light isn't meant, I realized, simply to shine things away, but to reveal the hiding places of that which no longer serves our evolution.

Without being fully conscious of it, I still carried an old pattern deep within, and as a result, repeated stories about my mother, the church, my childhood, my husband. I was a happy, upbeat, loving person, yet judgment crept into my conversations like a cunning thief. At some level, there was a part of me that still felt like a victim—driven to recount my past by some underlying need that I wasn't in touch with.

As my daughter, Maridel, and I worked on the book project together, the pain of our lineage emerged from the shadows. The most satisfying experience I'd ever had with my own mother was long after her death when I'd placed her in an empty chair and pummeled her with painful questions about my childhood. Her unforgettable response of good intentions—motivated by a desire to protect and love—was a gift I never thought I'd receive in this world. We'd been unable to have that experience in the flesh, but at least had achieved it in spirit.

It was different for Maridel and me. We'd shared many intimate moments and loving times in our years together. Her own spiritual awakening had been the model for mine. I had often joked that the reason my transformation took so long was that I had to give birth to the answer and then wait for her to grow up. Yet for many, many years, there had been a tension between us that often made being together painfully uncomfortable. Unlike her usual self, she was sharp and critical toward me. Unlike my usual self, I would shrink back in an attempt not to offend. Sometimes we would rise above it, and ease back into the sunny warmth of mutual enjoyment, but it never lasted long. Occasionally, we acknowledged this predicament, but didn't understand it or know how to address it. Both of us had our misgivings about embarking on the book project together, but they were overshadowed by the clear feeling of rightness. I think we both hoped this shared endeavor would help us transcend our difficulty. Ultimately, it did, but not in the way we imagined. Instead, the project brought our nemesis to a head and then to a crossroad. We couldn't finish the book without excavating our pain.

On the way to the airport after an especially challenging visit to Maridel's, she broached the subject, adding her apology to one I had offered the day before. "I know I'm difficult for you to be around," I had said to her.

"Mom," she said, glancing my way as she drove, "I know I'm difficult for you, too. I don't know why I react to you the way I do, but I want you to know that it's been painful for me. I just don't know how to stop doing it. I'm not myself when I'm with you."

"I'm not myself either. I feel like I'm always trying to be so careful about what I say…like I can't relax."

We spent the rest of the ride talking about our feelings. I felt that just sharing like this might dispel the strain between us, but Maridel was sure that it would take more than talk. "I think it's deeper than that. It feels older than just the two of us."

I understood her to say that she didn't want to talk about it again and though we parted lovingly at the airport, I felt compelled to do something on my own—different from what I'd done before. A few weeks later, I did one of the most difficult things I'd ever done: I called Maridel, and after expressing my love for her and my deep pride in who she is, set a boundary. "I don't want to come back to Sacramento or have you come to Boise unless it's to talk about our relationship. I'm not going to let myself be treated that way anymore."

She accepted my pronouncement calmly, clarifying that she wasn't unwilling to *talk* about it—just believed it would also take individual work on both our parts to actually change it. It was relieving to take action on my own behalf. After so many years of trying to please and placate others, it felt good to be self-respecting and make my own needs important.

Unwittingly, I had opened the door that had been barred to us for many years. A few days later, Maridel called with a response to my proposal. Her voice was shaking, deeply emotional, but the words were straightforward.

"Since you called about setting a boundary on our contact, I've begun to realize the root of my reactions toward you. Over and over through the years, I've tried to set boundaries with you when we were together—trying to curb your recurring stories about Dad, what your mother did to you, and about your childhood. Repeatedly, I've stopped you and said, "Mom, please don't tell me that again," or "I've heard that many times."

"Yes," I acknowledged, "you did."

"But it was to no avail. You continued to do it no matter what I said—and that's where my anger's been coming from. And even though I know setting a boundary was taking care of yourself, it infuriates me that you want to set a boundary with me when you never respected mine!"

Her honesty was painful, but also freeing. We were finally making some progress.

"I also see now that your fixation on the past was triggering my own past—all the negativity of the church mixed with spirituality. All the confusion I felt as a child when people said they were Christians, but were so critical and negative."

She paused. I could hear the tears in her voice and feel them in my eyes.

"What I needed to do, Mom, and didn't do, was sit down with you and honestly express how your stories and judgments were hurting me—especially the ones about Dad. I just didn't have enough awareness until now of why I was so angry. I just kept trying to control myself in your presence, but my defenses were so high that I reacted to almost everything. So you were the emotional abuser for years and I felt like the victim. Then it shifted to you as the victim and me as the abuser."

"Yes, I see that," I said, the truth of our intertwined pain suddenly clear.

"So if setting boundaries was the answer to our difficulty," she continued, "things would have changed a long time ago. It's a matter of *each* of us taking responsibility for both sides of the coin and speaking the truth of what we're experiencing."

When we hung up, it was as if a bright blue patch of light had opened in a hopelessly overcast sky.

A couple of days later, I called her back and asked her to repeat what she'd said. I wanted to hear it again and take notes

Fortunately, she had made her own notes and could accommodate my request. Taking it in a second time, I felt such movement in my being—like an impossible knot had at last been unraveled and was dangling free. We agreed to each work on ourselves and continue sharing our insights. "I'm just not sure how to stop the behavior that has become such a deep habit," I told her.

"It seems like you can't help it," she said. "Like it's compulsive."

"It is. I tell myself that I won't keep repeating and referring to the past, but I still do." I could see it in my sister, Rhea, too—how over and over she kept telling me the stories of how she'd been hurt by my mother. I realized with chagrin that in my own way, I'd been doing the same thing.

This relationship was the one that most reflected the remains of old darkness, of clinging to the debris of the past, but it wasn't the only one. For some time, I'd been aware that I was prone to telling my stories in my group of women friends. Shirley, Victoria, Dinah and I had met for years to trust each other with the inner workings of our lives. Sometimes I came away from our meetings in a state of deep vexation, having succumbed to repeating my old stories. I didn't think of it as being a victim—in fact, that's the last thing I identified with. But now I could see how that perpetual thread of being the injured party had woven its way into the tapestry of my thoughts and hence, my talk.

A few months after the pivotal conversations with Maridel, my sharing group was scheduled for one of our weekend getaways to McCall. The beauty of these retreats was that while we had great fun together, our laughter was complemented by great depth of sharing. The first evening, when one of our members shared a relationship challenge, I responded by telling the story of my most hurtful moment in my life with Arnold—a story they'd heard before. The room fell quiet and Victoria's face took on a piercing gaze.

"Addie," she said. "What is it going to take for you to let that go?"

I was dumbfounded—not that she had asked me such a thing, but because I saw more starkly than ever how compulsive my behavior was. I didn't want to be negative. I didn't want to keep telling stories about my deceased husband and mother, or about the church. Yet I kept doing it. How could I find a way to stop?

What followed next is impossible to put into words. I can describe the outer event, but it was the *inner* one that made the crucial difference. Victoria, gifted counselor that she is, drew a picture for me. I can still see her: her arms lifted, bent at the elbows, fingers almost touching. "This is your life in the past," she said, indicating the arm on her left. "It is over." She nodded toward the other arm. "And this is your life now," she said with calm certainty. "You're free, Addie. None of those old experiences have any power over you except what you give them by keeping them alive. *Why* are you keeping them alive?"

I suddenly flashed on something Maridel had said to me in one of our breakthrough conversations. "Maybe it feels like telling your stories is the only way you can be honest about your pain, but it isn't. You can speak directly and truthfully about your *own* experience without the stories and without making other people wrong."

Now, with Victoria's help, I could see it! Intellectually, I'd understood it many times before from books I'd read, talks I'd heard, and conversations I'd had. But this time, I *felt* it. This time it resonated throughout my body, and I felt an old barrier give way. This need to keep resurrecting the past in order to expose my pain was, I saw, so counterproductive. I could just tell the truth of my feelings. It wasn't about all of "them" and what they did. It was about *me* and my willingness to let the remains of my suffering go.

When I awoke the next morning in that cabin in McCall, the beauty of lake, mountain and trees were a reflection of the elation I felt. In that room, with Victoria's face fixed on mine, and her voice inviting me to step completely out of my story, something had changed. The old tales now seemed like things I'd been dragging around the way a child clings to an old, threadbare blanket with its stained and torn repertoire of memories. I'd laid that blanket down and while I knew I might, in a moment of habit, pick it up again, I also knew it would no longer feel like salve to my ancient wounds. I couldn't wait to get home and call Maridel.

It's been almost a year since that powerful epiphany in the safe surround of my friends and I am continuing to live the change of that moment. The strain is all but gone in the relationship with Maridel. Our talks on the phone are not only lighter, but more real. When she came to visit me after a year apart, we had another in-depth conversation about our relationship, taking it deeper than before. She shared honestly, but without judgment, that she hadn't trusted me emotionally for many years.

I asked for instances and she supplied them.

"But just as we were reflections for each other in feeling victimized, the same is true here," she said. "I'm seeing how I don't tell my emotional truth in relationships either—which is why I'm doing that now with you. I want to learn to tell the truth without making either of us wrong."

We had at long last reached the bottom of our anguish. There would still be the matter of telling each other the truth when issues arose, but I felt confident in our ability to do so. Confident that we had not only given each other a miraculous gift, but had as she said, "broken the spell" of mother-daughter relationships in our ancestral line.

My relationship with my daughter, as important as it is to me, is still the microcosm of the greater story. The miracle is that the deepest healing of my life came at the age of eighty-nine… the result of a choice I made to follow guidance that made no sense to me. How many women of my era have the opportunity to unearth and dissolve such a deep-seated pattern? How many are able to take that chance when it arises? Whoever they are, I am blessed to be among them. This healing is now reflected everywhere—in my relationships, in my dealings in the world, and in the hours I spend alone. It's in the quality of my life day to day. I feel compassion for my parents, for my husband, and gratitude to the church because I now see them as reflections of the consciousness I came into this life with and the issues I had to face in order to be whole. I feel love for myself—for taking on the challenge to move from dark to light and bring heaven to earth in this lifetime. I feel an overwhelming gratitude to Spirit for guiding me, even in the darkness of the early days, for keeping the flame of my spiritual restlessness alive, and ultimately, leading me to *this* day in which I long for nothing.

My legacy is that I have been a link in repairing the generational chain, not just in my own line and not just between mothers and daughters, but within the greater lineage of women's souls. In the latter half of my life, I found my way to the peace I craved as a young woman and therefore, hold out the torch for other women of all ages. And here in this last house, my spirit is more alive and fulfilled than at any other time in my history and as a result, I cherish the privilege of both living and dying consciously.

I still stand at my sink and look out on the Boise Mountains. It is holy ground for me. I not only received a life-changing message there, but found the courage to follow it. And in that act, my years of seeking, reaching, and growing have come to bountiful fruition. The truth has, indeed, set me free.

Epilogue

Addie Woodcook's 90th birthday celebration and book launch was held in October 2010 at The Center for Spiritual Living in Boise, Idaho.

A Tribute to My Mother

by Maridel Bowes

Since I was a little girl, I have admired my mother's grace, her elegance and style. I was always proud of her at school functions where she was not only present, but a presence. I loved the way she led the church choir, taught Sunday school, and went about her other duties: with great warmth and her own particular blend of confident command and a gift for cajoling. She brought out the best in others and it was clear to me from an early age that she was much loved.

Despite the "mixed blessing" of growing up in a parsonage with two overcommitted parents, I was secure in my mother's love and in the knowledge that I was important to her. When something really mattered to me, she was my ally. At five, when my brand new hat—embroidered with my name—blew off my head on a ferry ride, she sympathized with my heartbreak and got me a new one. In Junior High, she acquired my Dad's permission for me to take the lead part in the school play—even though it involved dancing, which was forbidden by our religion. She made the wedding dress of my dreams—too expensive to buy—by putting together three patterns and tapping the pool of her ingenuity. These things stand out because they reflect a larger picture: of a mother who sees and loves her child.

Yet beyond all these treasures is a far greater one. Above all else, I admire my mother for her spiritual resilience, her passion to know God, and desire to keep growing in truth. This is what has made her extraordinary transformation possible and her legacy a healing one.

My mother and I have had deep struggles, as so many mothers and daughters do. But because of her commitment to her own evolution, and her willingness to choose soul over safety, I have not been left to make peace with our relationship by myself. We have done it together. I am grateful for all my mother's gifts, but her spiritual awakening and path of continuing consciousness, transcends them all.

Maridel Bowes